G.E.M.S.

G.E.M.S.

DAPHNE VALCOURT

To order additional copies of this book, contact:
Xlibris
1-888-795-4274
www.Xlibris.com
Orders@Xlibris.com
803923

Contents

Dear Reader,

This is my personal legacy to my daughter and to those of you whose lives I may have touched. Growing up, I have had many mentors to teach me these life lessons, but I have also had to learn some the hard way. I am therefore gifting these lessons to you for the time to come when I may not be around. These valuable life-changing and inspirational lessons are supported by bible-based teachings and are shared as a source of encouragement to you on your personal journey. It is my hope that in reading these lessons, you will develop faith and self-confidence; build resilience through spiritual intelligence and develop enough courage to follow the path that leads to your success and mental health.

Acknowledgements

This book is dedicated to my parents and maternal grandmother; also, to the late Dr. Wesley Plummer, who prayed fervently for the success of this book. Sadly, he passed before its publication.

Acknowledgements go to Dr, Pastor Simone Lord Marcelle who started me off on the book publishing journey. Brother-in-law Patrick Folkes, aerospace engineer who even though a self-professed atheist, took time to read the entire manuscript and requested his own copy. Licensed Clinical Social worker Andre Hoover for his endorsement, my sister Beverly Stephenson, professor and former council woman of Spanish Town, Jamaica and Sharon Terrelonge, nurse practitioner specializing in holistic health for their observations and my daughter Sarah for her thoughts regarding cover design.

My gratitude goes to my husband Serge, educator and poet and my sister Joan, retired banker and entrepreneur for their ongoing support and to Allison Francis - a sweet soul whom I have come to regard as my personal angel, for her constant encouragement and urging to write, finish and publish this book. Finally, I thank God for His amazing love, favor and guidance throughout the years.

To My Precious Gem,

This is my personal legacy to you as you launch out in life. This book has taken me over ten years to write so guard it carefully. It contains powerful and inspiring life lessons that you will not learn in any one book. In the ancient traditions, life lessons and words of wisdom were passed down from one generation to the next through the oral tradition, but modern technology (television, electronic games and gizmos, and social media) has replaced the oral traditions - resulting in important life lessons not being passed on. I have written this book so that these life lessons and impactful stories will not be lost or forgotten. In times of crisis, most people tend to revert to a more primitive form of existence to seek for strength, but conceivably, if the life lessons were never learned then there would be nothing to revert to; it is then that they give up in defeat. This book has valuable life lessons and research discoveries, which I call "G.E.M.S" (an acronym for God and goals; Education; the Mind and Self-control). You must read this book and learn from the life lessons shared. These lessons will help give you direction and secure your anchor during the storms of life. This book will help you become spiritually intelligent in the face of life's challenges - and there will be many challenges in your journey of life. You must take time to read and reread this book. There are profound nuggets of wisdom in each life lesson that you must learn, unearth and never forget. Your success in life depends on it. These life lessons will lift you from the depths of despair – the dunghill of life and strengthen your faith in God. You will be encouraged to reach for new heights in attainment - soaring like the eagle and arriving ultimately at your desired haven-success and peace of mind!

Affectionately, Mommy

Foreword

Listen to a Father's [Mother's] instructions: "Forsake her not, and she shall preserve thee: love her, and she shall keep thee. Wisdom is the principal thing; therefore get wisdom: and with all thy getting get understanding. Exalt her, and she shall promote thee: she shall bring thee to honour, when thou dost embrace her....." Proverbs 4: 6-8 (KJV)

In your hand is a unique book full of powerful life changing GEMS that are dedicated to your success, mental health and spiritual growth. My initial title for the book was *"Up from the Dunghill"* and was aimed at providing a spiritual response to adversity, but realizing the intersection of science, mental health and spirituality, overtime its scope has expanded to combine bio-psychosocial science and scholarly research with intrinsic life lessons learned along life's pathway - hence the title and acronym GEMS. It is my hope that the contents will serve as a mentor to help guide you through adversity; offer new insight on coping with life's challenges and provide you with the encouragement you need to become the confident and successful person that God intends that you should be. Most importantly, you will understand that God has a purpose for your life and that even adversity can turn out to be your pathway to achieving incredible success.

I am particularly grateful to those who have shared their insight and knowledge to benefit others and to my mother and maternal grandmother for the life lessons they were able to share with me; now I am passing these lessons on to you. The insights shared have helped me and many others obtain freedom from a "caged bird mentality." By a "caged bird mentality" I mean ideas, thoughts, behaviors and relationships that are crippling and can prevent you from becoming your personal best. These nuggets are shared to give you hope if you are in the depths of despair and the courage to stand up again if you are feeling knocked down. It is my hope that it will help move you from your lowest point, to accomplishing your greatest good - soaring like the eagle. *This book is not a substitute for seeking professional guidance,* but it may help you to recognize when you need to do so.

You will find that the contents include my life experiences and the shared spiritual experience and yearnings of individuals past and present who have struggled against enormous and extreme social, emotional and material circumstances that had placed them at a disadvantage in life and yet they were able to bounce back or rise to incredible success. Their stories have been an inspiration to me, and I am sharing them for the sole purpose of illustration. This does not suggest that I agree with all their decisions, life choices or spiritual beliefs. The aim of this book is to go beyond being motivational to provide you with spiritual nourishment for the body, mind and spirit and sound insight for successful daily living. You can only benefit from reading and re-reading this book.

I have quoted extensively (with permission), from one of my favorite authors, Ellen G. White, who lived from1827-1915. Growing up in the Seventh-day Adventist church, I have seen people use her name to control others. They would say "Sister White says this" or "Mrs. White says that" as the final authority to quiet the enquiring mind - so much so that there are individuals who are dismissive of her writings and do not read her work. Some even speak ill of her and her writings. This is unfortunate because there is much inspiration that can be gained from her writings. Ellen White is a prolific writer whose formal education ended when she was only nine years old and yet she has written over 40 books and numerous manuscripts on a wide variety of practical topics. Much of her work, especially the book Desire of Ages testifies of the love of Jesus. I have found her devotional writings when read in conjunction with the Bible to be truly inspirational and a blessing in my life. In some of my darkest moments of self-doubt and uncertainty, her writings have provided me with incredible insight and comfort. The quotations shared were excerpted from her work, with permission from her estate and are my interpretations - intended only to inspire and encourage you on your spiritual journey. I have also quoted from various versions of the Bible, but mainly the King James and the New International Versions. Unless otherwise stated, the quotes are from the King James Version or New International Version.

I am not a theologian so my spiritual beliefs about God and my relationship with Him are based on my personal experience of God; the lessons learned from attending Sabbath School and from my maternal grandmother, a kind and loving God-fearing woman. I also studied religion at the Oxford University Advanced [A] level in England. My second doctoral degree in Christian Psychology obtained from seminary in the US has further served to enhance my understanding of theological concepts and insight in human behavior; however, I have spent much time in my own personal search for an understanding of the purpose of life, adversity, consciousness, the meaning of success and in exploring different religious faiths and belief systems in an effort to find answers for the many life questions that have puzzled me. I have learned since that my brain is filled with many spiritual beliefs and disbeliefs that are based on my knowledge, cultural exposure, life experiences and my relationship with God. These experiences result in the values I hold and the choices I make about what I believe and what I ignore. My beliefs and experiences also help to determine my level of spirituality and my emotional and intellectual responses to life's challenges.

I am an avid reader and a receptive learner, so I cannot remember all the sources, authors, pastors, teachers, or friends from whom I have gained insight. Therefore, I am here and now giving full acknowledgement and appreciation to all in case I overlook anyone.

Introduction

I was encouraged to write this book by my family and friends. My sister Joan, her husband Patrick and my husband Serge were especially encouraging. However, it was the continual urging of Allison Frances, an elderly lady with a spattering of grey that frames her face like a halo, a warm smile and the most angelic face that has kept me motivated to write. I don't know much about Allison except that she grew up in an orphanage and she heard me speak once at my home church and told me that I ought to write a book and that it will bless many - especially the despairing. Each summer, for several years Allison frequented my home church and at each visit she would ask for her copy of the book. Each time I would humor her in response, "Oh, it's coming soon." However, it took me a while to put pen to paper until I came across a Bible verse in Acts of the Apostles, which says: b*ut rise, and stand upon thy feet: for I have appeared unto thee for this purpose, to make thee a minister and a witness both of these things which thou hast seen, and of those things in the which I will appear unto thee; (Acts 26:16)*. My daughter's disillusionment with God during her pre-adolescent years, after losing three of her young friends - one died in a tragic car accident and the other two through chronic medical conditions, which afflicted them, all before the age of 10 provided me with added impetus to do research and write this book.

The life lessons shared are many and cover a myriad of topics such as cognition and beliefs, faith and adversity; mental health and relationships; success and money matters. Every case example, illustration, story and analogy are based on lessons learned along life's pathway and shared to help strengthen, encourage, and inspire you to be the best *you* that God intend that you should be. This is not the usual banal "success" or motivational book. I have read many of those books and have found them to be encouraging, but most are devoid of a spiritual foundation and does not counsel against practices, beliefs and behaviors that might sabotage your success or even prevent you from maximizing your potential. The propagation of the idea of sitting back and manifesting riches through supernatural forces or dishonest means is also foolish and panders to the minds of those who believe in achieving success without effort. The wise man Solomon admonishes against laziness: *"He becometh poor that dealeth with a slack hand: but the hand of the diligent maketh rich."* (Proverbs, 10:4). He also warns that *"An inheritance may be gotten hastily at the beginning; but the end thereof shall not be blessed."* *(Prov. 20:21).* I believe this to be true based on my years of experience in working with adults and teens who became criminally involved. I saw firsthand that individuals who committed criminal acts or engaged in illegal activity to make money would appear to be flourishing materially and even live a lavish life style, but after a while their lives would be cut short or they would lose it all through imprisonment, drug dependency, government confiscation, poor money management or death. Living and working in large cities, it was common to know or hear of individuals who were involved in illegal drug activity getting shot over a drug deal gone badly. Many were poor teenagers that drug cartels used as runners; these "kids" would get killed over "skimming off the top" of their drug sales and using the money to buy flashy brand name clothing and jewelry as a way of strengthening their fragile egos.

The life lessons to be learned from this book are many and because I want to help you remember them, I am introducing you to the acronym **GEMS**:

G represents ___God, Goals and Giving___. There are many gods in this world, but you must know what you believe and decide which god you will worship, and in which god you will anchor your faith. It is possible to make a god of yourself, your spouse, your children, your jewelry, your possession, your achievements, your job or even certain beliefs. Just be mindful that these gods will eventually let you down because they are byproducts of the true source. There is only one true God, the one who is creator. Revelations 4:11 says: *"Thou art worthy, O Lord, to receive glory and honour and power: for thou hast created all things, and for thy pleasure they are and were created."* Why worship the byproduct of creation rather than the source? It is like worshipping a few carats in diamond when the *White Dwarf Star* (discovered in 2004 by astronomers and nicknamed *Lucy* after the Beatles song *Lucy in the Sky with Diamonds),* equals a diamond of 10 billion trillion, trillion carats. The creator God's resources are limitless. Ps 50:7-15 says: *Hear, O my people, and I will speak; O Israel, and I will testify against thee: I am God, even thy God. I will not reprove thee for thy sacrifices or thy burnt offerings, to have been continually before me. I will take no bullock out of thy house, nor he goats out of thy folds. For every beast of the forest is mine, and the cattle upon a thousand hills. I know all the fowls of the mountains: and the wild beasts of the field are mine. If I were hungry, I would not tell thee: for the world is mine, and the fullness thereof. Will I eat the flesh of bulls, or drink the blood of goats? Offer unto God thanksgiving; and pay thy vows unto the most High: And call upon me in the day of trouble: I will deliver thee, and thou shalt glorify me..* You must daily acknowledge **God** as your creator and submit to Him all your plans, dreams, fears, aspirations and your life **Goals,** realizing that **"**There are many devices in a man's heart; nevertheless the counsel of the Lord, that shall stand." (Prov. 19:21)

You must set **Goals** in life in order not to wander through life aimlessly, for if you aim at achieving nothing in life, you will achieve nothing. When a dart player plays darts, he aims for bull's-eye; similarly, in life you must have targeted aims and **Goals**. Setting **Goals** will motivate you to move forward in life. In establishing your life **Goals**, be sure that your **Goals** are clearly defined, are achievable, and are realistic enough to be reached within a certain time frame. Having a belief in an all-powerful God, knowing what you want to achieve in life and establishing **Goals** to achieve them will help you become successful. Success in any line demands a definite aim; you must also focus intently on achieving that aim for *"without goals, and plans to reach them, you are like a ship that has set sail with no destination,"* says clinical psychologist, Fitzhugh Dodson. Finally, as God blesses you, you must be willing to **give** back: *But he that knew not, and did commit things worthy of stripes, shall be beaten with few stripes. For unto whomsoever much is given, of him shall be much required: and* *to whom men have committed much, of him they will ask the more.* (Luke 12:48). **Giving back** to God, to your family and to those less fortunate will lead to even greater blessings and ultimate success.

E requires that you embrace an ***Educational experience*** **t**hat will prepare you to establish yourself as a productive human being, but you must be **Enthusiastic** about doing so. The wise man Solomon, from his own life experience stresses repeatedly in the book of Proverbs, the importance of acquiring wisdom: Proverbs 4:7 says: "Wisdom is the principal thing; therefore get wisdom: and with all thy getting get understanding.." Proverbs 23:23 says: "Buy the truth, and sell it not; also wisdom, and instruction, and understanding." and Proverbs 13:20 reads: "He that walketh with wise men shall be wise: but a companion of fools shall be destroyed." *Dullness and ignorance are no virtue,*" says E.G. White. She goes on to say: "*The highest culture of the mind, if sanctified through the love and the fear of God, receives His fullest approval. All who engage in the acquisition of knowledge should strive to reach the highest round of the ladder. Let students advance as fast and as far as they can; let the field of their study be as broad as their powers can compass; but let them make God their wisdom*" (E.G. White, Fundamentals of Christian Education, p.47). You must make the most of your time and opportunities to develop intelligence and a balanced character. *The intellect should be cultivated, the memory taxed. All intellectual laziness is sin, and spiritual lethargy is death* (E.G. White, Gospel workers p.18). You cannot achieve success if you are not prepared to make the effort to achieve it. **Education** requires effort and decided mental application. My Jamaican grandmother used to say, "if you want good your nose has to run." In other words, success comes with struggle and effort. In your struggle and effort to achieve, you must show **Enthusiasm** and a positive mental attitude. **Enthusiasm** says Dale Carnegie is a little-known secret to success. I would say, *Education* is the ladder to success, but *Enthusiasm* is a vital rung on the ladder that leads to success. Another rung on the ladder of educational success is *curiosity* or **Enquiry**. All great discoveries and research came because of curiosity and Enquiry. Albert Einstein, who developed the theory of relativity and the equation E=mc2, which is noted to be one of the two pillars of modern physics (alongside quantum theory) once said: "*I have no special talent. I am only passionately curious.*" My own masters and doctoral degrees resulted from enquiry or I should say my curiosity and a desire to get answers to perplexing life questions that puzzled me. **Enthusiasm** and **Enquiry** are key rungs that will help you maximize your potential as you pursue higher education.

Pursuing higher education with a goal of getting a degree is a good goal but knowing how you plan to use the degree will be an even better goal. I Thessalonians 4:11 says: "…And that ye study to be quiet, and to do your own business, and to work with your own hands, as we commanded you." Think creatively of how you can utilize the knowledge you have gained from pursuing higher education to help you become financially independent, fill a need, solve a human problem and be a blessing to humanity. When your curiosity and enquiry lead you to pursue something that is of interest to you, you will be more enthusiastic about making a success of it.

M represents **the *Mind, Mental Health, and Money Matters***. According to neurobiologists, the brain receives information through our five senses: Sight, smell, touch, taste, and hearing; whereas the **Mind** is the activity part of our brain which thinks, feels, perceives; acts and determines how we understand and respond to life's events and challenges. The mind and the brain are terms sometimes used interchangeably to mean the same thing, but they are not one and the same. In basic terms, the brain is the physical aspect and the mind is the mental. Like the computer (although humans are way smarter), there is hardware and software. Similarly, the brain is the structure that consists of physical matter - cells, blood vessels and nerves, with specific functions that are located within regions of the cerebral cortex. Each area can make computations and store the information it needs. There are also neurons and synapses - the electronics of the brain. The mind is like the software - the thought that resides in the brain and handles such things as your emotions, memories and dreams. The average human brain is said to house over 100 billion nerve cells (*neurons*) with each connected to 10,000 or so other cells. These nerve cells connect with one another via electrical and chemical signals known as neurotransmitters. Neurotransmitters then communicate and transmit signals from one nerve cell (neuron) to the next. When the communication is disrupted a neurotransmitter, imbalance is likely to result. Everything we do – all our movements, thoughts, and feelings – such as: depression, anxiety and other mood disorders are thought to be causally related to imbalances with the neurotransmitters. That is why colloquially speaking a person can "lose his or her mind" in the same way that you can lose electrical connection. I have seen many individuals lose their minds through drug induced psychosis. **You must protect your mind from harmful substances**. Jesus, the Savior was so protective of his mind that even on the cross, writhing in pain from physical torture, and dehydrated and dying of thirst after having walked the long road to Golgotha, carrying a wooden cross and having not had anything to eat or drink since his last supper with his disciples (approximately 15 hours without food or drink), refused the wine vinegar and gall mixture intended as a narcotic or sedative to dull his senses (Matt. 27:34).

A mind is a terrible thing to waste is a well-known slogan, which was developed by the advertising company Young & Rubicam to promote the United Negro College Fund. Unfortunately, certain destructive life style practices and life events such as trauma can so distress, cripple and destroy the mind that it becomes wasted. Like the computer, you must protect your brain and be careful to input data into your mind that will be useful upon recall. Avoid seeing, hearing, tasting or touching anything evil like you would avoid a killer virus. Philippians 4:8 says: "Finally, brethren, whatsoever things are true, whatsoever things are honest, whatsoever things are just, whatsoever things are pure, whatsoever things are lovely, whatsoever things are of good report; if there be any virtue, and if there be any praise, think on these things." You can repair or renovate your mind through a study of the Bible and by putting away destructive thoughts and practices... *From a study of the Bible, your mind can be expanded, elevated, and ennobled. If you are, like Daniel and become hearers and doers of the word of God, you may advance as he did in all branches of learning. Being pure minded you will become strong minded. Every intellectual faculty will be quickened. You may so educate and discipline yourself that all within the sphere of your influence shall see what you can be, and what you can do, when connected with the God of wisdom and power (E.G. White. Ministry of Healing, pp. 464-466).*

Money – **is** a token of exchange which plays a central role in your life. Money can improve your opportunities and your quality of life; without it you cannot meet your basic need for food, clothing and shelter because "money answers everything" (Ecc.10:19). However, how you obtain money and how you feel about money will determine if you control it or if it controls you. Be careful that money doesn't control you.

Money controls you when it defines who you are, and you have sleepless nights worrying about not having enough. If money controls you, it has become your master, which means you are a slave to it. When you are a slave to someone or something, you become totally dependent on that person or thing. Jesus pointed out that "No man can serve two masters: for either he will hate the one, and love the other; or else he will hold to the one, and despise the other. Ye cannot serve God and mammon." (Matt. 6:24). You must understand how money works, but you must choose not to make a god of it, for ultimately whatever controls you, or your decisions, is your master or your God. There are enough scriptures to suggest that God wants you to be free from bondage in every area of your life - including money; therefore, you must **Master Money-Matters; know how Money works and how to save, budget and invest your Money**, for whatever you are able to master can no longer have control over you. In the United States, the motto "In God we trust" is imprinted on all paper money. According to history, this motto first appeared on silver coins in 1864 during the American Civil War, when the country was divided over the abolition of the slave economy in the south versus the growth of industrialization in the north; fears were percolating over the Republic of American being shattered so in response, the motto *"In God We Trust"* was imprinted on coins as a reminder to the American people to trust in God rather than in the monetary system. In Jamaica there is a saying that "one pound of fret cannot pay one ounce of debt" so do not worry about money; instead, start thinking creatively about how to make money and how to invest it so that you can become a financial blessing. It is "the love of money" and not money of itself that is the root of all evil. Money in the right hands can do much good and create opportunities for yourself and others. Solomon, a wealthy man himself once said: "He that trusteth in his riches shall fall; but the righteous shall flourish as a branch." (Proverbs 11:28) and "He that hath a bountiful eye shall be blessed; for he giveth of his bread to the poor." (Proverbs 22:9).

S represents the one ingredient that can make or break you as a successful human being, which is ***Self-Mastery or Self-control***. Self-control is being able to manage your feelings, attitude, behavior and responses. Proverbs 25:28 says: "He that hath no rule over his own spirit is like a city that is broken down, and without walls." Your potential increases with self-discipline when practiced.... *An ordinary mind, well disciplined, will accomplish more and higher work than will the most highly educated mind and the greatest talents without self-control.* — (E.G. White. Christ Object Lesson, p. 335). Self-control in the face of adversity is like a solid house built with cement blocks and a firm foundation that can withstand hurricane winds. In the world of computer, it is like a firewall. A firewall is a network security system that monitors and controls network traffic. The purpose of a firewall is to establish a barrier or a wall between a trusted, secure internal network and any outside network that is assumed not secure or trusted. Similarly, you must establish a firewall against triggers that will cause you to lose self-control. You must monitor your thoughts, behavior, actions and associations. You must take personal responsibility for your emotional response to slights and hurts, and how you react without blaming others for your own lack of self-control. My grandmother would sometimes say: "If you spread your bed, you must lie in it." In Chinese culture, Confucius thinking sees self-control as commanding the greatest influence in life. Virtue and self-control are both a personal quality and a requirement for leadership, individual dignity, communal solidarity, and political order more so than wealth and power. Confucius thinking came about when China was in total disorder and people had no control over themselves; now such thinking has become a way of life for the Chinese. The following are three meaningful quotes from Confucius to live by: *"Respect yourself and others will respect you." "Behave toward everyone as if receiving a great guest;"* and *"Ask yourself constantly, what is the right thing to do?"*

If you never finish reading this book, I wish for you to imprint this acronym "GEMS" in your mind and learn as much as you can about each word represented. However, because I expect you to continue reading, for sure, you will learn a lot more on your journey through this book. Enjoy the journey.

PART I

GEMS FOR THE JOURNEY

Your 1st Gem

KNOW WHAT YOU BELIEVE

"LORD, the God of our ancestors, are you not the God who is in heaven? You rule over all the kingdoms of the nations. Power and might are in your hand, and no one can withstand you" (II Chron. 20:6 NIV). "We must go back and reclaim our past so that we can move forward; so, we understand why and how we came to be who we are today." ---------Ancient Akan principle of Sankofa

Your core beliefs are the lens through which you view yourself and the world around you. Cognitive behavioral specialist, Mark McMinn describes core beliefs metaphorically as a tumor that starts from childhood and grows within throughout life. Ultimately, those beliefs shape the direction your life will take, how you perceive yourself, the relationships you form and the decisions you make. Some of these core beliefs become convictions. Knowing what you believe is therefore your first and most important GEM.

Behavior & Beliefs: Knowing what you believe and what you believe about yourself are fundamentals of a healthy mind, for when your belief is not consistent with your behavior you will experience discrepancies or what psychologists refer to as cognitive dissonance. In life we should seek for consonance or consistency between what we believe and how we live. Knowing what to believe however is often confusing and can be frustrating because we live in a world where there are many beliefs, religions and philosophies. Knowledge abounds and is easily accessible through electronic media; as a result, it is quite easy to develop cognitive dissonance by deciding there are just too many beliefs so it's not worth believing in any one thing and reconcile to just sticking with what you know; you may even rationalize your behavior although you know it to be wrong. Because you begin to form your beliefs about yourself and life from an early age, these beliefs may remain with you into adulthood or until such time that you begin to question them or recognize that what you have believed is not in sync with what is true or what you have experienced. Reflecting on my personal experience of growing up in Jamaica for example, I recall that the lessons I learned about England and America from text books and television were vastly different from my personal experience of living in these countries. Similarly, certain beliefs and myths that I grew up with, through my study of history, anthropology, biology and neurology, I now know not to be true. When your beliefs and reality collide and what you had believed to be true is no longer valid, it is then that the need to search for truth and understanding begins.

Christian Beliefs: I grew up with Christianity as fundamental to my core belief system. Overtime, however, as I studied history and the various sciences, I began questioning aspects of Christianity that did not make sense to me as a person of color. Christianity is ranked the largest religious belief system in the world, which started in the Afro-Asian region with Jesus and mushroomed in Europe with many Christian martyrs. Through picture books and the legacy of colonialism, I grew up associating Christianity with white Europeans. Every picture of Jesus and other biblical characters were portrayed as white and European, so inevitably I developed a Eurocentric view of Christianity until I came across a painting of Jesus by a Chinese artist who portrayed Jesus as Chinese. This led me to question and to recognize the influence of European art on our perception of Jesus. Art was used by the clergy in medieval and Renaissance Europe as part of worship and to educate the unlearned, not only in Europe but also in the colonies. As a result, Eurocentric images of Christ and Christianity have prevailed.

Living in Europe and traveling to other parts of the world, I was surprised to find that Christianity as a religion was on the decline among Europeans and North Americans but growing rapidly among Africans and Asians. In line with the beliefs of the Akan people of Ghana, "it is good to take from the past what is good and bring it into the present." It's as though the Afro-Asian region is reclaiming its history by embracing Christianity, which it once rejected.

Based on my research, the decline of Christianity in Europe started with Rationalism, which is the belief that reason is the path to knowledge; its decline progressed with Darwinism – the belief in the evolution of species by natural selection, followed by New Age religions. Philology – a study of the language of the bible as a mere book about history, poetry and parables also contributed to the decline. A strong evidence of the decline of Christianity can be seen in the decline in formal church attendance. It's as though what the Afro-Asians are giving up, the Europeans are embracing or adopting and vice versa. This can be seen in the increase among Europeans in the wearing of nose rings, tongue and belly piercings; the stretching of the ear lopes and other Middle-Eastern and African practices.

Historically, after slavery, people of color living under the influence of colonialism did not redefine themselves in relation to Christianity; instead, they embraced Christianity in its European form and added their own flavor to the worship experience; it is not surprising then that even among people of color, there has been a noticeable decline in church attendance. With increased access to knowledge, there are some who have dismissed Christianity outright as the "White man's religion," in part because of the European influence and the incongruence between Christian beliefs and the legacy of un-Christ like behaviors and beliefs perpetrated by colonizers in the name of Christianity. Mahatma Gandhi who experienced apartheid in South Africa is noted to have said to Stanley Jones, a missionary: "I love Christ it's just that so many of you Christians are not like Christ." Take the Atlantic Slave trade for example, in order for Christians to engage in human trafficking, which was a financially lucrative venture for the colonizers, it was necessary to dismiss, rationalize and come up with all sorts of laws, theories and bible based distortions such as "the curse of Ham;" and "slaves submit to your masters" not to mention the unscientific conjectures of social Darwinism's –"survival of the fittest" – all to appease the conscience and justify the inhumane treatment of one group of people by another for financial gain. The Fugitive Slave Act of 1850 is a classic example of a grossly inhumane action, which was incongruent with Christian beliefs. Ellen White in her work *The Progressive Years (Vol-2, P.34)* referred to it as the *"unconscionable law of the land, calculated to crush out of man every noble, generous feeling of sympathy that should rise in his heart for the oppressed and suffering slave."* Harriet Beecher Stowe's novel "Uncle Tom's Cabin" provides a fine portrait of the cognitive dissonance that Christian slave owners experienced in their efforts to condone and legitimize slavery. Although Christian slave owners believed slavery to be wrong in principle, they maintained its institution because of its economic benefits to themselves and to the church. John Newton, famously known for writing the song *"Amazing Grace"* was a notorious alcoholic slave trader who continued to engage in slave trading for several years even after his conversion experience. Newton rationalized his slave trading until one day he became so violently ill that he had to give up trading. Sometimes when you are living a conflicted life style, it may take a life changing, crippling or near-death experience like that of Saul (whose name was changed to the apostle Paul) a persecutor of Christians who was blinded in his quest to annihilate Christians, to jolt you back to your senses to achieve consonance.

In both Saul and Newton's cases, through their life changing conversion experiences, their eyes were opened to the evils of their ways and both became popular preachers of Christianity. Indeed, it was the Psalmist David that said: *The statues of the Lord are right, rejoicing the heart. The commandment of the Lord is pure, enlightening the eyes* (Psalms19:8). An understanding of the life and mission of Christ and a desire to develop a Godlike character based on God's commandments of love – love for God and love for your fellow men and women leads to cognitive consonance and harmony between what you believe and how you should live and treat others.

Truth Versus Pretense: Another area in which cognitive dissonance may show up is in pretense. It is possible to pretend to be what you are not to impress others or to give an appearance of success and achievement. "Fake it till you make it" is a common catch phrase that encourages inauthentic lives. Sadly, we also live in a world where hypocrisy and moral evils exist. Solomon wrote in Eccl. 4.1: *I returned and considered all the oppressions that are done under the sun: and behold the tears of* *such as were oppressed, and they had no comforter; and on the side of their oppressors there was power; but they had no comforter.* Oppressive situations such as abuse, and domestic violence often lead to pretense – the wearing of a false persona as a survival mechanism – smiling when you are hurting on the inside. The poet Paul Laurence Dunbar captures this beautifully in his poem *"We wear the mask that grins and lies"* to explain how African Americans were able to survive the oppressive Jim Crow era in America. For African Americans, outsized power left them with little choice but to live a life of pretense. Is it any wonder that the wise man Solomon says: *"All things have I seen in the days of my vanity: there is a just man that perisheth in his righteousness, and there is a wicked man that prolongeth his life in his wickedness." (Eccl. 7:15).*

Your desire in life should be to live a life of congruence and authenticity – being true to yourself and being willing to question your truth; being familiar with your conduct from day to day and the motives which prompt your actions without allowing pressure from peers, association, and the need to impress or obtain popularity to dictate your action. *And ye shall know the truth, and the truth shall make you free. (John 8:32).* When you are not being true to yourself, it is like watching a video that is not synchronizing with the audio. Such inconsistency will show up in other areas of your life – drugs, alcohol, sexual deviance, eating disorders, excessive shopping, unbalanced thoughts, and all sorts of addictions. I cannot tell you what to believe, but I will share what I have discovered in my own journey.

<u>Perception & Beliefs</u>: Your beliefs are formed based on the mental input received through your cognition, understanding, and mental impressions – your perception. Your perceptions can result in beliefs that are limiting or expansive. The question to you is, are your beliefs empowering you to be the best *"you"* that you can be or are they limiting you? Are your beliefs walled around you like iron bars that block your path and prevent you from achieving success, or an open door of possibilities ushering you into new paths and encouraging you to become the best *"you"* that you can be? Do you have a "can do" self-motivating attitude or are you trapped behind a perceived road block of "can't do" crippling beliefs? If a crisis occurs in your life, do you ask, "Why me?' Or do you say, "I need to understand what happened." Honesty with your self is important because: *A double minded man is unstable in all his ways, (James 1.8).*

If you have limiting beliefs about yourself, you must seek to find the etiology or root cause. Ask yourself where did this "can't do" belief come from? In science, to understand the etiology or root of a problem you must examine the three "C's" – *Cause, Correlation* and *Consequence*. First, you start by formulating some thoughts about where the problem began. Was it at home, at school, or in the community? Who told you that you cannot succeed? Who told you that you were a stupid moron or a worthless good for nothing? Now, ask yourself: What was going on at the time, in my life? What was the prevailing thinking of those around me, in my home, in my family, in my school, in my community and the society at large? How was I treated? What feelings did the experience generate in me? How did I respond? How do I feel now as I reflect on the experience? What is true of me now and what is not true? Understanding whether your beliefs are preventing you from succeeding or empowering you is important because the beliefs you formulate about life will guide your responses and decision making. Your beliefs will frame your perspective on life, guide how you view life, the associations you choose, and how you respond to life's challenges, successes and failures; therefore, the clearer you can be about your beliefs, and the more honest you are with yourself, the more satisfied you will be in your decision making and behavioral responses to road blocks and life's challenges.

Your Temperament Type: Your temperament type is another factor that influences how you respond to life's challenges. According to psychologists and temperament theorist, there are four distinct temperament types: Melancholy, Choleric, Sanguine, and Phlegmatic. More recently a fifth known as the Supine was added by the *National Association of Christian Counselors*. Each of these temperaments has driving needs that influence behavior; there is a need for *affection*, a need for *inclusion* and a need for *control*. The intensity of the need is influenced by the specific temperament type. The *Melancholy* tends to be introverted and a loner, with a fear of rejection. Their estimation of themselves tends to be low and, figuring that others do not like them, they may put up a defense by rejecting others first; they are creative, highly organized with high morals, but they are more prone to bouts of depression. The *Supine*'s self-estimate is also low, but they try to gain acceptance by going out of their way to be "nice" to others and in doing things for others; they are more prone to be a people pleaser, although at first appearance they may appear "stuck up." The *Sanguine* is extroverted, loves attention and enjoys being the "life of the party;" they are charming, outgoing and are great at sales or entertaining. However, they do not handle rejection well and their self-esteem crashes if they experience rejection. Yet, because of their outgoing nature they bounce back quickly and keep going. They are also more prone to engage in risk taking behavior with a tendency to exaggerate the truth. The *Choleric* is the "leader"-type and enjoys being "bossy." They have a need to control others, but do not like to be controlled. They are highly motivated by their goals, are great leaders and will use people to accomplish their goals. However, they can be cold, cruel and heartless in their dealings with others. The *Phlegmatic* is peaceful at heart, great mediator and very laidback with a low motivation for change. This lack of motivation is one of the reasons they put things off and do not accomplish all that they can achieve in life. They may even be perceived as lazy. Understanding your temperament is important because it can lead to a deeper self-awareness and therefore better decision making, as well as more fulfilling relationships, and better career choices.

<u>Mind, Body, & Spirit Connection:</u> The mind, body and spirit connection are important dimensions that help determine who you are and have a major impact on your spiritual growth and ultimately your beliefs. If you are not physically well, it's hard to feel mentally and emotionally motivated and if you are never still, always busy, you cannot spiritually connect with God; eventually you will wear yourself out physically and emotionally and disconnect from God. *Be still, and know that I am God: I will be exalted among the heathen, I will be exalted in the earth. (Ps 46:10)* is a reminder that we need to stop and chill out from time to time and connect with God. God created man in perfect balance, but disobedience has caused an imbalance in all three dimensions. It is His desire to bring you back into perfect balance. Neuroscientists have found that if you spend time in meditation and focus on your most positive, loving, and compassionate belief – your spirituality - it enhances the cognitive performance of your brain and helps to create mental balance by improving the control of your emotions, impulses, thoughts and movements. You will increase your natural ability to show compassion toward yourself and others, which in turn help to suppress anxiety, depression, anger, and fear – mental health issues that you must overcome to become successful in life. Your spirituality is critical to your mental health and overall wellbeing but paying attention to your spirituality means more than just going to church. You can become addicted to church attendance because of the emotional high it gives without having a meaningful relationship with God. You could also become a "foxhole Christian" – running to God only when you are in trouble and abandoning him when all is well. Having been a church going person for most of my life, I do not see organized religion as synonymous with spirituality; rather, I see organized religion as the institution that promotes spiritual beliefs. Research suggests that religion came out of man's genuine and innate need to come together to worship.

Choosing a Belief: Choosing a spiritual belief can be a challenge given the existing plethora of religions and religious beliefs, to which people ascribe: There are those who believe in pantheism (nature is god), polytheism (many gods), and those who believe in monotheism (one god); then there are those who believe in Humanism (a creator god without supernatural powers) and the atheist who do not believe in a god at all. The works of Karl Marx and Ludwig Feuerbach promote Communism and suggest that religion is an illusion that binds aspiration and that man can only become great by rebelling against God. This view, which was built on resentment against God, has helped to lay the foundation for atheism and various movements that reject a belief in God. Indeed, atheism may find a belief in God to be too simplistic a view, but sometimes it is the simple things of life that confounds the wise. 1 Corinthians 1:25 says: *"Because the foolishness of God is wiser than men; and the weakness of God is stronger than men."* Physicalism is another belief system. It offers that the universe is composed of everything known by physics. Physicalism however cannot explain the unpredictability of the mind or the development of neurological and psychological disorders.

A Belief in God: The books of I & II Chronicles provide a history of mankind from Adam to the kings of Israel. In II Chronicles 20:20, King Jehoshaphat when faced by two opposing armies, reminded the children of Judah and of Jerusalem that their success and prosperity would result from their belief in God: *"…Believe in the Lord your God, so shall ye be established; believe his prophets, so shall ye prosper." (II Chron.20:20).* I believe in a personal God who knows me as an individual; however, having this belief is not enough. According to James 2:19, believing in

God is good, but even demons (those who are locked in evil and rebellion against God) believe in God and tremble at His power; therefore, having a consciousness of God's presence and a transforming relationship with Him based on faith is more important. Your spirituality is about having an individual relationship with God based on your faith in Him. It is taking time out to build a personal relationship with someone you cannot see - for *God is a Spirit: and they that worship him must worship him in spirit and in truth.* (John 4:24), but whom you accept by faith, *and worship in spirit and in truth.* Worshipping a God, I cannot see is not a hard concept for me to accept because I grew up without my parents from birth until I was 13 years old. My parents lived in England and I in Jamaica. In those days, my grandmother did not have a telephone so my only means of communicating with them was through letters. From the promises in the letters I received, I had faith that one day I would see them again. Sometimes they delayed responding to my letters, but I never lost faith that I would hear from them. As I grew older, I learned to transfer my dependence upon my parents to God - my heavenly father.

The Spirit Within: Accepting God as your heavenly father means being able to transfer your dependence from things or people that you can see to a God you cannot see, but whose spirit consciousness (the Holy Spirit) dwells within you. *The kingdom of heaven is within you,* says Jesus. It is your choice whether or not you respond to the Spirit within. *The Holy Spirit is an effective helper in restoring the image of God in the human soul (E. G. White, The Faith I Live By. p.52).* If you constantly ignore the spirit's promptings, eventually you will stop responding to it altogether. It is as though your mind has been seared with a hot iron or you have developed a callous response. *"Quench not the Spirit."* Paul says in *1 Thess. 5:19.* In doing so, you will then look to external things to fill that need or to regain that spirit consciousness. It is then that you are more likely to turn to cigarettes, alcohol and drugs; hallucinogens such as LSD (Lysergic acid), DMT (Dimethyltryptamine), cannabis, marijuana, mushrooms etc., to alter the neurochemistry of the brain and help change your mood and heighten cognition and perception. Whereas, just by you simply submitting your will to God and choosing to respond to the Holy Spirit - your God consciousness - you will develop a personal connection with God and make amazing new discoveries. Enoch, Moses, Samuel and Elijah are examples of individuals who were keenly aware of the Holy Spirit or that "still small voice." As you sit in

silence or in meditation, and in a study of God's words, the "still small voice**,**" will be heard.

When Jesus said the kingdom of God is within you, this is precisely what He meant. His disciples had a hard time grasping this concept; Jesus even referred to them as dull because they looked constantly to external sources for happiness - to bring changes in their lives; to obtain relief from oppression, to obtain power and prestige instead of looking to God's spirit within to equip them with His power so that His name can be glorified in them. It was at Jesus' baptism —an inward decision to show outwardly a changed life and a total commitment to the mission of soul saving that the Holy Spirit descended upon Jesus as a dove and he experienced Pentecost. Similarly, it was not until the disciples began to look internally, acknowledging their faults and character flaws and were on one accord in their belief and mission of soul saving that the Holy Spirit was outpoured upon them and they experienced Pentecost. It was at Pentecost that they received the gifts of the Holy Spirit and began to speak in different languages (not gibberish) so that others present could understand the message of Jesus. It was at Pentecost that they finally understood Jesus' counsel and mission of discipleship and launched their ministry.

It was said that Enoch walked with God, meaning he had a consciousness of the presence of God (the Holy Spirit) in and with him. This connection with God opens a powerful channel that leads to a transformation of the mind, emotions and actions. Paul wrote a detailed account in Romans 1:19-25 and 2 Thessalonians 2:11&12 of the consequences of failure to have a spirit consciousness anchored in God. He points out that it can lead to delusional thinking, poor choices and all sorts of mental health problems, along with deviant and aberrant behaviors.

From my own personal experience and observation of others, when one develops a connection with God or a Holy Spirit consciousness, an amazing transformation takes place, which is quite different from becoming a nominal member of a church or having an intellectual understanding of the Bible. You can become a nominal member of a church and continue to live a destructive lifestyle and even create much havoc in the church. Whereas, when you are in a personal connection with God, through prayer and meditation, the destructive lifestyle and behaviors you once relished and engaged in becomes distasteful; you will not have a desire for them anymore because your goal is to become like God in character. *Sinful thoughts are put away, evil deeds are renounced; love, humility and peace, take the place of anger, envy and strife. Joy takes the place of sadness and the countenance reflects the light of heaven.... The blessing comes when by faith the soul surrenders itself to God. Then the power which no human eye can see creates a new being in the image of God. The Holy Spirit strives with everyman. It is the voice of God speaking to the soul (E. G. White. The Desire of Ages, p.173).*

The patriarch Jacob whose very name means deceiver or "con artist" is an example of an individual whose life experienced a transformation because of his personal connection with God. On one occasion, Jacob spent a whole night in prayer and meditation; Jacob wrestled with God earnestly, until he experienced both a blessing and a spiritual rebirth. His name was changed from Jacob the "con artist" to Israel, a prince of God. A relationship with God and staying connected with Him changes even your character flaws. Staying connected with God is therefore the secret key to maintaining a balanced life because like Kings Saul and Nebuchadnezzar you can easily lose that spiritual connection – thinking yourself to be a god or that you do not need God, you will eventually become mentally unbalanced and will look to things, people, power, prestige, or substances (drugs and alcohol) to create balance.

Disobedience and Sin: Disobedience or a refusal to respond to the spirit's promptings – often referred to as *sin*–a moving away from God, will result in a severance of your spiritual connection with God and a progressive downward slide, which is not immediately apparent. Before Adam and Eve disobeyed God, they had a personal and open relationship with God; but because of disobedience, they could no longer face God. Disobedience results in feelings of guilt and shame and these feelings can lead you to either respond to the spirit's promptings by submitting in humility to being on the wrong path and asking for forgiveness, as did David after the prophet Nathan pointed out to David his evil act of committing homicide in order to justify the abuse of his power in stealing another man's wife; or you can maintain a stubborn resolve as did Adam and Eve's first born son Cain, by separating and distancing yourself from God in resentment, to the point where you begin to justify your wrongs. The behavior then becomes sociopathic. A person with sociopathic tendencies or an anti-social personality disorder (meaning he or she has no sense of shame, guilt or feelings of remorse over wrong acts committed; does not follow the golden rule and does not care about the feelings of others), can commit a wrong act, lie, kill, and steal and feel quite comfortable in doing so. Such individuals will even blame the victim or those who oppose them as the ones at fault. I saw such behavior and attitude among some gang involved individuals in New York City, reminiscence of Al Capone, the child of Italian immigrants who became a notorious Chicago gang leader of the Prohibition era; these individuals presented a smooth polished exterior, always stylishly dressed and even gave gifts to the poor, but they had no conscience about killing anyone that dared to cross their path or were seemingly in competition with them. They were like Cain who killed his brother Abel and had no remorse over doing so. After killing his brother, *And the Lord said unto Cain, "Why art thou wroth? and why is thy countenance fallen? If thou doest well, shalt thou not be accepted? and if thou doest not well, sin lieth at the door. And unto thee shall be his desire, and thou shalt rule over him." (Read Gen 4: 6-7).*

Because of Cain's refusal to accept that he did wrong, he separated himself from God and became a wanderer. Wandering from God suggests a rejection of anything God commands and a resorting to secularistic or atheistic beliefs and ungodlike behaviors. Wandering in disobedience may also lead to engagement in all types of self-destructive beliefs, practices and behaviors that can become as curses in your life. In Cain's case, God asked for a blood sacrifice, but Cain willfully decided to disobey and pleased himself by offering a grain sacrifice. Yet when his sacrifice was rejected, he became angry, jealous and resentful to the point of killing his own brother.

You cannot choose to live a life style that is contrary to God's will and commands and expect to enjoy the benefits of a close spiritual connection with Him. Light and darkness cannot coexist. An openly rebellious child does not enjoy a close relationship with his or her parents. Similarly, sin or disobedience separates from God and with separation comes deviance. The further we drift from Godly principles, the more deviant we become. It is true that God sends His rain on those that have a relationship with Him and those that do not; indeed, a loving parent will always make provision even for a disobedient child. In a democracy, we enjoy the benefits of certain policies of an elected government, whether we support that party or not. However, you should choose to enjoy a personal relationship with God based on love and obedience and not on the benefits. Deuteronomy chapters 28-31 outlines all the promised blessings and curses that result from both obedience and disobedience: *I call heaven and earth to record this day that I have set before you life and death, blessing and cursing; therefore, choose life that both thou and thy seed may live and; that thou mayest love the Lord thy God and that thou mayest obey his voice (Deut. 30:19 & 20).*

A Connection with God is a Life-Giving Power. Failing to connect with God is like having electricity in your home and not turning on the switch. If you don't turn on the switch, you will grope or wander in darkness and cling to anything or anyone that gives you a sense of security. Therefore, the goal of spirituality is to restore one's personal relationship with God through self-surrender and obedience. Obedience and doing what are right leads to restoration and righteousness–meaning right doing; *For as many as are led by the Spirit of God, they are the sons of God. (Romans 8:14).* Association with like-minded individuals that share the same desire to grow in obedience helps to promote and maintain those beliefs because of the encouragement provided to one another.

Why So Many Beliefs? Some of the reasons that there are so many beliefs, philosophies, religions and cults are because of religious conflicts, disagreements and disappointments experienced by individuals. Usually, an organization, religious group or a church is formed when like-minded individuals unite together. The organization, church or group may break up or splinter when one individual or a group of individuals begin to differ in their perspective and views. Sometimes certain influential individuals may experience disappointment in their expectations of God and develop new ideas or beliefs about God and influence others to do the same. The age of Enlightenment and the rise in Humanism proliferated after the bubonic plague, which came to be known as the "Black Death," had wiped out 200 million people between Europe and Asia in the 14th century. Because of this expansive devastation, some philosophers and intellectuals abandoned their belief in a supernatural God because in their eyes, God failed to save people supernaturally from death and diseases. Disappointment in God can impact in whom or what you choose to believe. A religious young man I know quite well decided there was no God, after going to church one Sunday and upon returning saw his home go up in flames. He could not understand why God did not protect his house while he was in church, praying to God. Because of his anger and disappointment with God, he has since declared that money is god, for in his eyes, his family had to find money to rebuild their house. Many atheistic beliefs have resulted from disappointment in God or disappointment in individuals who have been entrusted with positions of power in the church and have abused that power.

The Seventh Day Adventist church was born out of a great disappointment experienced by some 10,000 Baptist believers who hung their faith on the predictions of William Miller, a charismatic Baptist preacher who believed from his study of Bible prophecy that the second advent of Jesus would appear in 1844. When Jesus did not return, many gave up their belief in God, but a small group of believers went back to studying the Bible and from their study, they determined that Miller had misinterpreted the prophecies of Daniel chapters 7 & 8. This group of believers maintained their faith in the second advent of Christ and came to be known as Adventists.

Cultural and Familial Influences: The genre of music that is used for the worship experience; familial traditions, cultural preference, associations, friendships and occupations are also factors that could possibly influence the style of worship and even contribute to the splintering of a religious group. These differences may account for reasons why some churches or places of worship appear to be more spiritual or more conservative than others. In California and New York, I frequented different churches within a two-mile radius and saw these differences to be quite apparent. I also saw in England, where a whole congregation of white people abandoned a church when people from the Caribbean began obtaining membership in large numbers. It was as though two different cultures and approaches to worship collided and could not coexist in the same church. The white people's approach to worship was brief with less time spent engaging in praise and testimonies and less socializing in church; while the people from the Caribbean had longer worship services and spent more time in church praising and bonding around their shared cultural experience as strangers in a foreign land. These differences led to cliques and possibly contributed to the separation.

Be Very Careful of Cults: My grandmother used to say, "misery loves company" and usually cult leaders are individuals in rebellion against God and make of themselves a god. They desire only to be worshipped. A cult leader is like a captain in a ship on water who drills a hole in the bottom of the ship with everyone on board. Usually a cult has one leader - a sociopath who commands a following and strict adherence to a rigid set of rules; or is a narcissist who engages in "gas-lighting" or covert manipulations. Often these individuals are extremely charismatic and lead by the cult of personality; they vilify and berate those who dare criticize them and through subtlety and the use of hypnotic language and double binds trap vulnerable individuals in no-win situations to the point of insanity and self-destruction. I recall visiting a neighboring Seventh Day Adventist church in England, just after graduating from university, and meeting followers of David Koresh's Branch Davidian at the church; they were secretly recruiting new members and invited me and a friend to have lunch with them. These people were very charming and professed to have a "higher light," but were impatient and dismissive of anyone who did not agree with them or dared to point out the error of their ways. It is important to remember that God does not force your will, choice or judgment, nor does He take pleasure in slavish obedience. He gives you free choice. *He desires that the creatures of His hands shall love Him because He is worthy of love. He would have them obey Him because they have an intelligent appreciation of His wisdom, justice, and benevolence… The principles of kindness, mercy and love taught and exemplified by our savior [Jesus] are a transcript of the character of God (E. G. White, Great Controversy, p.541).*

Beliefs & Organized Religion: Organized religion or church attendance can help you grow spiritually as well as help you nurture and maintain your spiritual beliefs. My favorite worship service is Wednesday night prayer meeting. I also enjoy Sabbath school - otherwise referred to as "the church at study" in the Adventist church. Fellowship and a study of the Bible nourish your mind and spirit, which ultimately leads to lifestyle changes because. ….. *For the word of God is quick, and powerful, and sharper than any two edged sword, piercing even to the dividing asunder of soul and spirit, and of the joints and marrow, and is a discerner of the thoughts and intents of the heart* (Heb. 4:12).

Worship with others that share a common goal benefits the soul. This is one of the reasons that self-help groups work so well. Without support and nurturance, before long, you may become spiritually weak or relapse into old behaviors or habits. Think of a log wood fire, if you remove one stick from the fire it will eventually go out but left in the fire it will keep burning. Therefore: *Not forsaking the assembling of ourselves together, as the manner of some is; but exhorting one another: and so much the more, as ye see the day approaching. (Hebrews 10:25).*

It is estimated that there are over 4,000 religions in the world and in my study of some of the more well-known and not so well-known religions, I have learned many important life lessons: From Judaism, I have learned the blessing of resting or refraining from my usual course of business on the Sabbath in acknowledgement of the creator God. From the Buddhist, I have learned the importance of practicing meditation, temperance and balance. According to the Buddhist, prayer is talking to God, but meditation is allowing God to talk to you. From the Animist, I have developed an appreciation for nature as the medium through which nature's God speaks to us. From the Hindus, Dama, Karma and Dana: Dama meaning self-control, Karma-you reap what you sow and Dana-share what you have with others. From the Sikhs, the importance of family rituals and the mental health benefits of refraining from indulgence in any form of intoxicant such as alcohol, narcotics or other substances; from Scientology – knowing how to know or obtaining knowledge can free you from self-doubt, insecurities and despair; from the Catholics, the mental health benefits of confessing one's sin and the healing power of forgiveness. From the Mormons - the power of the collective consciousness, patriotism and Bible study; from the Mennonites - justice, simplicity, community, and mutual aid; from the Episcopalian – The Eucharist as a perpetual reminder that Christ suffered crucifixion for all people regardless of their place of birth, ethnicity or national origin and that at the foot of the cross all people are equal. From the Salvation Army, charity and the mental health benefits of being charitable; from the Baptist - Baptism by emersion as symbolic of a spiritual birth and a public confession of a life style change; from the Methodist - faith and good works go hand in hand, but it is God's grace that sustains the believer; from Islam - the importance of prayer and reverence to God as the supreme being; from the Coptic Orthodox Christians - faithfulness under persecution; the Jehovah's Witnesses - the importance of witnessing or sharing one's faith to help those who might be searching for meaning at a point when life may seem totally meaningless; from the Pentecostal - the importance and power of praise and thanksgiving to change things when the odds are against you; from the Rastafarian - the health benefits of eating clean as opposed to unclean foods and of course, a knowledge of my royal

African roots; from the Allen African Methodist and Episcopal (AME), mutual aid and self-help in the face of racial discrimination, and from the Seventh-day Adventist - the importance of developing one's mind through education, the body through healthful living, and maintaining a spiritual connection with God through prayer and a personal study of the Bible.

Having learned all these lessons, I have also come to realize that simply ascribing to a religious belief becomes meaningless if it does not transform your life into something meaningful....*The darkest chapters of history are burdened with the record of crimes committed by bigoted religionists...The same danger still exists. Many take it for granted that they are Christians, simply because they subscribe to certain theological tenets. But they have not brought the truth into practical life...if it does not make them sincere, kind, patient, forbearing, heavenly minded, it is a curse to its possessors, and through their influence it is a curse to the world. The righteousness which Christ taught is conformity of heart and life to the revealed will of God (E.G. White, The Desire of Ages. P. 309-310).*

Jesus & the Bible: While I have gained much knowledge from the many religions and beliefs explored, I have chosen to allow the Bible to serve as my guide and Jesus Christ as my supreme example of how I must live and treat others. In line with Pauline teaching, I see Jesus as the visible personification of an invisible God. His death on Calvary fulfilled the plan of salvation for humanity. Through Christ's death and his shed blood, I do not need to offer sacrifices of lambs for my sins. Controlled by the mind of Christ and infused by his spirit, I can choose to consecrate my life daily in developing Christian character.

After Christ's death and resurrection, Christianity spread throughout the Roman Empire, Greece, Asia Minor, and Egypt and many distinctly Jewish practices concerning circumcision and foods considered unclean –ceremonial laws were eventually dropped. The Saturday Sabbath, although practiced since creation was also changed to Sunday to accommodate the Pagans who were Sun worshippers. Emperor Constantine who converted to Christianity in 312 AD and the Council of Nicaea, sought to bring about religious unity among Christians and Pagans through various compromises. Their compromise had a profound influence on the books that were included in the Bible, and the substitution of holy days such as Christmas and Easter for the pagan holy days occurring at the same time. The Romans celebrated the birth of the sun God on December 25, so Constantine introduced the worship of "Christ-mass" instead. The compromise of the pagan holy days provided heightened economic activity and was rejected by some protestant reformers. Since then however, because of the focus by Christians on Christ birth and his death, these holy days have come to be regarded as Christian holidays and traditions in many Christian churches; ironically, these celebrations are banned in some Muslim and atheistic countries because of the association with Christianity. Despite these compromises, I do not see the Bible as an epic fiction or in the words of one atheist, "whimsical totems and taboos of the demons and deities who emerged with us from our cave-dwellings at the end of the Paleolithic Era." Rather, I see it as a powerful God inspired book that can elevate the mind. Indeed, it is the one book known to have transformed many lives.

Creation, Evolution & Life Form: I do not consider the biblical creation story allegorical because quite simply, as an artist creates a master piece or an inventor an invention, I am convinced that for all things created there is an original creator; something cannot come out of nothing. When I look at the mathematical precision of human organs and the beauty and wonder of nature in general, I can only conclude that there must be a "God" of superior intelligence who is the original creator and master mind behind such awesome design. *Great is the Lord and greatly to be praised; And His greatness is unsearchable.... All thy works shall praise thee, O Lord; and thy saints shall bless thee. They shall speak of the glory of thy kingdom, and talk of thy power (Psalm, 145:3, 11, 14).*

Even Charles Darwin, a naturalist who formulated the theory of evolution had to admit, some 20 years after the publication of his seminal work *The Origin of Species*, that there were still aspects of evolution that puzzled him. Chief among these was the flower, which he referred to as "an abominable mystery" and "a most perplexing phenomenon." I accept certain aspects of evolution resulting from mutation, amalgamation and genetic drift, but in line with the Bible, I believe that originally, things were created in an orderly fashion and mathematically designed rather than in a haphazard fashion. Believing in a creator God may sound simplistic and trite, but for me, the weight of evidence in nature and my personal experience of the miracle working power of God in my life and shared in this book is enough to strengthen my faith and belief in God. It was the Psalmist David who said: *The fool hath said in his heart, There is no God. They are corrupt, they have done abominable works, there is none that doeth good. Ps.14:1.* Furthermore, I would prefer to believe that I am the product of a master artist and a created being than the by-product of a fish or an ape. Believing that I evolved from an animal does absolutely nothing for my sense of self-worth, how I relate to others or the estimate that I place on myself. It certainly does nothing to help me realize my potential or help me become all that God intends for me. It was Thomas Carlyle that said: *Let each become all he was created capable of becoming.*

I believe in a supreme being, who is omnipotent, omnipresent and omniscient. Some people call Him Yahweh, Allah, Guru, or higher power; I call Him heavenly father, creator God who knows everything about me; Jehovah, the one who is in total control; the God of Abraham, Isaac and Jacob, my provider; the one who loves me unconditionally, despite my imperfections, failures, shortfalls and downfalls. I believe that He along with His team (He said let us) created life form. Evolutionary biology explains how things evolve through mutation, amalgamation or genetic drift, but it does not explain where the very first living cell or life form came from or why one species of bird or fish does not change into another species. Indeed, there are over three million species on earth, and they have all stubbornly remained within their own specie.

The Beginning: According to the Bible (Genesis 2:7-14) and confirmed by anthropologist and archeologist, life on earth began in the North African region - where the River Nile ran through the Garden of Eden located somewhere near Ethiopia. Natural disasters however, such as tsunamis, glacial storms, earth quakes, famines, hurricanes and volcanic eruptions have resulted in population drift, interbreeding or even a cut-off in life form in certain locations. After Hurricane Sandy devastated certain parts of New York - flooding buildings and shutting down power lines, I visited South Street Sea Port and was amazed at how desolate the place looked. I imagined then what it must have been like after Noah's cataclysmic flood. The devastation of the flood in Noah's time wiped out people and animals, moved landmarks out of place and upset rivers and valleys. It was as though a world had ended and mankind (Noah and his family) were starting a new beginning.

Aristotle and other major thinkers do not believe there is a "beginning" and I must admit that I cannot explain "the beginning" because by implication, there is more than one beginning. Evidently God and other beings existed before he created planet earth since he said, "Let us make man." Therefore, planet earth, which is estimated to be about 6,000 years old, is just one of His amazing created masterpieces in the universe; other life forms could have been created millions of years before God created planet earth. Recently astronomers at NASA discovered seven earth-sized planets orbiting around the constellation Aquarius; they are estimated to be 39 light years away and warm enough to have water or life form. I like the statement by Jewish scholar, Reb Jeff, which suggests that the world has a beginning, but it is a beginning that has never ceased. The important point then is not for you to be concerned about the beginning but rather your reason for being here. Moses did not write the creation story to tell you exactly when life form began, but rather to explain that you are here through purposeful design and not by chance or happenstance. You are included in God's amazing masterpiece and you were created for His glory.

There is much that we do not know about creation and efforts made by scientist to *penetrate into the future world* and to have the secrets of eternal mysteries disclosed have proven futile....*The imagination may summon its utmost powers in order to picture the glories of heaven, but "But as it is written, Eye hath not seen, nor ear heard, neither have entered into the heart of man, the things which God hath prepared for them that love him." (1Corinthians 2:9; E.G. White, In Heavenly Places p.366).* We should not doubt God's word because we cannot understand the mysteries of His creation. *"In the natural world we are constantly surrounded with wonders beyond our comprehension; should we then be surprised to find in the spiritual world also mysteries that we cannot fathom? The difficulty lies solely in the weakness and narrowness of the human mind."* — Ellen G. White, *Education*, p. 170.

When I was a child and lived in the beautiful island of Jamaica, my understanding of the world was limited to my experience of living in Jamaica and what I had read in books; then I travelled to Europe and to the United States and other parts of the world and my world view expanded. Similarly, my knowledge of God and his creative power is based on what I have read, what I have seen in nature and what I have experienced and heard over the years. I have never seen God, but I cannot imagine a world without a creator God. Indeed, there is an innate desire in everyone to worship something. I choose to worship the creator God rather than the things He created. Without a belief in God, I would have no real moral compass. I would simply do what instinctively feels right, which would be guided by my circumstances rather than a set of beliefs couched in a moral code of conduct.

The Biblical Code of Ethics: Each professional organization has its own code of ethics or morals to live by; the 10 Commandments, given to Moses by God is seen as the code of ethics or moral code of conduct for humanity. As I reflect on the experience of African Americans who were enslaved for hundreds of years and then abruptly given their freedom without a leader, without guidance, and without an inheritance - drowning in despair and chaos - I can only imagine the challenges that Moses faced, in leaving Egypt with over 600,000 people who had been enslaved. Conceivably, without any established rules of conduct, Moses' effort in leading an unruly mob striving for power amid freedom, must have been absolute bedlam. Their wayward, raucous and idolatrous behavior after Moses went up into the mountain to commune with God is an example of the challenges Moses faced in leading them. Is it any wonder that upon his return and observing their behavior, his old righteous anger problem resurfaced and rose to the point of his reacting by breaking the first edition of the 10 Commandments?

Codes of ethics are formed to address problem behavior and the Ten Commandments became the rules of conduct for the unruly Israelites, which provided guidance and order out of chaos.

The Ten Commandments found in Exodus 20:1-17 teaches important relationship skills. It teaches how to relate to God, to material things and to others. Thomas Jefferson referred to the Ten Commandments as "the law to which man is subjected by his creator." From the Ten Commandments, I have learned how to build a personal relationship with God and how to live with and treat others. Without the commandments, if I were to accept evolution as the basis for my belief, then I need only rely on animalistic instincts to dictate my behavior and my treatment of others. I would also have to trace my ancestry back to animals. I prefer to believe that I am a descendant of created human beings for...... *And the Lord hath avouched thee this day to be his peculiar people, as he hath promised thee, and that thou shouldest keep all his commandments; And to make thee high above all nations which he hath made, in praise, and in name, and in honour; and that thou mayest be an holy people unto the Lord thy God, as he hath spoken. (Deut. 26:18 & 19).*

It is this belief that God is creator and that ownership belongs to Him that serves as the core of my spiritual belief. As a core belief, I accept that God is all powerful, sees everything, knows everything and does everything well and for a purpose. Even disappointments work for my good. This belief has sustained my faith in difficult times, given me mental stability and clarity and has helped me to cope with life's challenges and adversities. In the grand scheme of things, I accept God as creator and nature as His lesson book. I also trace my ancestry back to his created beings. If you believe this, you too can walk with pride and with your head held high because in the words of the Apostle Peter: *"But ye are a chosen generation, a royal priesthood, an holy nation, a peculiar people; that ye should shew forth the praises of him who hath called you out of darkness into his marvelous light;" (1Peter 2:9).*

God's Master Plan: My personal perception of God is that of a loving parent who makes preparation for the arrival of a newborn. God created the earth with everything needful for life form: air, water, light, gases and plants for food. Everything was done with precision and order. Like a master painter or craftsman, no detail was missed. Even the very whirlwind has its place in gathering the autumn leaves at the end of autumn. God gave us nature, which is ultimately all that we need to survive, and He did all this before He created humans and animals to inhabit planet earth. Like a loving parent, who prioritizes the needs of his children, God makes preparation for His children. He makes preparation for you too. Every day is a new day filled with His love and endless possibilities. I do not see God as an autocratic dictator or a passive and permissive creator. God gives His created beings the power of choice, but He also establishes limits and boundaries through His commandments, and He does it out of love (for our own good); He also outlines the consequences when we deviate from His commands. Yet, when we become deviants, He doesn't give up on us. In the same way He went looking for Adam and Eve after they disobeyed and for Cain after he killed his brother, His love for us is unconditional and He seeks always to restore us to Himself. He says: *"I love them that love me; and those that seek me early shall find me. Riches and honour are with me; yea, durable riches and righteousness. My fruit is better than gold, yea, than fine gold; and my revenue than choice silver." (Prov. 8:17-19).*

Sin is another concept whose roots I cannot fully explain except through the eyes of a loving parent with a teenager who is in total rebellion and is unresponsive to counsel, structure and guidance. It is said that *...And there was war in heaven: Michael and his angels fought against* *the dragon; and the dragon fought and his angels, And prevailed not; neither was their place found any more in heaven. And the great dragon was cast out, that old serpent, called the Devil, and Satan, which deceiveth the whole world: he was cast out into the earth, and his angels were cast out with him. (Rev.12:7-12).* A child is not born rebellious, but over the years, his *"will"* takes over as in Satan's case. I worked for many years with teens in rebellion whose parents had given up on them. They were all angry with their parents for real or perceived wrongs done to them and harbored resentment against their parents. These teens would create havoc in the home and outside of the home until the parents had to surrender them to the authorities. Some of these parents simply "washed their hands" of their rebellious teens, but there were others who having tried everything, had to allow experience to be their teen's teacher and through unconditional positive regard establish a redemptive plan for the child - meaning they would only accept the child back if or when he or she decides to change his or her rebellious ways. I see sin and salvation in the same light. Sin or disobedience destroys lives, but obedience leads ultimately to salvation - a life of freedom from destructive behaviors and practices. For Christians, Jesus [Michael] is all part of that redemptive plan. He is like the older sibling who steps in to help fight your spiritual battles when turning from a life of disobedience becomes too difficult. I do not see God's relationship with his created beings as dictatorial, one sided or didactic. It is reciprocal and unconditional; therefore, if I genuinely love God and believe that He loves me unconditionally, then I must show my love through reciprocity and by heeding His commands. *If ye love me, keep my commandments. (John 14:15).*

In working with children and in observing my own, I have observed that a child who feels loved unconditionally is not hard to discipline because obedience comes from knowing that whatever commands or discipline the parents give are not grievous and are given out of love. The Ten Commandments that God gave to Moses are all about God's love for humanity. The first four commandments are about showing your love for God, the last six are about showing your love for others. Of the 10 commandments, the fourth is a reminder and the fifth is a promise.

The fifth commandment begins the series of six commandments that provide counsels on how to treat others. The first of the five starts with an admonition that you must show love for your parents - your family and in so doing, you will be rewarded. Your first honor, however, should go to God. Malachi 1:6 says: *"A son honoureth his father, and a servant his master: if then I be a father, where is mine honour? and if I be a master, where is my fear? saith the Lord of hosts unto you, O priests, that despise my name. And ye say, Wherein have we despised thy name?* It is interesting that only the fourth commandment, which is among the first four, stands out as a reminder to honor God on the seventh day. Ex 20:8-11 says: *I am the Lord thy God, which have brought thee out of the land of Egypt, out of the house of bondage. Thou shalt have no other gods before me. Thou shalt not make unto thee any graven image, or any likeness of any thing that is in heaven above, or that is in the earth beneath, or that is in the water under the earth. Thou shalt not bow down thyself to them, nor serve them: for I the Lord thy God am a jealous God, visiting the iniquity of the fathers upon the children unto the third and fourth generation of them that hate me; And shewing mercy unto thousands of them that love me, and keep my commandments. Thou shalt not take the name of the Lord thy God in vain; for the Lord will not hold him guiltless that taketh his name in vain. Remember the sabbath day, to keep it holy..* A reminder to keep the Sabbath day Holy suggests that the Sabbath existed before the Ten Commandments. I can only remind my child of a task if I had instructed her previously to do the task.

According to the book of Genesis in the Bible, after creation was completed God rested on the seventh day. Biblically, the only day of the week that was given a name was the seventh day – the Sabbath. The Anglo Saxons gave names to the days of the week based on the names of their gods and the planets, starting with Sunday – the sun god, followed by Monday - the moon and so on, but to remember the Sabbath Day is to acknowledge God's creative power and keep afresh in your memory, His unconditional love for you. We honor our national heroes on a given day as a sign of gratitude for the sacrifices they made for us, so why should we not take one day out of the week to honor God our creator? On the 7th day Sabbath, I refrain from secular work and activities in order to worship God and "delight" in the Sabbath. God knew what he was doing when he gave us the 7th day Sabbath; studies on the mental health benefits of worshipping on the Sabbath have found it to provide a structure for emotional expression, help to reduce anxiety and improvement in overall mental health. Through this very act of worshiping on the Sabbath, God also promises a special blessing. He says: *If thou turn away thy foot from the sabbath, from doing thy pleasure on my holy day; and call the sabbath a delight, the holy of the Lord, honourable; and shalt honour him, not doing thine own ways, nor finding thine own pleasure, nor speaking thine own words: Then shalt thou delight thyself in the Lord; and I will cause thee to ride upon the high places of the earth, and feed thee with the heritage of Jacob thy father: for the mouth of the Lord hath spoken it.(Isaiah 58:13 &14).*

Putting Stuff into Perspective: My belief in God helps me to put my very existence into perspective. I see life as a journey and heaven, or the earth made new as my ultimate destination. It is by faith that I hold this belief because I have never seen God or heaven. This is where this book is different from other "success" books you may have read. This book is not about accumulating 'stuff" (material blessings). Rather, it is about being a blessing through the "stuff" that God provides for your enjoyment while on this earthly journey. If everything comes from God, then there isn't anything that you need that He cannot supply because: *And it shall come to pass, that before they call, I will answer; and while they are yet speaking, I will hear.* (Is. 65:24). I am also learning not to cling too tightly to the stuff that He supplies because for sure I will not need them in death or in the earth made new. When I left Jamaica for England, all I could take with me was a suitcase (a tan colored 'grip' as we called it then) and when I left England for the United States, I was only allowed two pieces of check-in luggage. All the "stuff" I had accumulated over the years, I had to give away or leave behind. Upon arrival in the new country, I soon forgot about all the old stuff that I left behind and began accumulating new stuff, which soon became old – a brand new car is considered used once the title is handed over to you and you drive it out of the show room. The question is - how much "stuff," do you really need in life to feel satisfied? My many camping trips with Pathfinders into the woods and sleeping under a tent and in a sleeping bag, without the creature comforts of life and just a few essential items of clothing and toiletries in a duffle bag has taught me that I really do not need much "stuff" to be happy. I can understand why Agur says in Proverbs 30:8 *"…Remove far from me vanity and lies: give me neither poverty nor riches; feed me with food convenient for me"*

This book uses the Bible (many versions) as the foundation for understanding God's awesomeness and His power to change, wonderfully change, the most difficult of circumstances. He can improve your mental health and bring blessings, honor, riches and favors –features we call success - into your life. Since God is your creator, He knows enough about you to know what is best for you. If you are submissive to Him and trust Him, He will decide what "stuff" to remove from

your life, and what to allow. As you submit to Him, He can help you
become spiritually intelligent and live a rich and rewarding life. This
does not mean you will not experience heartache and disappointment,
but because you trust God implicitly and are obeying His will even
disappointments will work for your good. This book is therefore a
confirmation of the infinite power of God to do for you more than you
can ask or think. Essentially it is about getting up after being knocked
down; it is about bouncing back after life has struck you some extra
difficult blows. And, it's about obtaining your deepest desires consistent
with God's will, because *the desire of the righteous shall be granted. (Prov.10:
24). Every saint who comes to God with a true heart and sends his honest petition
to Him in faith will have his prayers answered (E. G. White, Testimonies, Vol.1,
p.120-121). And, behold, I am with thee, and will keep thee in all places whither
thou goest, and will bring thee again into this land; for I will not leave thee, until I
have done that which I have spoken to thee of. (Gen 28.15).*

Your Constructive Action Plan Learn the Ten Commandments
found in Exodus 20 and let them become the guide to your code of conduct.
The following is an abridged version of the Ten Commandments. The
first four are instructions and a reminder to love God and the next six
to love your fellowmen - starting with your family. If you accept and
follow the first four commandments as the rule of law for your life, like
the patriarch Joseph you will not break the other six because all ten
are inseparably linked. You cannot love God and love your neighbor
as yourself and then commit adultery because you would first consider
your love for God and your love for your family before choosing to sin.

An Abridged Version of the Ten Commandments

1. *Do not have other gods.*
2. *Do not create or set up anything or person to worship as a god.*
3. *Honor and respect God's name.*
4. *Remember to keep the Sabbath day holy.*
5. *Honor your parents to have a long and productive life.*
6. *Do not murder anyone*
7. *Do not commit adultery.*
8. *Do not steal.*
9. *Do not lie and perjure yourself.*
10. *Do not covet or envy.*

Your 2nd Gem

YOUR LIFE'S JOURNEY

Trust in the Lord with all thine heart; and lean not unto thine own understanding. In all thy ways acknowledge him, and he shall direct thy paths. (Prov. 3:5 & 6). The road to success is not a smooth way over which we are borne in palace cars, but it is a rugged path filled with obstacles which can be surmounted by patient toil" (E.G. White Testimony Treasures, p.605).

The phrase "life is a journey and not a destination" is popularized and quoted often as though it is fact; but think for a moment, if life is a journey without a destination, aren't we simply wandering through life aimlessly? If you don't know where you are going how will you know which road to take or when you have arrived? Life is not just a journey; it is both a journey and a destination or a series of destinations with one ultimate destination. What you determine to be your ultimate destination will depend upon your spiritual outlook on life. I think Steve Jobs, founder of Apple computer puts it best before his passing when he said, "No one wants to die, even people who want to go to heaven don't want to die to get there, and yet, death is the destination we all share. No one has ever escaped it." Indeed, there are two realities of life that we all must face: The first is our birth and the other is our death. Unfortunately, nature is not too selective about who become parents and therefore you do not have a choice about the circumstances under which you start out on life's journey. You do have a choice however; about the route you choose to take. You may have started out on life's journey under unfavorable circumstances that are beyond your control, but once you can exercise choice and are able to make decisions about your future, you can begin to change course and create your own path.

<u>Suicide is Not Your Option</u>: Some individuals have chosen to end the journey prematurely by taking their lives, but this is a foolish choice because who knows what tomorrow will bring. Change can happen overnight. If you have a disease, a remedy for the disease can be announced at any time because scientists are always conducting research and each day new discoveries are made. If a relationship has ended, you may find someone better. If you lose all your money or fail your exams, you have a mind; you can try again or start another business. If your misdeeds will lead to you receiving jail time and bring shame and embarrassment to your family, they will forgive you eventually and you will have a life lesson to share. Don't give in to the shame and hurt feelings. Ask instead: What can I learn from this experience and how can I use my experience to be a blessing to myself and others? Indeed, if anyone ought to have chosen suicide it was the patriarch Job, who lost everything in a gut-wrenching way; he lost his health, his wealth and his family, but he chose to maintain a steadfast faith in God instead of opting out on life.

The story was told of a man who invested in a business that failed. He went to a park and sat on a park bench and was contemplating suicide when he was approached by an elderly gentleman. He shared his story with the elderly man and in response the elderly gentleman took out his check book and wrote him a check for a large sum of money. "Now go and start another business, but only use the check if you desperately need it," the elderly man counseled. The suicidal man became hopeful again; he went off and started another business, which was phenomenally successful. To his surprise, he never used the check that the man had given him. He returned to the park to find the man, share his success story and return the check. He soon learned from his inquiry that the man was demented and often wrote worthless checks and gave them to people, but he had no money. While the check had no worth, it gave the suicidal man much needed confidence to believe in himself again and restore his hope in the future.

In most cases, being suicidal means, you are in pain and you want the pain to end; you feel your situation is hopeless and you cannot see any way out or things changing for the better. It is not your life that you want to end, but the powerlessness or pain that you feel. The problem with suicide is that it is not reversible; the pain you are experiencing however can be treated or managed. If you feel like you are in a deep hole, God can airlift you out. Your circumstances can change for the better. Don't cheat on life. The story was told of two frogs that fell in a bucket of milk. One frog just gave up and died while the other thought of his family and reasons to live and kept jumping up and down to get out. Eventually his repeated efforts resulted in the milk churning into butter and a base formed for him to jump out.

Don't Give in to Hopelessness: If God had called you by name and said to you that your present ordeal would lead to you becoming a huge success, would you still want to give up? Perhaps not; it is your surrendering to hopelessness that leads to despair. Bees navigate naturally towards the sun so if placed in an open glass jar with a light at the bottom of the jar it will gravitate towards the light and will remain focused on getting out by way of the light until it perishes, while if you do the same with flies, the flies will find their way out in a quick second. Yet bees are more productive than flies and considered even more intelligent; flies on the other hand, while less intelligent are more resourceful, willing to change direction and explore new ideas. Similarly, as smart as you are, unless you are willing to accept change, see things differently and explore new options, like the bees you will remain stuck in a state of hopelessness. If like the fly however, you are willing to explore your options and the alternatives available in the face of life's challenges you will be more likely to succeed.

Move from Fear to Faith: The story of the patriarch Job is that of a man who had every reason to commit suicide. Even his self-indulgent wife encouraged him to curse God and commit suicide. Job lost his business, his children, his home and to top it all his health; sores, maybe cancer - skin lymphoma caused by a weakened immune system (because we all have cancer cells that can be activated under stress and a lowered immune system) began eating away at his body.

Indeed, having lost everything, Job had every reason to end it all, but in his pain, he said: "Though they slay me, yet will I trust in Him." In other words, although he had lost everything, he still had hope. He believed in an all-powerful God who had given him everything he had. He said, "the Lord gives, and the Lord takes away." He also had faith that whatever spiritual warfare he was in, God would fight the battle for him; as a result, God honored his faith and restored his wealth with twice as much as he had before. His "cancer" disappeared, and his health was restored. He was also blessed with a new family. A study published in the Southern Medical Journal in 2004 associated personal faith with better health outcomes such as improved immune function, lower death rates from cancer, less heart problems, lower blood pressure, lower cholesterol and even better health behaviors such as less cigarette smoking; more exercise, and better sleep. You could say Job's move from fear of the things which came upon him to implicit faith in God fired up his immune system and helped restore his health. Moving from focusing on death to focusing on life begins in the mind. It begins with thinking right and living right. In the words of Paul, you must become *And be not conformed to this world: but be ye transformed by the renewing of your mind, that ye may prove what is that good, and acceptable, and perfect, will of God." (Romans 12:2)*. David wrote, "What *time I am afraid, I will trust in thee. In God I will praise his word, in God I have put my trust; I will not fear what flesh can do unto me." (Psalm 56:3, 4)*.

When you were born you received a birth certificate, but it did not have an expiration date on it. Death is the ultimate end of the road on this earth for everyone because we all have a warranty on life with an unknown expiration date. Not knowing the expiration date should help dictate how you live your life and how you embrace your end. You are on this earth for a purpose and not to live for yourself alone. I remember as a child my grandmother told me the story of a man who came up on hard times and had lost everything; all he had left was one banana. He decided to eat the banana, climb the tree and take his life. After eating the banana, he dropped the skin on the ground. To his surprise, a man came along, picked up the skin and began eating it. Observing someone in a worse shape than he, the disheartened man came down from the tree and decided to go on and live his life with purpose. Your situation may be bad, but there is always someone who is in a worse situation than you are. I gave a homeless person at a New York City subway station begging for food a sandwich. He thanked me and promptly gave it to another homeless person, saying "he hasn't eaten yet." If you can accept this fact, then there is absolutely no reason to give up on the journey of life prematurely. You must continue the journey. Choose life over death and stop dying and start living.

You are on This Earth to Glorify God: How does ending your life prematurely bring glory to God or to anyone else for that matter? How does taking your life help a starving, emaciated or abused child who has no one to love or care for him? Take a trip to a developing country and see the face of that poor starving child with putrefying sores to the corners of his mouth due to pellagra and a swollen stomach due to malnutrition; what can you do to help? Stop focusing on yourself for a moment and begin to think how you could make a difference in this child's life. Jesus is your example. Upon his crucifixion he said: *"I have glorified thee on earth: I have finished the work which Thou gavest me to do…I have manifested Thy name."* (John 17:4-6). Your life should bring glory to God, not to yourself. What are you doing to make that happen? The Apostle Paul was a persecutor of Christians, but after his conversion experience he was satisfied with his life and in looking forward to his new tomorrow declared: *"I have fought a good fight, I have finished my course, I have kept the faith: Henceforth there is laid up for me a crown of righteousness, which the Lord, the righteous judge, shall give me at that day: and not to me only, but unto all them also that love his appearing." (2 Tim. 4:7-8).*

Knowing there is an end in view, you must not live your life aimlessly, in a vacuum, or leave everything to chance or randomness. You must seek to create your own path on your life's journey. Yes, the path of life will be rough sometimes, mountainous with peaks and valleys. There are some huge potholes too, but that's the reality of living in a world where good and evil exist. You must equip yourself with aims, goals, purpose, character and an abundance of faith and courage. You must also learn from those that have created paths and have left footprints behind. This book is littered with names of individuals that have been an inspiration to me. As you reflect on their lives, give some thought to what your obituary will say about you at your funeral or better yet, write your own obituary and begin to live your life accordingly. In the words of Henry W. Longfellow: *Lives of great men all remind us we can make our lives sublime, and departing, leave behind us footprints on the sands of time. Footprints, that perhaps another, travelling o'er life's solemn main, a forlorn and shipwrecked brother, seeing, shall take heart again. Let us, then, be up and doing. With a heart for any fate; Still achieving, still pursuing, learn to labor and to wait.*

Creating a Path: A road can only be paved after a path has been made, so seek to create your own path rather than follow someone else's trail. I read a story of a man who was driving along a country road and lost his way. It was a very dark night and he could hardly see ahead so he decided to follow behind another car; suddenly the car in front came to a halt and the poor lost soul found that he had followed the driver into the man's car port. There is nothing wrong in following someone if you are lost and you know that you are lost; indeed, it is smart to follow the guidance of someone (a parent, mentor, counselor or coach) who can steer you back on course until you find your way. Once you have found your way however, you can begin to create your own path by monitoring your thoughts, words and actions. Your thoughts precede your emotions, words and actions so you must be careful about how you channel your thoughts. Consider even now if your thoughts are catastrophizing, envious or uplifting.

In the book of Genesis, the very first book in the Bible, we have the case of Cain who was born to Adam and Eve, the first created couple. Cain did not have peers, neighbors, grandparents, aunts and uncles or the media to influence him negatively and yet he killed his brother. Conceivably, Cain's actions were influenced by his own festered evil thoughts. In the journey of life, you must carefully guard the way you think because your thoughts will influence the steps you take and the path you create or fail to create for yourself. In his book *As a Man Thinketh*, author James Allen notes: *You are today where your thoughts have brought you; you will be tomorrow where your thoughts take you.* You may not be able to predict the obstacles that you will meet on your life's journey, but how well you handle those obstacles and your interpretation of them will determine whether you make it successfully to your desired destination. I invite you to learn from some of the valuable life lessons here shared. These are helpful GEMS that can transform your life and help you achieve your highest purpose.

Facing Life's Travails: There are many advantages to living in a society that is technologically and digitally advanced. One example is communication and the other are travel. It is possible to be in one country and have a conversation digitally with someone in another country. Social media, for example makes it possible to see and speak in person. In preindustrial times when businesses were conducted from one's cottage in a little town, communication was limited to the town crier. The cottage industry also meant travel to work was limited to the local community, but technological advances have made it possible to live in one state and commute to work in another - and all in a single day. When I was a teenager in London, we would take the overnight ferry to Paris but today you can live in London and work in Paris because the Eurostar can take you from London to Paris in just a few hours. One of the disadvantages however is that travel eats up much of the work day. For many years, while living in New York City, I travelled each day - sometimes by car, sometimes by train and sometimes by bus, from my home in the borough of Queens to my place of employment in Westchester County. This amounted to five hours of commute each day by public transportation. By car it was anywhere from an hour to two hours, round trip - depending on traffic. I used the travel time by train and bus constructively to read, but as I reflect on my daily travels, I cannot help but see similarities to the travails of life.

As a new immigrant to New York, I did not know my way around, so the first time I traveled to Yonkers in Westchester, I sought help with directions. I used a road map and mapped out my route, but I also exercised caution and asked those who knew the way, for their ideas about the best possible route to take. Once I had learned the best route, making the daily journey became easier. Most days it was possible to travel for miles on the parkway or the expressway on smooth tarmac; but at some point – sometimes unexpectedly, I would meet construction and the road would narrow and cause a build-up of traffic – especially on the Whitestone or Throgs Neck Bridge. When you are stuck on the bridge, there is absolutely nothing you can do but wait for the traffic to move. At other times, there might be a detour or an accident just before getting to the bridge. Sometimes I would see drivers who anticipate being stuck on the bridge make a sudden detour before entering the bridge. Admittedly, a few times I have done the same, but soon, experience taught me that if you are unfamiliar with the route you are taking, and you don't know your way around, you could find yourself ending up on a one-way street that takes you further away from your destination, or maybe even a cul-de-sac or a dead end. By the time you find your way back on course, you are further behind than where you first exited. Sometimes though, that change of course proved to be a much better route.

My traffic encounters from Queens to Yonkers is a reminder that there will be times on your life's journey when life's occurrences will seem like gridlock, sudden detours and dead ends. A death in the family, a divorce, a lost love, a lost job, a pregnancy or a major accident can cause a radical change in your life circumstances. Remember, it's not the end of the road. If at times you feel totally lost, don't get discouraged, lose faith or give up in frustration. Getting lost, feeling betrayed or feeling let-down by someone is your opportunity to make new discoveries and uncover new truths about yourself. Your life changing occurrence may just be the opportunity you need to change course. Daymond John, the successful designer of FUBU clothing line, in sharing his life story Magazine pointed out that after enjoying incredible financial success and spending his money foolishly, it took losing his money and his friends to learn to simplify his life and rediscover what financial success really means.

Exercise Caution in Making a Major Life Changing Decision:

Be aware that making a major life changing decision will steer the direction that your life will take. Choosing whether to attend college or not, deciding on a career path, deciding on a life partner, purchasing a home; choosing to get married or divorce, or bringing a child into this world are all examples of major life changing decisions that can influence your future for better or worse. You must first seek counsel so that you can make wise decisions and have as few regrets as possible. If you have decided to take chances in life, you must first weigh the decision and be prepared to accept full responsibility for the consequences or outcome without blaming anyone or asking, "why me?" One way to limit your regrets is to first seek wisdom from God through meditation and a study of His words – the Bible and obtain counsel from those with knowledge. *Acquaint now thyself with him, and be at peace: thereby good shall come unto thee. (Job 22:21).* Isaac in choosing a wife spent much time in meditation. It is interesting also that Isaac's father, Abraham chose his oldest servant – Eliezer, which suggests Abraham chose a man of wisdom to go in search of a wife for Isaac. The servant in turn did not rely on his own wisdom, he prayed: *And he said O Lord God of my master Abraham, I pray thee, send me good speed this day... (Gen 24:10-14)*: Essentially Eliezer asked God to guide his decision making. A wise decision is always a well-informed decision. I like the statement by Ellen White in the book *Adventist Home*, which states: *If those who are contemplating marriage would not have miserable, unhappy reflections after marriage, they must make it a subject of serious, earnest reflection now. This step taken unwisely is one of the most effective means of ruining the usefulness of young men and women. Life becomes a burden, a curse. No one can so effectually ruin a woman's happiness and usefulness, and make life a heart sickening burden, as her own husband; and no one can do one hundredth part as much to chill the hopes and aspirations of a man, to paralyze his energies and ruin his influence and prospects, as his own wife. It is from the marriage hour that many men and women date their success or failure in this life, and their hopes of the future life (AH. P. 43).* You must choose also to act from principle rather than impulse. According to the wise man Solomon, amid counsel there is safety; plans go wrong for lack of advice; and many advisers bring success (Prov.11:14 & 15:22).

Coping with Feeling Stuck: On your life's journey, you will experience setbacks like drawbridges, struggles like uphill climbs and disappointments like steep declines. There will be inevitable mishaps or unexpected delays that will leave you feeling like you are stuck on a bridge suspended in air. At times when finances are low, and you are just trying to make it day by day, you will have unexpected crises that seem like a tire blow-out or a long drive on an almost empty gas tank - hoping to make it to the next gas station, only to find upon arrival that the gas station is closed or under construction. At that point you are at a total loss as to what to do. Indeed, it is when your back is against the wall that all you can do is pray and pray some more. I like the acronym PUSH [pray until something happens]. The story of Jonah is a reminder that God is everywhere. He will never leave you or forsake you. Jonah was thrown from a ship into the ocean. His body was supposed to be food for whales, sharks and marine creatures, but instead, God used the very same marine creature – according to Jesus, a whale - to swallow Jonah and act as transportation to take him back to shore. God is omnipotent, omnipresent and omniscient. He is all powerful, He is everywhere, and he is all knowing. He has the answer to every trial or difficulty. He can make a way out of no way. He can make the impossible, possible. He can use the negative circumstances that are working against you to bring you to your desired haven. He has promised to prepare a table for you in the very presence of your enemy. Imagine a king's table prepared for you! Just trust him with all your plans, yours dreams, your fears and your aspirations. He will come through in awesome ways. *Delight thyself also in the Lord: and he shall give thee the desires of thine heart. (Psalm 37:4).*

Indeed, in life you will meet obstacles that halt your journey or frustrate your plans. You will experience unforeseen events that seem like you are hitting a series of red lights, stop signs, pot holes or reckless drivers that cut in front of you- seemingly from nowhere to interrupt your path; it is like being involved in a major accident or a small fender bender. There will be times when you will feel like you are stuck in a ditch and all the revving of the engine and reversing back and forth will not get you out without a helping hand. I was at Camp Victory Lake in upstate New York and observed a young man who thought his car was stuck in the grass and the mud, so he kept revving back and forth in frustration and was just spinning his wheels until an elderly gentleman said to him: "Release your hand brake son;" upon doing so the young man was free to move forward. Doing the same thing repeatedly and getting the same negative results is foolish. You must question your actions to determine if change is needed. Sometimes it is your own actions or inactions that might be holding you back. Other times you just need to release the problem to God. Just "let go and let God take over."

Your circumstances may even lead unexpectedly to a crisis that feels like you just hit a wet spot on the road and are having a major spin-out; or worse yet, you are about to cross a bridge to your destination and the bridge explodes right in front of you - just as you are about to cross. The trauma of the experience can leave you shaken or broken; yet, it is all part of the journey. Similarly, in life, there will be times when life may go smoothly for a while, but then unexpectedly things will happen, and changes will come. People will double cross you; family will disappoint you, tragedy will strike, or your business might go belly-up. There are life lessons to be learned from these experiences. Don't give up in despair. God has promised: *Thus saith the Lord, which maketh a way in the sea, and a path in the mighty waters... Behold, I will do a new thing; now it shall spring forth; shall ye not know it? I will even make a way in the wilderness, and rivers in the desert. (Is. 43:15,19).*

Deprogramming of the Mind: The children of Israel left Egypt and journeyed for the Promised Land. As slaves they were programmed to think, behave and expect certain treatment. They were told when to get up, when to eat, and when to sleep. Choice was taken from them. In leaving Egypt, first they had to go through the Red Sea to reconnect with God by exercising faith in Him and then through the wilderness to take time to rebuild a personal relationship with God and with nature in order to experience that inner peace that nature provides. This deprogramming of their minds was essential to help them unlearn the ways of being slaves in order to reclaim their identity as children of God.

Sometimes adverse circumstances come your way so that you are forced to go back to God and for Him to reclaim you as His own and free you from the bondage of evil. When you return to God in faith, angels that excel in strength are there to help you, for the angels of the Lord encamp around those that fear Him and deliver them. In leaving Egypt, things changed overnight for the Children of Israel. They moved from slavery to freedom in one night and likewise things can change overnight for you and for the better. Out of the blue you could come up with a brilliant new life changing idea or someone could suggest a brilliant new opportunity. President Gerald Ford did not campaign for national office when he was handpicked by President Nixon to replace Vice President Spiro Agnew, who was forced to resign due to a financial scandal. In fact, Ford was considered an afterthought. After eight months of being in office as vice president, the Watergate scandal broke and Ford became United States president. You could say the position was thrown into his lap. In Psalm 42:11 David said: *"Why art thou cast down, O my soul? and why art thou disquieted within me? hope thou in God: for I shall yet praise him, who is the health of my countenance, and my God."* You have absolutely no idea what blessings await you tomorrow, so hold on. Don't quit.

<u>Don't Give up on the Journey –Miracles Still Exist:</u> At times though, you may feel like you are going nowhere fast or you don't have the energy to go on. My own life experience is a testament to that. It is during these rough spots on life's journey that you may begin to question if there is a God or like the patriarch Gideon you may even become cynical, wondering if all the miracles you have read about are for real or if God even exist. Just remember, it is just as irrational to believe that God does not exist. Personal tragedy and disappointment can lead to skepticism, but in the same way that God came through for the Gideon of the Bible, He can come through for you. Gideon wasn't from a rich or powerful family; in fact, his family was among the poorer tribes. Gideon himself acknowledged it. He couldn't hide behind a famous family name. Yet, God told him to go in the strength that he has. That strength was his faith in God, which wasn't much and yet God said he would be with him. As a result, Gideon saw the miracle working power of God. God still works miracles today but there maybe life-lessons that you need to learn during times of difficulties.

Your faith may be weak, and you may feel like giving up, but don't give up. Don't quit. Stay the course. Whatever little faith you have, God will strengthen and help you to accomplish incredible feats. You don't need a whole lot of faith – just faith the size of a mustard seed, which is only 1-2 millimeters in size – a small ink dot or pin head. Adversity can be your greatest blessing and your opportunity to make a change. There is a God. There have been times when I have questioned God's existence, such as when I am living right and doing right, and nothing seems to be going right or an innocent child gets killed, or is physically or sexually abused by an adult, but I have seen that if you stick with God, he will reveal his miracle working power as he did with Pastor George McKinney. In a local newspaper article and confirmed by Pastor McKinney, it was reported that each year for a number of years, Pastor George McKinney of San Diego hosted a pool party for children and families without any incidents, but during one of these parties, the children were playing dead man float and as fate would have it, one child drowned despite all efforts to save him. Pastor McKinney wrestled with God about this senseless tragedy and began having visions of an alert bracelet which gives signals to a life guard or a parent that a child is in trouble and invented the AJADD, named after the deceased child. This device is aimed at helping to save the lives of young children who according to the Center for Disease control are at the highest risk of drowning. Out of one tragedy came an opportunity to save the lives of many. Harold Kushner, a rabbi, in his book *"When Bad Things Happen to Good People"* tells his own story about his son Aaron who suffered from a rare disease called progeria, "rapid aging" and the rabbi's own disbelief and confusion about how the world is supposed to work. He was not a selfish or dishonest person, yet he was struck by tragedy. It was out of this devastating experience of watching his son age before his very eyes that he was able to write an encouraging book which has brought comfort to millions.

Feeling Like You are in a Pit: The patriarch Joseph went to the field to bring food for his brothers, wearing a fancy coat of many colors given to him by his father. He must have felt on top of the world in his designer coat. He had no idea how his life was about to change. Out of jealousy, his gang banging brothers placed him in a pit – a hole used for waste disposal; their evil scheming was supposed to have been the end of Joseph, but God had a greater plan for him. God moved upon his brothers' hearts and had them remove him from the pit. Joseph must have felt hopeful when they removed him from that pit, but the worst was yet to come. They sold him as a slave instead of leaving him to die in the pit. In this case the brothers were not acting out of concern for Joseph by removing him from the pit. They were acting in their own selfish interest. At times in life, even self-serving individuals can bring about your deliverance by happenstance. As if things couldn't get any worse, while a slave in Potiphar's house, Potiphar's seductive wife cried rape after Joseph refused her overtures and Joseph ended up in prison for a crime he did not commit. From the prison however, he was promoted to Pharaoh's palace, where he became a blessing to Egypt and to his own siblings that betrayed him.

You might feel like you are in the pit of your experience, but deliverance will come. Don't give up on your faith in God when tragedy strikes, or disappointments come. There are GEMS to be discovered from that very experience. Don't give up on God. Joel 2:21 says: *"Fear not, O land; be glad and rejoice: for the Lord will do great things."* I suggest you give up on God when someone can build a computer with precise algorithms that can match your DNA data storage system and has enough artificial intelligence to predict the flexibility of your mind. I suggest you give up on God when you can figure out the distance between the depths of the sea and the highest heavens or when you become your own creation. Until then keep believing, don't give up on your faith in God or take forbidden paths to find answers. Whatever you are going through now, might just be the preparation you need for something amazing that is coming your way or the protection you need from some worse ill that could befall you; you must trust God to help you get through it. It is said that God doesn't take you to the sea to drown you, but to see how well you can swim. Stay the course. Don't give up. Prep yourself and pass the test. *Fear thou not; for I am with thee: be not dismayed; for I am thy God: I will strengthen thee; yea, I will help thee; yea, I will uphold thee with the right hand of my righteousness. (Is. 41:10-16). Blessed is the man that trusteth in the Lord, and whose hope the Lord is. (Jer17:7; ICB).*

God's Ironies: For sure, God does not leave you to plough through life's adversities alone. He can bring irony out of evil and success out of defeat. Take the story of Moses for example, Pharaoh was envious of the success of the Hebrews and feared they would one day take over Egypt, so he ordered Shiphrah and Puah, two Hebrew midwives to kill all the new born Hebrew baby boys in Egypt; but these midwives could not in their good conscience adhere to Pharaoh's cruel command to take the lives of innocent babies. In response, they defied the king's orders. When Pharaoh saw that his decree did not result in his evil plans, he ordered that all the new born male children be thrown into the River Nile. Jacobed, mother of Moses could not allow her son to be killed. I can only imagine her personal struggle to protect her child from harm; so, she hid him for as long as she could. Ironically, pharaoh commanded that every male child that is born to the Hebrews be cast into the Nile river and, Jacobed obeyed the king's command by placing her son in the Nile. However, she exercised wisdom in her obedience to an evil command by doing everything in her power to secure her child's life. You could say she reached a point in her struggle with injustice when all she could do was just let go and let God have His way. She had no idea what the outcome would be, but she trusted God to come through for her child. In so doing, God turned things around in an amazing way. It should not have been a surprise for Pharaoh's daughter to see a baby in the Nile. After all, her father had given the edict, but God honored Jacobed's faith by arranging circumstances beyond her expectations. The child whose life should have been snuffed out by order of the king became the grandson of the very man who ordered him killed! And to top it all, his own mother was paid to care for him. Now if that is not an amazing irony, I don't know what is! In the book of Esther, Haman schemed to kill Mordecai and all the Jews in the land, but after Esther fasted and prayed and stepped out in faith-allowing God to have His way – she said: "If I perish, I perish" Haman ended up escorting Mordecai through the street in a parade and hanging from the very gallows he built for Esther's cousin, Mordecai.

If you allow God to direct your path, He can make your enemies your footstool, as he did with Mordecai. He can turn your rough roads of adversities into avenues of possibilities, as He did with Daniel and his companions who were placed in the fiery furnace. He can change your negative experience to a positive outcome - as He did with David who was persecuted relentlessly by Saul and yet He replaced Saul as king. God can turn your little into much, as He did with the small boy's lunch of five barley rolls and two small fish; and He can move you from your lowest point (the dunghill) as He did with Hannah, who was childless to become a mother of many. *The road may be rough and the ascent steep; there may be pitfalls upon the right hand and upon the left; we may have to endure toil in our journey; when weary, when longing for rest, we may have to toil on…. when discouraged, we must still hope; but with Christ as our guide we shall not fail of reaching the desired haven at last (E. G. White, Thoughts from the Mount of Blessings p.140).*

My Personal Journey: I will share some of my early life experiences to illustrate God's guiding hand in my life and his amazing miracle working power even in those times when I wondered if God cares or even exist. I was born in Jamaica, West Indies in very humble surroundings. From my birth to aged eleven I was reared by my maternal grandmother and great grandfather. At birth, my mother began hemorrhaging so my grandmother immediately assumed care taking responsibility of me. Like so many other West Indian children, whose parents migrated to greener pastures in search of a better life during a period of chronic economic imbalance in the Jamaica labor market, my parents migrated to England when I was about 18 months old, leaving me and my older sister in the care of my maternal grandmother. As grandchildren, my sister and I enjoyed the affections and attention of our grandmother and great grandfather.

My grandmother was affectionately called "Nanny" by my sister and the name stuck. The man I came to know as my great grandfather, she called "Ta-Ta" and this pet name also stuck with him. Ta-Ta was blind, but he was so self-sufficient you would not know it. He died when I was about seven years old. He was from Scotland and was my step-great grandfather. I was told he was the son of Catholic missionaries from Scotland and he fell in love with my great grandmother Adina, a real beauty of mixed African and Arawak Indian heritage. My grandmother's biological father, apparently worked on the Panama Canal, which was built between1904 and 1914; my grandmother was born in 1905. I was told my great grandfather would often return home bearing gifts. He also invested in buying land. He died when my grandmother was about 10 years old. Ta-Ta subsequently met my great grandmother and they had two sons - both of whom died at an early age. My grandmother had two children, my mother, Florence and my uncle Jackie, but their father also died when my mother was about 10 years old. Ta-Ta therefore became a surrogate father and grandfather, and a wonderful support and provider to the family until his death. Ta-Ta owned much land. My most vivid memory of my childhood was that of growing up carefree; we lived on a long stretch of land - over an acre, which was surrounded by over 12 different fruit trees; sugarcane, peanuts, a bee apiary and animals such as chickens, turkeys, pigs, goats, cows, donkeys, and dogs. Mango season was my favorite time of the year because I would pick and eat mangoes from the mango trees in our yard. Ackee and breadfruit were staples and sweetsops and jackfruit were available for snacks.

My Grandparents Made Lifestyle Changes: Although my great grandfather was blind, he was considered a wise man by people in the community. He had served in the police constabulary before losing his sight so many people often stopped by to see him or seek him out for advice. I also remember seeing a white Catholic priest in a clergy collar come to our house on Sundays to give Ta-Ta communion. The two would chat for hours sipping freshly brewed coffee. I don't drink coffee because of the high caffeine content and because it is a legal psycho-active drug and a central nervous system stimulant; on the occasions I have tried beverages with caffeine, I have experienced palpitations and a piercing headache. I therefore abstain from caffeine altogether, but the aroma of coffee always reminds me of Ta-Ta. The Sunday chat sessions continued until Ta-Ta and my grandmother became Seventh–day Adventists and the visits stopped. The coffee drinking also stopped because Adventists discourage the use of harmful substances and alcoholic beverages. Ta-Ta loved his coffee, so he substituted parched dandelion seeds for coffee beans. After they became Adventist, to my delight, my grandparents got rid of the pigs they owned. In a child's eyes those pigs were huge. They were some ugly, smelly enormous hogs. My grandparents disposed of the pigs because according to Leviticus chapter eleven, pigs are classified among the unclean animals that should not be eaten, possibly because their meat is known to be a carrier of diseases such as the trichinae larvae; pork is also extremely high in cholesterol, which clogs up the arteries and results in heart disease. I can remember the glee I felt when they hauled those squealing hogs away; I was no longer afraid of passing the pig-pen or having to hold my nose because of the stench from their sty. My grandmother planted aubergines (egg plants), tomato, pumpkin, corn and bell peppers in what used to be the pig-pen; it was such a delight to wander about the very colorful vegetable garden. To this day, I love to visit vegetable stands and peruse over the assortment of vegetables and even try the unfamiliar.

My Grandmother the Savvy Business Woman: My grandmother was a very savvy business woman who created multiple streams of income in order to survive; she grew ground provision - yam, dasheen, sweet potatoes, breadfruit and bananas; she took care of the animals that my grandparents owned, (although there were always extra hands to provide help in exchange for food or shelter) and she sold livestock and dairy produce. In addition, she had rental properties and was also a skilled potter who sold the pots she made to supplement her livelihood. I remember on one occasion seeing my grandmother build a kiln in the yard and then placing the pots she made in the kiln. When she removed the pots, not one of the pots came out whole. All the pots had cracked under the heat and some came out in pieces. She was so dejected. When I asked her what had happened, she used the experience to teach me several object lessons. She said the pots needed to dry slowly and evenly before going into the kiln to prevent stress on the clay. Without going through this process, she said, the clay is likely to crack under the firing. In this case, she had an order for pots and was trying to cut corners by drying the pots quickly in the sun. "Learn from this experience" she said. Looking back, there were many GEMS to learn from that one experience; there were lessons on patience, paying attention to details, doing a job well, resilience under difficult circumstances and allowing God to be the potter of your life - GEMS that are covered in this book. I hope you will take some time to ponder over the lessons you might also learn from the potter's experience. *If it do evil in my sight, that it obey not my voice, then I will repent of the good, wherewith I said I would benefit them. (Jeremiah 18:10).*

My Grandmother's Death: My maternal grandmother was a loving woman who demonstrated her love by wanting the best for her grandchildren. She especially valued education and often used her last dime (literally) to make sure my sister and I had our reading books for school. In my time, we had to pay for our text book - the Rainbow Readers. I can recall my grandmother being as proud as punch – righteously proud when at eleven years old I got baptized at the Spanish Town Seventh Day Adventist Church and in the same year passed the first hurdle of life for an eleven-year old child in Jamaica – the dreaded

Common Entrance Exam, which at the time, many in Jamaica saw as the gateway to success. The results of those who passed the exam were published in the *Gleaner*. In my case it was a scholarship to St Jago High School. My success was a proud moment for me, not to mention my grandmother and my class teacher, Mrs. Dorothy Lawrence. I was a pupil at Crescent Primary School and in the year that I received the Common Entrance scholarship, it was the same year that I also received first prize for the best all-rounder pupil in my class/Junior 5-Al. My prize was the book "The Lady with the Lamp". I did not own many books, so I must have read that book about Florence Nightingale and her heroic work with wounded soldiers about two or three times that summer. I have kept that book till today – over 40 years.

I started attending St Jago High school in September of the same year and wore with great pride, my linen green tunic with its razor-sharp pleats that had been starched crisp and pressed. Like most other girls, keeping our pleats in place became a ritual. I remember carefully folding my pleats in place before sitting down. The school instilled pride of appearance and good grooming through daily inspection of our clothing and as a result, as students we walked with pride. I was my grandmother's pride and joy with a self-esteem that was running high. Then one fateful day on November 11, tragedy struck. It was during a week of prayer series at Fairfield Road Mission, that my grandmother went to an early morning prayer-meeting and while praying she fainted. She recovered soon after, walked home and went straight to bed. Upon returning from school that evening, she was still in bed, which was most unusual for her. She was always busy watering and pruning her vegetable garden in the evenings. Surrounded by friends and church members she asked if I had eaten and then said she was going to church. Everyone laughed, not realizing the seriousness of her condition. In our presence, she breathed her last breath and died. I was sitting next to her on her bed and, her death came as a frightful shock to me. It was so sudden and so unexpected. She was only 62 years old and in my 11 years of knowing her, I had never seen her sick in bed. Suddenly my idyllic carefree world of being cushioned by a loving grandmother was turned upside down. My parents had not planned for my care in the event of my grandmother's death. Their plan was to return to Jamaica after accruing enough money and had not considered any eventualities.

From this experience, I have learned the importance of arranging guardianship of my child in the event of tragedy.

My Foster Care Experience: My grandmother's sudden death left me without a guardian. I wondered why God could take my grandmother from me, leaving me without a caretaker; but even in this tragedy, God was working out a master plan. My neighbor, Mrs. Smith whom I called affectionately, Miss Nezie was present in the room when my grandmother died and took guardianship of me. I lived with her family for a year before joining my biological parents in London, England. I had known the Smiths all my life and often played with their children. My parents also grew up with them. Being in a familiar setting helped me cope with the loss of my grandmother.

In reflecting on my life experience, although unsettling and traumatic for a child, I can see how this experience helped prepare me for my work with children who have experienced abuse and neglect and are placed in foster care or adopted. Indeed, my personal experience in kinship care and living with the Smiths helped me develop a special empathy for children who end up in foster care or get adopted. The Smiths had a lovely home and all the creature comforts that my grandmother did not have. The Smiths' children were also kind to me and treated me like another sibling. Christmas in their home was memorable. They had a real live Christmas tree with colorful pepper lights. That Christmas all eleven children - their seven plus the three others that lived with them decorated the tree with cotton buds and exchanged gifts with one another. The gifts were simple hair slides and pencils - nothing expensive or elaborate, but the act was memorable. Living with them also meant there was always someone with whom I could interact. However, despite all the creature comfort and kindness of the Smiths, it did not quench my longing to be with my own family. I wanted to belong somewhere. I looked forward with yearning for the day that I would live with my own family. According to psychological studies, people have a need for constant, positive, personal interactions with others and to know and experience a bond that is stable, where mutual concern for one another exists and the attachment continues. It is this longing for a promised bond that can sometimes lead to alienated youths becoming gang involved or to individuals joining religious organizations and even cults.

Church Attendance: The Smiths were not Adventist, but during my stay with them, I continued my attachment with my church and the ritual of attending church on Saturdays. In the Adventist church there are Sabbath School divisions. There are divisions for children, youth and adults - with each division following a thematic study of the Bible during a thirteen-week quarter. This thematic study guide is referred to as the Sabbath School Quarterly and is used among Adventists throughout the world churches. It also serves as a connecting link for members. It's like having family all over the world. It is possible to attend an Adventist church in any part of the world and besides language barrier, participate in the lesson study. My grandmother always purchased a Quarterly for me and was insistent that I read my Quarterly to her on Friday nights. This simple weekly exercise helped to improve my spiritual intelligence and etched in my mind some amazing Bible stories of faith and courage and many object lessons. These Bible stories remain indelible reminders of God's power to change things and His loving care for His children. From these stories, I had an assurance that in the same way that God cared for the Patriarchs of old, it is the same way that He cares for me. Now as an adult, I can see where my childhood experience has helped to nurture a positive mental attitude and the spiritual intelligence needful to deal with life's challenges. The church that I attended became my extended family and I looked forward to attending each Saturday (Sabbath). Every Saturday I would walk to the Fairfield Road Mission, where I always felt supported and at home.

The habit of attending regular church services, especially Sabbath School and Wednesday night prayer meeting has remained a constant in my life and has helped to steer my life in a positive direction. When I joined my parents in England, I learned that my father was Catholic and my mother Baptist, but neither one attended church except for funerals, weddings or baby dedications. Upon arrival, I told my parents I was a Seventh Day Adventists and that I observe the Sabbath and certain dietary restrictions. My mother was not incredibly happy about my being a Seventh Day Adventist and made it known; she even tried to discourage my attending church by giving me chores to do on Sabbaths, but this did not discourage me. I would do the chores and then go to church. It was some ten years later, just after I graduated from Whitelands Teachers' College, the University of London, that she became a member of the Greenwich Seventh Day Adventist Church in

Greenwich, London. My father on the other hand was supportive of my church attendance. He saw it as a positive activity for a female young lady to engage in and made it his duty to link me to an Adventist family, the Greens. The Greens owned the only West Indian grocery store in Brockley. My father did not know the Greens, but he was aware they were Adventists because their small grocery store was always closed on Saturdays with a notice *"Closed in Observance of the Sabbath."* Every Saturday morning, I would get up early and walk to the Greens' home so that they did not have to wait on me. In a short while, I learned the bus routes from my house on Wickham Road in Brockley to the Lewisham Seventh Day Adventist Church and made my own way to church independently.

Living in England: I had just turned thirteen when I arrived in London, England. I remember it was towards the end of the summer because I attended the annual Blackheath fair with my parents and my younger brother. The weather was also beginning to feel chilly and damp. My mother said I needed a coat and took me to Petticoat Lane market in London's East End where Cockney Londoners peddled their wares. I had never experienced anything like it. The crowd was thick and vendors on soap boxes engaged in fast talking chants common to auctioneers as they compete for the attention of customers. There among the bustling crowd, we scoured the market to purchase a coat. I still remember that soft tan leather coat with a crew neck that buckled at the neck. It felt so snug and so warm, but it did not compensate for my desire to be back in the sunshine and warmth of Jamaica. Leaving the sunny island of Jamaica to retreat to the confines of being indoors on cold dark winter days was difficult for me. I longed for the sunshine and the freedom of the outdoors, but winter seemed long and dreary. Many evenings, after doing my homework, I would often retreat to painting pictures of hibiscus, palm trees and blue seas. Then one dark winter's evening, my dad brought home two chirping birds (canaries). He said they were called budgies. I'll never forget the excitement the two brightly colored chirping budgies brought to our home. It was the new addition to our family and a welcome distraction from the cold weather and missing Jamaica. We gave the budgies names –Leslie and Joey, and we took good care of them, but in-spite of our protective caring, those birds were always restless and tried several times to escape from their cage. Being air borne creatures, it seemed their only desire was to escape the confines of a cage. Each time we released them to fly around the room, they headed for the window. Sometimes in their desperate effort to escape, they darted into the clear glass window with such brute force that they fell to the floor. Our only choice was to pick them up and put them back in their cage.

Adversity & Disappointments: Like our trapped caged budgies, sometimes in life you may find yourself in adverse situations, which may or may not be of your choosing. You may feel knocked down by circumstances and disappointments; you are at your lowest point and feel like you are just spinning your wheels and going nowhere fast. Each time you see a glimmer of hope and you leap forward, your hope is shattered, and you are right back to where you started, or in an even worse condition. You try everything to move forward, but your efforts end in failure. Like the bird that heads for the window, you can see where you want to go, but there is a sealed glass ceiling that prevents you from moving forward. You feel that God has forgotten or forsaken you. You feel knocked down. You are in a state of despair. Depression sets in and you just cannot see your way. You feel caged in or like the patriarchs Hannah and David you feel like you are on the dunghill of life and don't know what to do. Truly, behind every cloud is a silver lining. Behind the disappointments you face, God has a master plan that will work for your good, and He will do it in His time and for His glory. *For the vision is yet for an appointed time, but at the end it shall speak, and not lie: though it tarry, wait for it; because it will surely come, it will not tarry (Habakkuk 2:3)*

Before God created Adam and Eve, he prepared a home for them and supplied all their needs. Know therefore that whenever you are going through adversities, God has already made a way for you. Don't allow the cobwebs of anger, disappointment, defeat or discouragement get in the way of your blessing. The story was told of a young man who felt he could never please his father, whom he considered to be a very demanding and overly religious man. He wanted a car and his father promised him a brand new one if he graduates from college with a degree. Upon graduating from college, he went to his father expectantly, hoping to get the keys to a new car, but instead, his father handed him a large new leather-bound bible as his graduation gift. The young man threw the Bible down in anger. He was feeling disappointed that he had worked hard but had not pleased his father. He was angry that his father had not fulfilled his promise. He stormed out of the house and vowed never to return. When his father died, he returned home at his mother's pleading. Upon returning home, the young man observed sitting on the mantle-piece, the leather-bound bible that his father had given him. He picked up the bible and there inside was an envelope with his name written on it. He opened the envelope and inside was a note and a check dated the day of his graduation. The note read: "Son I am so proud of you, now buy the car of your dreams." He was devastated. He allowed his anger at his father to get in the way of his blessing and the opportunity to build a relationship with his father. Don't allow God's apparent delay in answering your prayer to get in the way of your blessing. God is your heavenly father. *For I know the thoughts that I think toward you, saith the Lord, thoughts of peace, and not of evil, to give you an expected end. (Jeremiah 29:11).* In your prayers, echo the prayer of the Psalmist David: *Remember me, O Lord, with the favour that thou bearest unto thy people: O visit me with thy salvation; (Ps 106:4); Help me, O Lord my God: O save me according to thy mercy: That they may know that this is thy hand; that thou, Lord, hast done it. (Ps 109: 26,).*

Your Windows of Opportunities: My budgies' deepest desire was freedom from their caged existence and one fine day, their wish was eventually granted, and their window of opportunity came. God can fulfill your deepest desires or help you find a way to cope with your situation to the point where it works to your advantage. My hours of painting pictures on dark winter evenings in London led to my art teacher, Mr. Nicholls spotting my artistic talents and providing me with a portfolio. He told me to keep every piece of artwork securely in my portfolio. Eventually I developed my artistic abilities to the point of receiving an A grade in the Advanced level (A –Level) Oxford General Certificate of Education (GCE) Examination, a Major County Award, and a coveted place at London's prestigious Chelsea School of Art. Indeed, my portfolio came in handy for my entrance interview to art school. Who would have thought that an adverse situation could work to my advantage?

God can use your adversities and disappointments to open seemingly sealed doors of opportunities. He can help you to soar to new heights in attainment, but you must be prepared to take that first step of faith. I recall that each time we released our budgies from their cage they headed straight for the window, only to end up back in their cage. Then, one warm sunny day, their desire was granted. My mother had opened the windows in the house to welcome the summer sunshine into our home. The lace curtains shielded the opened windows. Being unaware that the windows were open, I opened the bird cage to change the sand paper and had let the birds out; by the time I realized my mistake, it was too late! The budgies bolted for the window - only this time it was open, and the birds made their quick escape. The budgies never gave up on their desire to escape and eventually their window of opportunity came, and they seized it. It was Michelangelo that said: "The greatest danger for most of us is not that our aim is too high, and we miss it, but that it is too low, and we reach it."

What are your deepest desires that keep eluding you or your highest aim that you cannot reach? Does it feel like you have crossed a bridge that leads to a wall or climbed a ladder that is too short? Do you feel crippled by your circumstances or morass in your despair? Has life served you a curved ball? Whatever your situation, you can get up again and soar like the eagle. The weight of evidence included in this book is your reminder that if God worked for me and for others like me, why should He not work for you? God still answers prayers. *Commit thy way unto the Lord; trust also in him; and he shall bring it to pass.* (Ps. 37: 5-7). You may not know how or when God will come through for you, but rest assure that God will come through for you in His time and in His way. If you are facing adversities, disappointment or challenges this minute, tell yourself, "I don't know how, and I don't when, but I know God is coming through for me." Repeat this statement until it is imprinted in your mind and expect God to work a miracle in your life. Meditate on the Bible Verses included in each section of this book, whenever the way seems dark and there just doesn't appear to be any way out. Study and repeat them as affirmative statements to help you get through each day. In doing so, you are reaffirming your trust in God and your faith in his ability to do for you more than you can ask or think. *And it shall come to pass, if thou shalt hearken diligently unto the voice of the Lord thy God, to observe and to do all his commandments which I command thee this day, that the Lord thy God will set thee on high above all nations of the earth: And all these blessings shall come on thee, and overtake thee, if thou shalt hearken unto the voice of the Lord thy God.. And all these blessings shall come on thee, and overtake thee, if thou shalt hearken unto the voice of the Lord thy God..Blessed shalt thou be in the city, and blessed shalt thou be in the field...Deut.28: 1-12.*

It is my prayer that in reading this book you will be inspired to move from accepting the ordinary to aspiring for the extra-ordinary; that you will move from a feeling of despair - like you are on the dunghill of life or caged in by your circumstances and can't see your way out, to accepting responsibility for your actions and moving forward in faith soaring beyond expectations and safely arriving at a wealthy place. May you recognize that God has a plan for your life and that he desires for you to soar like the eagle until you get to that wealthy place; although the road to get there might be steep, bumpy or full of pot holes, don't give up. God will carry you when you get tired and you feel like you just can't do it anymore. The words of this poem *(Author unknown)* are worth remembering:

> *The road to success is not straight.*
> *There is a curve called Failure.*
> *A loop called Confusion,*
> *Speed bumps called Friends,*
> *Red lights called Enemies,*
> *Caution lights called Family.*
> *You will have flats called Jobs.*
> *But, if you have a spare called Determination,*
> *An engine called Perseverance, insurance called Faith,*
> *A driver called Jesus you will make it to a place called Success.*

This is a picture of me as a toddler, my older sister, grandmother and great grandfather in Jamaica, West Indies

Your 3rd Gem

FLY WITH EAGLES

And be not conformed to this world: but be ye transformed by the renewing of your mind, that ye may prove what is that good, and acceptable, and perfect, will of God.12:2.

Your 3rd GEM is focused on the choices you make in life. Be incredibly careful about your choices, decisions and the associations you make today because these will affect your future tomorrows and have long-term spiritual, social, financial and psychological consequences.

Your Life Partner: You must be careful about the one you choose as your lifetime partner. It was the singer Bob Marley who said, if she [or he] is amazing she won't be easy and if she [or he] is easy she won't be amazing. Do not become sexually and emotionally connected with a life partner before getting to know the person's character. Failing to get to know the person's character will make it harder to disentangle yourself later after you discover character flaws that you cannot tolerate, and you desire to end the relationship. Seek counsel *before* you become engaged to someone or make preparation to proverbially speaking "tie the knot." Don't become engaged and then seek counsel. To do so is like putting the cart before the horse. Observe your intended partner's treatment of those that provide a service and to children and the elderly. Is it demeaning or caring? The treatment of others less fortunate tells a great deal about a person's character. Does he or she keep you away from your family or friends and speak negatively of them? Be aware that this is an unhealthy relationship and is done to isolate you from others and exercise total control over you. Many abusive relationships start in this manner. Be aware of the use of what Susan Johnson calls "demon dialogues" or putdowns. These will destroy your sense of self -worth.

It is said that your five closest friends reflect who you are at this point in your life so choose your associations carefully. You can associate without adapting the negative behaviors of those around you. I remember a young man with whom I grew up in church. He had a bright future, but he fell in with the wrong crowd and rather than be an influence for good, he chose to join them in smoking the drug, marijuana. Unknown to him, the marijuana was mixed with a toxic substance to increase the potency and the feeling of being "high;" this one-time experimental use was so damaging to him mentally that it contributed to his being diagnosed a catatonic schizophrenic. If he had not chosen the forbidden, his future might have turned out very differently.

Adam and Eve were given access to every tree in the Garden of Eden - except the Tree of Knowledge of Good and Evil. Life was good for them. They did not know shame and dishonor. Then one day they made one poor choice and that one poor choice resulted in their losing it all. If they had not chosen to eat the fruit of the forbidden tree, they would never have known evil. Similarly, if you choose to indulge in the forbidden - be it in an illicit relationship, crooked business deal, gambling or the use of illicit drugs - that one-time poor decision could steer you into paths that could influence the direction of your entire future into a downward spiral. If you have already ventured into forbidden paths, you do not need to keep going down the same destructive path. You can choose to stop and change course.

Overcome Bad Habits: Whatever you cease to feed must die eventually. I love to have plants and flowers in and around my home, but if I don't remember to water them, eventually they will die. If I don't eat, eventually I'll die. Similarly, if you don't feed a bad habit, it will die eventually. Make a conscious decision today to stop any self-destructive behavior and ask God to guide your life. *"Nothing is impossible with God. Nothing is so entangled that it cannot be remedied; no human relationship is too strained for God to bring about reconciliation and understanding; no habit so deep rooted that it cannot be overcome; no one is so weak that he cannot be strong; no one is so ill that he cannot be healed. No mind is so dull that it cannot be made brilliant. Whatever we need if we trust God, He will supply it. If anything is causing worry or anxiety, let us stop rehearsing the difficulty and trust God for healing, love, and power"* (Ellen G. White, Review & Herald, October 7, 1865).

Dopamine, which is a neurotransmitter of the brain, plays a major role in the problem of addiction because it triggers an emotional response at the very sight of a thing that brings you pain or pleasure - even before touching it. A dog begins to salivate when it sees food and the same happens with addictive behaviors. Just the sight, smell or person associated with the addiction can trigger a relapse. You must therefore avoid people, places or things that will lead you into forbidden and destructive paths. That is why Christianity is good for people in recovery because it encourages a lifestyle change. I heard a story about a man who had an alcohol problem who decided to change his ways and sober up. However, he had a habit of riding his horse into town and hitching it in front of the saloon that he frequented as an alcoholic. Although he had abstained from drinking, he continued to hitch his horse in front of the saloon. One day while under a lot of stress, he hitched his horse in front of the saloon as usual; only this time, he entered the saloon, ordered a drink and relapsed.

It's hard to change a bad habit if you continue to frequent or associate with those who are indulging in the same destructive behavior. *"Be not deceived: evil communications corrupt good manners."'* (1 Corinthians 15:33). Think of a fruit basket with apples. Just one rotten apple can diffuse enough acid gas to eventually destroy the entire basket of fruits, so be careful of your associations. Decide to change your course if you are heading in the wrong direction. It's never too late. Replace the negative behavior with a positive one. If you find your-self reverting to old feelings or starting to re-engage in old patterns of behavior, you can break or interrupt the pattern by doing something different. Get up, move away, breathe, exercise or focus on something else; go and visit an elderly or sick person. Try it. Think of your favorite fruit and see how quickly a shift occurs in your thinking. Best of all kneel and pray. Ask God for help. *Trust in the Lord with all thine heart; and lean not unto thine own understanding. In all thy ways acknowledge him, and he shall direct thy paths. (Proverbs 3:5-6)*

Understand the Two Forces at War Within: Whenever you find yourself slipping back into old negative habits or patterns of behaviors, it is important to remember that there are two forces at war within you - the sinful (the desire to do what is wrong) and the spiritual or the moral (the desire to do what is right). Paul describes it in Galatians 5:17 as the spiritual and the lustful. The lustful wants to do evil, which is just the opposite of what the spiritual wants. An old Indian chief told his son that there are two wolves at war within. One is good and the other evil. The boy asked, "so which one wins in the end?" The chief replied: "the one that you feed." If you grew up in an environment that was not governed by sound values, or morals in decision making, you may find yourself making decisions based on the circumstances in which you find yourself. This is known as situational ethics or in certain eastern countries, social ethics. In other words, the situation in which you find yourself or your social relationships dictate how you behave rather than your actions being prompted by sound moral principles. A young criminal in jail was heard bemoaning his fate, "I am so sorry" he kept repeating. A visiting priest observed the young man and thought he was being repentant for his wrongs and proceeded to reassure him of forgiveness. "God forgives you my son" the priest said. "No father," he responded "you don't understand; if only I hadn't sneezed. You see father, I am here today because I sneezed." If you constantly indulge in doing wrong (committing sin), before long, you will begin to rationalize or excuse your actions. You may blame your circumstances without taking personal responsibility. It may take someone else to point out your wrong to you, as in King David's case. After David had committed both adultery and homicide, it was Nathan the prophet who pointed out his wrong actions to him. Even then, David did not see himself in Nathan's parable until Nathan said, "you are the man." It is for this reason that Paul in his letter to the Galatians (Gal. 5:16-17,) wrote: *This I say then, Walk in the Spirit, and ye shall not fulfil the lust of the flesh. For the flesh lusteth against the Spirit, and the Spirit against the flesh: and these are contrary the one to the other: so that ye cannot do the things that ye would..*

Watch Your Thoughts: In Paul's letter to the Romans (Romans 6:11-14), he admonishes them to focus on, *whatsoever things are true, whatsoever things are honest, whatsoever things are just, whatsoever things are pure, whatsoever* *things are lovely, whatsoever things are of good report; if there be any virtue, and if there be any praise, think on these things. Those things, which ye have both learned, and received, and heard, and seen in me, do: and the God of peace shall be with you. (Phil.4: 8-9). Christ in the heart, Christ in the life, this is our safety. The atmosphere of His presence will fill the soul with abhorrence of all that is evil. Our spirit may be so identified with His that in thought and aim we shall be one with Him (E. G. White, Min Healing, p.511).* Do not allow your thoughts to run riot. Uncontrolled thoughts can lead to self-control problems and detrimental consequences. Your self-control problem might be hidden from others - such as lustful thinking or envy; or visible to others - such as impulsive over spending, gambling, and alcoholism, all of which could seriously impact your well-being and the well-being of your immediate family. Then there are problems of self-control that create victims of others such as sexual abuse, domestic violence, or criminal offenses that result in imprisonment.

When you give in to unwholesome thoughts or lustful desires, you are preventing God from doing amazing things in your life. God says in Jeremiah 29:11-13: For I know the thoughts that I think toward you, saith the Lord, thoughts of peace, and not of evil, to give you an expected end." Joseph did not give in to Potiphar's wife seducing behavior and her desire to become sexually intimate with him. If he had given in to her seduction, thinking no one would know, he would have remained a slave to her for the rest of his life. He would have stifled his own growth and thwarted God's awesome plan for his life.

Overcoming Addictions: A temptation succumbed, has the potential to lead to an addiction. That one sinful indulgence can lead to an addiction that consumes your life and negatively impacts your physical, mental, social, spiritual or financial well-being. Joseph resisted temptation and was imprisoned falsely, but he eventually went from being a prisoner to becoming the prime minister in Egypt. Now look at the lives of individuals in the Bible who gave in to sinful indulgences; what happened to their lives? Sampson, a judge in Israel had a sexual addiction to prostitutes and ended up losing his sight and died a tragic death; David's voyeuristic behavior led to his desire for Bathsheba and the killing of Bathsheba's husband. His sons, Solomon and Amnon were also sexual deviants. What-ever sinful indulgence you succumb to in life, will rule and eventually destroy your life. It is possible to achieve the things for which you aspire in life, but through lack of wisdom, or intemperance and addictions you make inappropriate choices and lose it all.

It is important to remember that sinful desires and practices are often clothed in deception and attractiveness to seduce you. Look at advertisements for alcohol and cigarettes; you don't see a bunch of drunken homeless persons staggering around with bloody wounds on their faces from having fallen over in their drunken stupor and hurting themselves neither do you see pictures of individuals with blackened lungs, emphysema and missing fingers from cigarette consumption. You see images of good-looking people laughing and seemingly having a wonderful time. The subliminal message is that alcohol and cigarettes will make you a fun loving and popular person and not destitute and poor. You must remember that a publicist job is to sell a product - regardless of whether the product is good for you or not. Advertisers appeal to you through various means —more often than not through the power of consensus —meaning everybody is doing it, which helps to normalize even something that might not be good for you; through urgency – you must make a decision now in order not to miss out on an opportunity; through bargaining -you have nothing to lose by trying and through the use of a catch phrase that resonates with the way you want to feel. Manufacturers pay a lot of money on market research to get consumers to buy products that may or may not be any good for them so guard the "avenues to your soul" – your senses and avoid being deceived.

Guard Your Senses: Appealing to the senses is another approach used by advertisers. I was having lunch at South Street Seaport in New York City and observed the promoters of a popular brand of alcohol promoting their product. They had beautiful displays of the bottles stacked together in pyramid shapes with the sunlight gleaming against the glass like stacks of diamonds. Then, to engage the public, an attractive entertainer, dressed in black, invited people – mostly tourist and lunch hour crowd to participate in a full day of interactive fun activities. The simple goal was to endear as many people as possible towards their brand of alcohol. It was amazing the large number of people that participated in their fun activities. Having participated in this fun activity, a positive feeling was generated, which connected them emotionally to the product; now each time they see that same brand of alcohol, they will associate it with fun and will be inclined to purchase it. You must realize that it is not everything that looks good is good for you. *Hear thou, my son, and be wise, and guide thine heart in the way. Be not among winebibbers; among riotous eaters of flesh: For the drunkard and the glutton* *shall come to poverty: and drowsiness shall clothe a man with rags (Prov. 23:19-21). The law of the Lord is perfect, converting the soul: the testimony of the Lord is sure, making wise the simple (Ps 19:7)".*

In the story of Adam and Eve, it was the serpent's attractiveness and seducing promises that seduced Eve. Satan appealed to Eve through her senses. The serpent told Eve that eating of the fruit would make her as wise as God and that she would not die. Eve was fascinated by a talking serpent and lingered in its presence. The serpent then connected her emotionally to the fruit by placing it in her hand to prove that nothing would happen to her. Satan deceived Eve through his subtle wiles. Satan's denial of God's directives is like saying that believing in God is a made-up fairy tale to keep you ignorant and submissive. In modern times it would be like Karl Marx referring to religion as "the opium of the people and the sigh of the oppressed creature, the heart of a heartless world, just as it is the spirit of a spiritless situation" or Charles Darwin who proposed that evolution started from a lower form such as a fish and progressed to a higher form –a person. Of course, there are some elements of truth in both theories: Religion does satiate some poor people and prick the conscience of some rich people and some things do evolve from a lower form, but these are not absolutes. Many individuals have given up on God because they accept these tenets as absolute truths and like Eve have bought into Satan's lie.

Eve's one poor choice resulted in the loss of the couple's Edenic home and a life of hardship. She did not die immediately, but from that lingering moment of indulgence she began to die spiritually, emotionally, and physically. My grandmother used to say: "It is not the same day that the leaf falls from the tree that it rots." In other words, you may not see the immediate result of your poor choices or decisions, but eventually it will show itself. Is it any wonder that Solomon, the son of David who himself succumbed to some foolish decisions, wrote in Proverbs 13:15, *Good understanding giveth favor; but the way of the transgressor is hard (KJV);*

Most of the drug addicts with whom I have worked have told me that they were introduced to drugs when they were feeling down, fearful of a situation or hanging with friends who were drug users or drug pushers who told them the drug would make them feel better. Most unwanted pregnancies and sex slaves resulted from the seducer whispering sweet nothing to a naïve girl [or boy] who was feeling unattractive and unloved. Satan was a celestial being. He was in the presence of God. He has superior intelligence. He and his angels were cast out of heaven because he wanted to usurp the authority of God. He is the arch deceiver and he has many followers who have sold their souls to him and indulge in practicing iniquity. Today we call these deceivers sociopaths or antisocial personalities, but whatever the term, they are one and the same – deceiving con-artists with a very flattering tongue. They are charming, deceitful, controlling and manipulative, and will use your vulnerability to serve their own purpose. They are like leeches and will even make you feel guilty about not giving in to their manipulations. Their only concern is for themselves. Their goal is not to help you, but to take from you. When you are no longer of use to them, they will toss you aside like a plastic bag full of garbage and go in search of their next victim.

Satan tried to seduce Jesus at a point when Jesus had been fasting and was most weak and vulnerable by appealing to human greed and a desire for power and control. Satan offered Jesus the wealth, power and riches of this world, but Jesus was not seduced. He was not "conned." He chose instead to follow the commands of God than to succumb to Satan's wiles. He was so in tune with the scriptures that he was able to use it as his defense. He chose not to be overcome with evil, but to overcome evil with good. It is through the spirit of God actuated by His grace that you will overcome the wiles of the evil one. Paul writing to the Ephesian church that was struggling with esteem issues because they were once Gentiles and therefore considered inferior - foreigners, aliens, and dogs pointed out to them that in accepting Christ they became joint heirs, royalty, members of one body and he encouraged them to grow in grace and in the knowledge of Christ and leave behind their past life of sensuality and impurity (Ep.4:17-19).

Make Lifestyle Changes: You must avoid people, places or things that will drag you down. It is like moving out of an apartment or selling a house. You must leave it broom clean so that you have absolutely no reason to go back. If the influence is external to you then you must not let the external influence leave any baggage behind. This will avoid their having any excuse to return. You must make a total life style change to avoid any excuse to relapse into old bad habits. This is where Christianity helps because it has the power to transform. When you become a Christian, you must make a conscious decision to make a life style change. That is one of the reasons people get baptized. Baptism is a public acknowledgement of a changed life. When you make a public decision to change, you are more likely to want to maintain that changed life style since people will hold you to it. You must also make it a habit to set aside time each day to study and memorize even one verse from the Bible. Bible verses will strengthen your faith and act as your defense during those times that the temptation to relapse will come your way. Jesus studied and memorized the scriptures and when temptations came at the point when he was most vulnerable, he was able to utilize scriptures to help him resist. You too can overcome, but if you neglect to adhere to these practices, you are likely to relapse into old addictions or be drawn into new ones. *Every athlete exercises self-control in all things. They do it to receive a perishable wreath, but we, an imperishable. So, I do not run aimlessly; I do not box as one beating the air. But I discipline my body and keep it under control, lest after preaching to others I myself should be disqualified (1Cor 9:24-27).*

Be careful about the genre of music to which you listen and the movies or social media material that you watch. Your eyes and ears – your senses are avenues to your soul. Guard them carefully because through the things you hear and watch you can be drawn back into old habits and negative behaviors. A song or a movie or even a smell from your past can bring you back in time and stir up the old memories and desires that you once had. It is for this reason that the Apostles admonish us to choose to think about things that are true, honest and of good report and avoid returning to old bad habits like a dog going back to its vomit. *As a dog returneth to his vomit, so a fool returneth to his folly (Prov. 26.11); But it is happened unto them according to the true proverb, The dog is turned to his own vomit again; and the sow that was washed to her wallowing in the mire. (2Peter 2:22).*

Exercise Self-control: You must learn to exercise self-control and self-mastery. Do not allow your emotions to dictate your actions. Act from principle or what you know to be right and not from impulse. Don't allow your personal biases or emotions to get in the way of your decision making. Studies have found that people with high levels of self-control and self-mastery enjoy better health, better relationships, and better finances. A study by Duke University of more than 1,000 young adults over three decades found that those who scored high on self-control tests as children were far more likely to enjoy better health and financial success as adults than those who did poorly on the self-control tests as children. It was the wise man Solomon in the book of Proverbs who pointed out that a person who cannot control himself is like a city without walls (Prov. 25:28). A city without walls is vulnerable to attack. Similarly, a person with poor self-control makes him or herself vulnerable to attacks. Be mindful that diet can play a big role in your ability to exercise self-control. It is said that the brain needs lots of energy in the form of glucose so if you are hungry or you are not able to metabolize glucose well due to lack of sleep, stress or bulimia you are likely to experience mild dysfunction in the prefrontal cortex. Psychologist Kelly McGoniga of Stanford University writes extensively about this. She states, "It's as if you have brain damage in areas you need to have self-control; and that turns you into the worst version of yourself." You will find yourself getting into rages easily and being impatient with others; you are also likely to resort to old destructive behavior. You must therefore watch what you eat and what you drink. Bulimia and anorexia are two forms of eating disorders that can upset your brain chemistry and your reaction to stress. These disorders can lead to paranoia, hallucinations and mood disorders. Alcohol too plays a big role in how you react to stressful life events. I have worked with many couples involved in domestic violence situations and I have yet to see a couple in a domestic violence dispute where alcohol was not involved. Alcohol affects the central nervous system and therefore affects how you respond to situations of stress. Be especially careful of wine tonics and iced teas with alcohol; observe for the percentage in proof of alcohol. Proof means twice the alcohol content by volume or the amount of ethanol there is in an alcoholic drink; even 5 percent (5%) proof – same amount in beers can have an impact on the central nervous system. Be responsible. Practice self-control; "Mastering others is strength. Mastering yourself is true power" says Lao Tzu. *Wherefore, my beloved brethren, let every man be swift to hear, slow to speak, slow to wrath. James 1:19.*

Set High Standards & Goals: The psychologist Nathaniel Branden in his book "*The Psychology of Self Esteem*" notes that the choice you make about your reality registers in your mind, for good or for bad: Either it confirms and strengthens your self-esteem, or it undermines and depletes it. Now, you may not have any choice over where you were born, the family in which you were born, or structural inequality, but how you think and respond to your circumstances will determine how high you will soar or how low you will fall. You cannot reach a higher standard than you think you can achieve. Set yourself a high standard and exercise wisdom in reaching for it. The July 2016 *Economist* journal cited a paper published by Simon Burgess, an economist at the University of Bristol, who analyzed the outcome of wife of President Obama, Michelle Obama's visit to Elizabeth Garrett Anderson public Girls School in London in 2009, where, about three-quarters of the girls are eligible for free school meals. Mrs. Obama told the assembly that she too came from humble origins and that she had worked her way up from a poor part of Chicago to the Ivy League, a top law firm and (with help from Barack) the White House: "I'm standing here…because of education," Mrs. Obama said. "I thought being smart was cooler than anything in the world." Burgess observed that the school's exam results in the years after Mrs. Obama's visits for 15 or 16-year-olds sitting their GCSEs did much better than girls in the previous year; from 2011 to 2012, for example, the boost was equivalent to each pupil moving from "C" grades to "A" grades. Those improvements were much bigger than the average increases in performance across London state schools, suggesting that the effects were specific to the girls at Elizabeth Garrett Anderson School.

A child knows that if a cookie jar is on the top shelf of a cupboard, it is pointless looking around on the bottom shelf for it simply because the top shelf is out of his reach. He will put effort into reaching the top shelf. He may get a ladder or a stool to get to the top shelf or ask for help because his goal is to get to the cookie jar. You must have an idea of what you want to accomplish in life before you can go after it. World renowned Olympic gold medalist Usain Bold says he sets himself goals each step of the way and works hard to achieve them. Once you have decided what you want to achieve, you must visualize the outcome and put effort into achieving it. Don't become distracted or discouraged by those who do not have your best interest at heart. In most games or sports a typical ploy is to distract your opponent by talking, laughing, belittling or criticizing; it's just a soundbite to send you into a confused frenzy. Be aware of distractions by those who do not have your best interest at heart. A dart player focuses on his target. He does not throw darts aimlessly on the dartboard. He aims for bull's eye, therefore if you aim at nothing you will achieve nothing. *Set goals big enough that God will be proud*, says author, Ken Blanchard. For every new term, venture or endeavor, you must stamp in your mind a mental picture of the goals you want to achieve in life and never lose sense of that image from your mind.

Succeed Through Failure: Never see yourself as a failure or consider yourself a failure just because you failed at something or at a task. Can you imagine telling an eagle, a cow, or a dog that it is a failure? You may fail at a task but failing at a task does not make you a personal failure. If you do fail at a task, like Henry Ford you should see failure as an opportunity to begin again more intelligently. If you mess up, you are not a failure; if you made mistakes you are not a failure. Mistakes can be corrected; that is why erasers, whiteouts and the delete button on the computer were invented. If you made a wrong choice you are not a failure. If you get fired or lose your job you are not a failure. People may refer to you as a failure, even close relatives may intimate that you are worthless, but you are not a failure. Austrian psychiatrist Viktor Frankl once said: "The one thing you can't take away from me is the way I choose to respond to what you do to me. The last of one's freedoms is to choose one's attitude in any given circumstance." Stop seeing yourself as a failure in life and do everything in your power to bring about the result you expect and leave the rest to God. Trust Him to come through for you in His time and in His way. The prophet Samuel must have felt like a total failure after the people – his own sons included - rejected him in favor of a king. Samuel then anointed Saul who turned out to be a total and utter disappointment. In his dejected moment, God did not leave Samuel alone. He reassured him that he did not have to mourn for Saul anymore because He had also rejected him. The psalmist David said: *For he shall deliver the needy when he crieth; the poor also, and him that hath no helper.. Ps 72:12.* God has promised to never leave you or forsake you, so shake off that dejected feeling which is sapping your energy and stalling your progress and get back on the journey of life. There are still new heights to climb, goals to accomplish and great feats to achieve. *"Through the provisions of divine grace, we may attain almost to the excellence of the angels". — (EG White, Mind Character & Personality Vol.1-p.9)*

When it was time for Solomon to take over the throne from his father David, he did not make assumptions about his potential to be a successful leader. He may have been the son of a king, but he knew the responsibilities required of him as king were enormous; he also realized the magnitude of the job and his lack of experience in governing a huge population of people. He wanted to be the best that he could be, but he felt ill equipped to do the job. In humility, he asked God for wisdom and knowledge – an understanding heart to judge the people and to discern between good and bad. In return, God answered his request and gave him riches and honor as well. It is important to note that the reward of riches and honor came after his request for wisdom and understanding. It is not surprising that in later years, Solomon wrote: *Happy is the man that findeth wisdom, and the man that getteth understanding. For the merchandise of it is better than the merchandise of silver, and the gain thereof than fine gold. She is more precious than rubies: and all the things thou canst desire are not to be compared unto her. Length of days is in her right hand; and in her left hand riches and honour. Her ways are ways of pleasantness, and all her paths are peace. She is a tree of life to them that lay hold upon her: and happy is every one that retaineth her. (Prov. 3: 13-18).*

Now Fly with Eagles: One of my favorite children's stories is that of the boy and the eagle's egg. There are many versions to this story, but I have added my own twist to it based on my own life experience to help illustrate my point. The story is told that a boy found an eagle's egg and not knowing what to do with it, he placed it under a hen about to hatch some chickens. When the hen hatched the eagle's egg, naturally it was an unattractive eaglet that looked vastly different from the cute little yellow chickens. Eagles must be taught to fly so without any flying instructions or anyone to help him, the eagle fluttered around like a chicken. He was different in size and shape, so he did not feel that he belonged. The other chickens called him ugly and inept. After all, he was an eagle. Why should he expect to be accepted? Before long, the eagle began to believe that it was ugly and would never be like the other chickens, so it retreated to a miserable and cynical existence. This version of the story did not sit well with me because it seemed to reinforce the notion of learned helplessness. As a person of color, I was fortunate enough to have spent my early years in Jamaica, a country that values education as a vehicle for upward mobility. In my elementary school, Crescent Primary, I can still recall the class motto that Miss Magnus, my 2nd grade class teacher wrote in colored chalk at the top of the chalk board: "If you can't be a pine on the top of a hill be a shrub in the valley but be the best little shrub by the side of the rill." She never erased that motto from the chalkboard for the entire school year and that motto has remained etched in my mind.

In my version of the eagle story, the eagle had a few options: First, he could accept being an ugly chicken and decide to use his size and looks to his advantage; after all, he had powerful wings and a strong beak and could possibly have become adept at warding off prey; second, he could have chosen to become a voice or an advocate for the chickens; or third, he could simply resolve that he was not a chicken and seek to find his own niche. I prefer to believe the third option. He knew he was not a chicken and he needed to find himself, so he began looking around at other birds to develop his own identity and find his niche. He didn't identify with the chickens and he was not accepted by the dove, the pigeons or the robins, but he refused to give up in despair; he just kept looking to find his identity. Then one day he looked up [instead of staying focused on looking down and around] and saw an eagle - way up high -gliding through the sky. It was a bald eagle. Its brown body and white head and tail made it easy to identify even from a distance. When flying, the bald eagle very rarely flaps its wings, but soars instead, holding its wings almost completely flat. The eaglet looked at himself and looked at the soaring eagle. He thought to himself: "that eagle looks like me. That's where I would like to be; that's where I belong." He prayed for wisdom to know what to do and began to learn the ways of eagles. He began by flapping his wings. Each time that he toppled over, the chickens would laugh at him. "Stop wasting your time," they would say. "You are just an ugly old chicken."

Despite their mockery and put down, he didn't stop trying or give up in discouragement. He remembered his class motto by Longfellow, *"The heights that great men reached and kept were not attained by sudden flight but they while their companions slept were toiling upward through the night."* Instead of practicing during the day, he began practicing flying at night while the chickens were asleep. A wise old night owl watching him practice each night encouraged him to keep trying and not to give up. As he practiced, his wings got stronger with each failed attempt. Then one day he flew beyond his limit and began soaring higher and higher. As he struggled to soar, a flock of experienced soaring eagles spotted him struggling against the wind and swooped down to help him up - supporting him with their strong wings until he could fly independently - higher and higher- soaring against the wind. This version of the story reinforces the notion that you do not have to accept a low estimate of yourself. You have options. I like the statement by Paul Arden, which says, "it's not how good you are that matters, it is how good you want to be."

You might face rejection or ridicule in your climb, but don't give up. Assess your skills and competencies and learn from the experience of others. Trinidadian, Sir Trevor McDonald, Britain's first Black television broadcaster who rose from humble beginnings to prominence in the British Broad Casting Corporation (BBC) and was knighted by the Queen of England said he practiced hard at public speaking and refined his English by listening to the British Broadcasting world service.

Work at Becoming Your Best You: You must work hard at becoming the best you that you can be and ignore those who try to thwart your efforts and put you down. Be on the alert for opportunities to improve yourself; accept help when it is given and ask God for wisdom to fill your lack. In the words of author Alan Loy McGinnis: *"The distribution of talents in this world should not be your concern. Your responsibility is to take the talents you have and ardently parlay them to the highest possible achievement."* It is said that "birds of a feather flock together." In other words, people who share the same values spend time together. Be sure that those with whom you choose to spend your time support your goal of self-improvement and have your best interest at heart. The Psalmist David in Psalms Chapter One counsels you to avoid the counsel of the ungodly and the seat of the scornful. Working in poor communities in London, California and New York, I saw firsthand youth who became gang and drug involved. Once caught up in the clutches of these groups, it was hard to break free. By repeated exposure and involvement, they eventually became numb to even criminal behaviors. You must avoid people, places and things that will destroy your sense of self-worth and stop you from being the best you that you can be. Remember the proverb, "If you lie with dogs you will come up with fleas."

Your education of course matters immensely; it serves as preparation for success, so work hard at developing the skills and competencies necessary for the position to which you aspire. If you are not socially connected and you are a college student, be sure to pursue an internship or a volunteer position and work as though you were a hired employee. In my undergraduate years at University in London, it was through my internship that my intern supervisor, Bridget Cramp a retired magistrate court judge saw my potential and encouraged my career path. As an intern, I worked hard and was always looking for creative ways to solve problems; my intern supervisor was so impressed with my work that she spoke to the right people on my behalf and doors of opportunity opened for me.

You Must Know Your Worth: How you see yourself will influence your perception of your worth and what you do with your life. *"The reality of life is that your perceptions—right or wrong—influence everything else you do. When you get a proper perspective of your perceptions, you may be surprised how many other things fall into place"* says *Roger Birkman*. Do not let someone else's editorial of you – be it positive or negative, determine your self-worth. Self-worth and self-esteem are terms that are used interchangeably, but they are not the same. My Jamaican grandmother used to say "alligator lays eggs, but him no fowl" – to translate, an alligator lays eggs, but it's certainly not a chicken. As far as I am concerned, self-worth is the value you place on your-self as a child of God. Like the psalmist David, you can look at yourself and say, "I am fearfully and wonderfully made." I saw a poster on a staff member's desk, which said, "God doesn't make junk;" this person is reaffirming her worth as a part of God's creation. Self-worth is not to be confused with pride. Pride is about drawing attention to ones' self and one's accomplishments or contribution as did the proud Pharisee who went into the temple and prayed (to paraphrase): "Lord look at me, I pay tithe and pray three times a day" in other words, "I am a good guy, so I deserve special favor." Self-worth is about knowing who you are and whose you are; where you came from and what you can and can do or contributing to this life. Self-esteem on the other hand is like an inflated balloon. Circumstances may increase, deflate or lower your self–esteem, but not your self-worth. Your self-worth is about knowing your worth or value. Like a precious piece of Waterford crystal glass that is used without care, you may be around people who do not know your worth and they may treat you in a way that lowers your self-esteem or the way you feel about yourself, but that doesn't mean your worth has decreased. Those around you may not know your worth, but you must know your own worth.

Mass culture can have an insidious impact on your self-worth because you can begin to believe you are "valued less than" if you don't match up; but you must resist being sucked in to this illusion – yes, it is an illusion because you can rise above it. The story was told of an African boy who was in a class of misbehaving children. Soon after the teacher left the classroom the entire class erupted into a disorderly mayhem. The African boy refused to join in. When the teacher returned and saw him still sitting in his seat, she asked his reason for not joining the rest of the class in their disruptive behavior. He said, I am a prince and a change in my circumstances, or my environment does not change who I am. He did not allow his situation or the behavior of others to dictate his behavior.

You do not need to conform to cultural behaviors that are unhealthy or destructive just because it is fashionable or because you want to fit in. Often the media uses the opinion of a handful of people – a focus group, to generalize of a larger group and to dictate how you should feel or think. Think for yourself. Don't compromise with wrong just to fit in or get recognition. Samuel was a foster child in the home of the priest Eli who had two sons Hophni and Phinehas. These two young men were alcoholics, sexually promiscuous and had total disregard for anything Godly. Samuel's own mother, Hannah was mistaken by Eli for one of the women his sons had sexually exploited, when he saw her in the inner court of the temple praying. Samuel could have developed resentment against his mother for seemingly abandoning him in such a negative environment and only visiting him just once a year. He could have acted out behaviorally by choosing to adopt the destructive path of his foster brothers - Eli's sons, but Samuel did not allow his environment to influence him. For every choice you make in life there is a consequence and despite his negative environment, Samuel eventually became a judge and a prophet in Israel.

Not everyone will recognize your worth or give you the respect or credit you deserve for your work or effort. Do not respond by becoming upset, arrogant or resentful. The book of Esther tells the story of Mordecai who discovered an assassination plot to get rid of the king; he disclosed this to the king and saved the king's life. One would expect him to receive all sorts of accolades and rewards, but he received nothing – at least not immediately. It was several years later that the king remembered and rewarded him.

Jesus made the comment that a prophet is not without honor except among his own people and kin, after his return to his hometown and his own people and kin rejected him. Consider this, if Jesus was not given the recognition he deserved from his own family, why should you expect to be treated any differently? Expect even those closest to you to try and treat you less than you are worth, but like a valuable piece of Waterford crystal, you must know your worth and forgive those who don't appreciate your worth or refuse to give you the recognition you deserve. Jephthah was born the illegitimate son of Gilead who had a liaison with a prostitute. Because of his illegitimate status, Jephthah's brothers ostracized him from the family. As is common with teens that feel abandoned by their family, Jephthah became gang involved. Later however, after the people of Gilead - his father's family were threatened by the Ammonites, his brothers, feared for their lives and turned to Jephthah for help - referring to him first as "a mighty warrior." Through his "street smarts," Jephthah was able to lead them to victory against their enemies. Suddenly, this rejected son became a judge in Israel. Even his name was mentioned in the Hall of Faith found in Hebrews Chapter 9. *Humble yourselves therefore under the mighty hand of God, that he may exalt you in due time:* (1Peter 5:6).

Be Careful how You Respond to Being in the Spotlight: Sadly, in Jephthah's case, being in the spotlight and gaining recognition and acceptance from his family that once rejected him went straight to his head; with his limited understanding of God's redemptive love and a history of gang involvement, he was most likely used to making oaths and pledges, and so he made a rash pledge to God, which cost him his daughter's life. You must be careful how you respond to being in the spotlight or to receiving accolades. Marian Anderson, the great African-American concert soloist, was reported to have been asked by a reporter about her greatest moment in life, to which she responded that her greatest moment was being able to tell her mother that they did not have to take in washing anymore for a living. She did not allow the illusive and dazzling effects of stage lighting, stardom and the tumultuous applause of presidents, royalty and her adoring fans to blindside her, neither did she allow newspaper editorials to define her. Marian knew her worth and that in the scheme of things, after the stage lights have gone out and the applause has stopped, she must face herself and the reality of her circumstances as a person of color in a segregated society. Marian knew that she was a great singer by craft but saw no need to dwell on her stardom or on her moment of being a celebrity in the spotlight. As my grandmother would say "lions do not need to roar." Achieving celebrity status, accolades and awards can inflate your ego or self-esteem to the point where you hunger for it and seek validation through it. I recall one famous politician who achieved wide acclaim and celebrity status as a result of a major crisis in his city; he self-confessed subsequently that the celebrity status heaped upon him as a result of the crisis gave him a hunger for recognition after the crisis was over. His frequent television appearances and the accolades received led to his loving the lime light so much that he reached a point where he began looking around for another crisis in order to remain in the limelight. E.G. White notes in Desire of Ages p.331 that: *In the heart of Christ, where reigned perfect harmony with God, there was perfect peace. He was never elated by applause, nor dejected by censure or disappointment. Amid the greatest opposition and the cruelest treatment, He was still of good courage. But many who profess to be His followers have an anxious, troubled heart, because they are afraid to trust themselves with God. They do not make a complete surrender to Him; for they shrink from the consequences that such a surrender may involve. Unless they do make this surrender, they cannot find peace.*

Affirm Your Royal Heritage: I like the *God's Word* translation of I Peter 2:9, which says: *But ye are a chosen generation, a royal priesthood, an holy nation, a peculiar people; that ye should shew forth the praises of him who hath called you out of darkness into his marvellous light;*As a child of God, you are considered royalty, a child of the king, so you do not need to be on the strain for recognition or achieving celebrity status. Your behavior should not become fodder for the media. By virtue of being from a royal household, you must know your royal status and carry yourself accordingly. I have friends from Africa, who are considered royalty in their own country, but outside of Africa they are not given the same respect or recognition they receive at home; as a child of God, you need not fear losing your royal status, you are royalty wherever you go. However, you do need to consider that what you might be capable of doing today might become obsolete tomorrow, which could shake your self-esteem if your estimation of yourself is tied up into what you do. Getting a degree might raise your self-esteem, but not getting a job after graduating could crush it. Knowing this, self-esteem (as opposed to self-worth) is not static. It changes like time and season. Today your skills might be in demand, but tomorrow technology or someone more skilled might replace you. Today you might be appointed president of an organization, tomorrow you might be *dis-appointed*. That is why it is important to invest in your education and a skill. Benjamin Franklin says, "An investment in knowledge pays the best price."

As with nature, you must grow and seek to always create or improve yourself. You cannot dwell upon yesterday's successes or the time when you enjoyed success in another place. This does not suggest that you should start behaving like a mouse on a gerbil wheel, forever studying and creating nothing. Once you have found your niche, you must seek to get better, diversify; create or invent something that can be a blessing to society or seek to reproduce yourself through new talent.

Passion Precedes Success: Successful individuals have a passion for what they do, and they seek to get better at it. Nick Vujicic from Australia has no arms or legs. He was born with a rare disorder called phocomelia, that has left him without all four limbs, yet he seeks to inspire others all over the world. His passion is a driving force for his success. Nick reports that during his childhood he struggled with depression and even attempted suicide, but one day he decided to concentrate on what he did have instead of what he didn't have. He decided that if he could not get a miracle in life, he could be a miracle to someone else and he began to use his life story to inspire many people. Muhammad Ali was known as "The Greatest heavyweight boxing champion of all time," but it took much effort and practice on his part. Ali also studied the science of boxing, during which he coined the phrase, "float like a butterfly and sting like a bee." By the time Ali was 18 years old, he had won several national championships and an Olympic gold medal. He made himself stand out from other boxers by adding his love for poetry, colored with boasting and rhyming. The talking and rhyming also became one of his artful skills at distracting his opponent. He used it so skillfully that it attracted considerable media attention both nationally and internationally. He was only 22 years old, when he won the heavyweight championship of the world. In his efforts to improve his skills, he developed a new style of boxing known as the "rope a dope;" where he let his opponent wear himself out while he rested against the ropes. When his opponent was tired, he made his attack. After winning his first championship, Ali went on to successfully defend his title ten more times. As a child, I did not like to watch boxing because it seemed a brutal sport, but I was never afraid to watch Ali; he was so entertaining and so skilled at his craft, he made boxing look like child's play.

Indeed, it is a truism that when people have a passion for what they do and strive to be the best they can be and are skilled at what they do, their work becomes like child's play and people cannot help but feel drawn to them. Whatever you do in life, do it to the best of your ability - be the best that you can be, and opportunities will come your way. As you strive to be the best that God intends for you to be, you will be in harmony with his will and your self-worth will soar. If you make Jesus your example, you will be qualified to fill any and every position that you may be called upon to occupy…. you are not to feel that you are a bond slave but a son [daughter] of God *(E.G. White, Sons & Daughters of God. p. 283)*.

YOUR CONSTRUCTIVE ACTION PLAN:

If you have made poor choices and decisions in the past, create an action plan to change your situation. Answer the following questions to help you in this process:

- Ask yourself: With whom do I associate? How do these people help or hinder me from becoming the best me that I can be?
- How do I see myself?
- Am I estimating my self-worth based on people's perception of me or am I estimating my worth as a child of God?
- Am I where I want to be in life now? If yes, Congratulations! If no, ask your-self the question, "what I should be doing to improve?" what I need to be doing to get to where I want to be?"
- Write down your desire as a goal. Be specific. Now write down the three obstacles to your completion of this goal.
- List three possible solutions to the problems identified.

My Goal is to _____

The three obstacles are:
1. _____
2. _____
3. _____

The three solutions are:
1. _____
2. _____
3. _____

Your 4th Gem

FINDING YOUR PURPOSE IN LIFE

When we walk to the edge of all the light we have and take the step into the darkness of the unknown, we must believe that one of two things will happen. There will be something solid for us to stand on or we will be taught to fly." ~ Frank Outlaw

In trying to discover my purpose in life I was struck by the following statement that was made by E. G. White: *"Many whom God has qualified to do excellent work accomplish very little. Thousands pass through life as if they had no definite object for which to live, no standard to reach. Such will obtain a reward proportionate to their works. Remember that you will never reach a higher standard than you yourself set. Then set your mark high, and step-by- step, even though it is by painful effort, by self-denial and sacrifice, ascend the whole length of the ladder of progress. Let nothing hinder you. Fate has not woven its meshes about any human being so firmly that he need remain helpless and in uncertainty. Opposing circumstances should create a firm determination to overcome them. The breaking down of one barrier will give greater ability and courage to go forward. Press on with determination in the right direction, and circumstances will be your helpers not your hindrances" (E. G. White, Christ Object Lessons p.256).*

The story was told of a rich westerner that went to a "paradise" island and saw a native swinging in a hammock. Each day the native got up, fished, ate, swam and slept in his hammock. "Don't you want a better life?" Questioned the westerner? "What does that better life look like?" The native asked. "Well look at me," replied the westerner. "I am a chief executive. I'm worth millions of dollars. I work 45-50 hours per week, I own a Rolls Royce and a Mercedes Benz, houses, boats and properties." The native listened "What's the purpose in all of that?" The native asked. "Well, those things are the luxuries of life. If you become like me, you too will get all the material things in life that you want," replied the westerner. The native looked at the westerner with a puzzled look on his face and asked, "And do you expect me to exchange my life for yours?" The native returned to his hammock, turned over and went back to sleep. The point here is that another person's ideas of success might not be yours. You must be clear about your purpose in life, what it is that you want out of life and what success means to you. Another person's purpose may not be yours. Often what you see in the media about an individual's lifestyle may or may not even be true. The job of a publicist is to increase the public's interest in his client, so don't allow someone else's story of failure or success in a given field dictate the path that you choose for yourself. You do not want to climb a mountain and reach the top - only to find that you climbed the wrong mountain. A seed or a nut grows into its own unique plant. It doesn't imitate another plant. You are your own seed. A mango seed doesn't grow into a pear tree. A dog doesn't imitate the meowing of a cat or a cow the braying of a donkey.

Nurture Your Own Seed: The many inventions that we enjoy today resulted from individuals that nurtured their own seed. They became creative in a field that interested them. Henry T. Sampson, the first African American to earn a Ph.D. in Nuclear Engineering in the United States, and a pioneer in the technology used in the cellular phone that has become such an indispensable gadget to us was observed to say: "What drives me is curiosity, I love to learn. To me, that's what living is." You can often discover your purpose according to what drives or irks you. Moses was riled up about the Egyptian's treatment of the children of Israel; little did he know that he would be called to lead the children of Israel out of Egyptian bondage! Rosa Parks was upset about the gruesome killing of 14-year-old Emmett Till, under segregated Jim

Crow and refused to go to the back of the bus. She was already sitting in the front row of the colored section of the bus and was told to give up her seat to a white male when the White section became full. Rosa Parks is quoted as saying, "I thought about Emmett Till, and I could not go back. My legs and feet were not hurting, that is a stereotype. I paid the same fare as others, and I felt violated." As a result of her stance she became a prominent leader in the civil rights struggle and helped to change the course of history for people of color in the United States.

If you want to succeed in life you must ignore the crowd and follow your passion. Just because a field of employment or business pays well, and many people are going into it doesn't mean it is the right field for you, or that you will survive or do well in it. You might pursue it temporarily to help you survive a financial downturn, but you should always seek to find your niche. Look at a fibrous plant with its roots tightly impacted and all clumped together in a pot that is too small. What happens to it? If it is not transplanted it will not grow and will die eventually. I have seen many individuals enter a profession or field of business because it pays well or because it brings prestige, only to end up miserable failures or drug and alcohol dependent. Oscar Levant, a noted pianist who suffered from mental illness and addictions, which cut short his life, said "it's not what we are, but what we didn't become that hurts." I like the statement by Jewish philosopher Martin Buber, which says: *Every person born into this world represents something new, something that never existed before, something original and unique…. there has never been anyone like him in the world, for if there had been someone like him, there would have been no need for him to be in the world. Every single man is a new thing in the world and is called upon to fulfil his particularity in this world…. Every man's foremost task is the actualization of his unique, unprecedented and never recurring potentialities, and not the repetition of something that another, and be it even the greatest, has already achieved.*

<u>Don't Envy Other People's Success, Create Your Own:</u>
Envying other people's success is foolish because you don't know what such individuals have done to get to where they are – the struggles they overcame, the compromises they made or the downside to their success. I like the story of the two chronically ill bed ridden patients in a hospital room with the screen drawn between them; each day, one patient would tell amazing stories of what he could see on the outside. The other patient soon became jealous of not being placed next to the window so

when his room-mate died he asked to be placed in his room mate's bed. He wanted to enjoy the same amazing scenes; to his disappointment, there was no window just a plain brick wall; the scenes described by his room-mate were all in the room-mate's mind. Learn from other people's successes as you seek to create your own path. You should seek to develop and exercise your own creativity rather than try to compete with another. Psychiatrist Viktor Frankl says it well: *"Everyone has his own specific vocation or mission in life; everyone must carry out a concrete assignment that demands fulfillment. Therein he cannot be replaced, nor can his life be repeated; thus, everyone's task is unique as is his specific opportunity to implement it."* Like the acorn that grows into an oak tree, you must grow into your purpose. Once you have discovered your purpose in life, your possibilities will become endless. Several individuals have inspired me to think this way. Steven Spielberg, the award-winning filmmaker decided early in life that he wanted to be a filmmaker, but not just any old filmmaker. He wanted to combine entertainment with a moral purpose and was able to tackle tough racial issues in his movies such as Nazism and Jim Crow. Marian Wright Edelman, social activist pursued a legal career in order to become an advocate for the poor. Bill Gates imagined a computer on every desk. "There is no more noble occupation in the world than to assist another human being - to help someone succeed," says Alan Loy McGinnis, psychotherapist and the founder of the Glendale Counseling Center in California.

The psychologist and author Richard J Leider sums it up best in his article *Lifestyles of the Rich in Purpose (reprinted with his permission).* "Purpose," he explains "is the deeper meaning we give to life, work and relationships. It is the "spiritual core" and it helps us to value and to find the aliveness in all of life's experiences. Purpose is hard to understand because it can't really be measured and it's hard to see. It is often a major life change that leads people to identify or rediscover the true purpose of their lives. A purpose is something you may discover, but it was already there. You've lived your life by it, perhaps without fully realizing it, when you do name it, you will know that you've "known" it all along. It's your lodestar, your personal compass of truth. It tells you, in any given moment, whether you're living your life "on purpose" or not. A purpose is not a goal. A goal is definable and obtainable. A purpose on the other hand is a direction like going West - no matter how far West you go, there's still more West to travel. A purpose is never achieved, but it can be used for choosing goals along the route. It is continually expressed in each moment that you are "on purpose."

Individuals who are in tune with their purpose can face life's challenges and crises with greater resilience. Each stage of the human life cycle from birth to death often results in a crisis. The birth of a child or graduation of a child from school or college may bring joy, but it may also bring financial and emotional crisis and marital break-up. Retirement or marriage may bring joy, but it may also bring emotional, spiritual and financial crisis. Aging parents who can no longer care for themselves can pose a crisis of change in a family. Critical life changes can knock you off your equilibrium and cause you to lose focus. Losing a loved one can create a major life crisis; but in all these crises, your ability to bounce back will be determined by your resilience, your own sense of purpose and how deeply embedded you are to your life's purpose and to your faith in God. To a person with a sense of purpose, a crisis is like a seed that has potential for new birth. Henry Sampson was not only an inventor of the gamma-electric cell – a key piece of technology for the cellular phone, but also during a period of crisis in his personal life, he became the creator of a documentary about African Americans in the film industry - a previously untold history of American blacks in film, television and radio. It was Norman Vincent Peale that said: *"I believe that deep within every crisis lies a seed that if it is properly used, it has the potential to solve the problem. Every problem we face contains the seeds of its own solution. Let's turn that statement around: If you don't have any problems, you don't get any seeds!"* - Norman Vincent Peale.

A seed contains an embryo, but the embryo does not move or grow by itself. It will remain dormant unless it is planted and allowed to germinate (sprout) within a certain length of time. Germination is the growth (or sprouting) of an embryonic plant contained within a seed. Thus, the seed must go through its own crisis of change before germination can take place. Germination only begins when a seed sprouts or comes out of dormancy. When a crisis occurs in your life, you must not retreat in despair. You have gifts that must come out of dormancy and germinate as a result of the crisis. I remember teaching parenting skills classes in the Bronx, New York. Many of the parents attending these classes were mandated by the courts to do so because they had been arrested for using excessive corporal punishment – breaking the skin of their children or they had been involved in a violent domestic dispute in the presence of their children. They resented being there and presented a tough hostile exterior as a defense mechanism. Some had not completed high school, so the thought of attending "classes" conjured up painful memories for them. Once they were able to work through their defenses, not only did they complete the parenting course, but also some decided to return to school and finish their education or learn a new skill. Their crisis created a new opportunity for growth in their lives. Whatever the crisis in which you find yourself, there is a lesson to be learned. Charles Colson who was imprisoned for his involvement in the Nixon Watergate scandal had a conversion experience while in prison. As a result of his imprisonment, he started prison fellowship and wrote numerous inspirational books on positive Christian living.

Plant Your Seeds of Opportunities: What are some of the defenses you are putting up that are stopping you from growing? Seeds of opportunities are all around you. There are seeds of promise that you must explore and plant. Sometimes like a tomato plant that has short dormancy life you must jump at an opportunity. Unless you do something about your gifts and talents, they will remain dormant. You must plant a seed to see result. No seed, no fruit. Stop looking at how bad your circumstances are and stir up the gifts that you have. The parable of the fig tree is a fascinating one. A fig tree is huge. It can be as tall as 300 feet and as wide as 200 feet. We are told Jesus went to the fig tree when figs were not in season expecting to find figs. When he didn't find any, he cursed the fig tree. Why go to a fig tree when figs are not in season and then curse it? It is an object lesson. In life, it is possible to achieve considerable success and simply stop growing or producing; or you reach a point in your life's journey where you stop trying and start making excuses for not accomplishing certain goals in life. You can learn from the fig tree and stop the excuses because all you are doing is bringing a curse on yourself. Begin to bloom where you are.

Make the most of all the opportunities that you have. A friend of mine hated her job but enjoyed crocheting. One day, on her way to the job that she hated, she sat on the train crocheting hats; a businesswoman saw her hats, liked them and placed a large order with her. Colleagues also ordered from her and before long she had a thriving little side business. Another friend was a science teacher who enjoyed teaching but hated the daily classroom routine. She decided to open a day care, which posed some challenges initially, but eventually grew into a hugely successful day care and after school program. I am reminded of a story that Dr. Elliston Rahming, Bahamian Ambassador to the United Nations shared with some young people at a youth retreat, at Camp Berkshire in New York. The story goes: Two young boys tried to trick an old wise man who knew the answer to everything. One boy decided to place a lizard in his hand and ask the wise man what is in his hand. The boys concluded that if the wise man identifies a lizard they would ask if it was dead or alive. If the wise man guessed correctly and say alive, the boy with the lizard in his hand would squash it dead to prove him wrong. When the boys quizzed the wise man, the wise man correctly identified a lizard in his hand. When asked if it was dead or alive the wise man said, "the answer is in your hand my boy, the answer is in your hand."

God asked Moses: "What is in your hand?" The same question is asked of you. What is in your hand? It's time to stir up that gift that is within you. Like Moses you are probably making all sorts of excuses - I have no gifts; I am not good at anything; I am such a failure. Then there are the "what ifs;" what if I try and fail? What if things get worse? My response to those questions is: "So what? Are you going to sit around and wallow in self-pity?" Acknowledge God as your creator and begin now by asking Him to stir up the gifts that are within you. God is a creator and you are a product of his creation. You are endowed with creativity. Start looking, reading and listening. I have encouraged and assisted many adults to go back to school and finish their education and they are much better off for having done so. If school is a challenge for you, you might want to look at what is creating the block. I certainly agree with L. Ron Hubbard that failure in any subject is due to a lack of understanding of concepts and word meaning. New knowledge will be anxiety provoking at first because your mind must adjust to the new information.

Embrace New Knowledge: As a student I was fearful of statistics until I attended Columbia University and had a Chinese professor, Dr. Ada Mui, who taught statistics. At the start of each class, Dr. Mui would utilize humorous comic strips and current events that were relevant to the subject matter; this association helped to make the study of statistics fun, relevant and easy to understand. As I grew to love statistics, I eventually obtained employment requiring the use of statistics. Don't be intimidated by new knowledge, especially in mathematics and the sciences. Sometimes you must go back to basics to master the subject matter. I recall a computer Excel instructor saying he grew up hating mathematics until he discovered Excel. It was in the process of learning about Excel formulas he said that the acronym for factoring (PEMDAS -parenthesis, exponents, multiplication, division, addition, and subtraction) made sense to him. In my study of pharmacology, a fellow student was intimidated by the scientific names of the prescription drugs and asked the professor how to pronounce the pharmaceutical names of the drugs and he replied, "with confidence." Embrace new knowledge as though you are learning a new language. Often, it is an encounter with a new word or technical words that are unique to the subject matter that stumps you and you give up. Don't give up. Instead, research the meaning of the word, break it up into syllables and keep trying. I completed a class in digital publishing at the New York University Continuing Education Program after hearing computer terminologies being used, to which I was clueless. I realized then that I needed to improve my computer knowledge and vocabulary. My main interest in taking the class was to obtain new knowledge and learn a new vocabulary; the final grade was not important to me. I also did a course in real estate, which proved invaluable when my home was being renovated. With the new knowledge, I was able to point out short cuts that the contractor was taking - like missing flashings from doors and absent leaders from drainage. The Bible verse: *My people are destroyed for lack of knowledge (Hosea 4:6)* is a reminder to maintain your quest for knowledge.

Learn from Germination: As with a seed, when you begin to develop your talents you will begin to see results; germination will take place. The interesting thing about germination is that there is a period in the process when nothing seems to be happening; the change is not immediate and visible, but you can rest assure a change is coming. Similarly, in life you will go through stages when it seems like nothing is happening; things might even become progressively worse. Don't give up in despair; germination ends after the plant gets its first true set of leaves and a seedling is formed. Once you begin to develop your talents you will see growth. You will see results. Age, ethnicity, poverty or social status cannot stop you. In the game of chess, mobility and material advantage result in victory in the end game. Without mobility you cannot neutralize your material advantage. Mobility is the key to the end game. Like the chess player, you must act and use whatever skills you have to move forward and bring about the result you expect. A position may have been closed to you, but God can orchestrate things to bring about a breakthrough and the position becomes open, as He has done for me. He can create a position where there was none, but you must have an aim in mind. You must think of achieving the unachievable and work to make your vision a reality. With God nothing is impossible. E. G. White in the book *Desire of Ages* says that God is well please when you make big demands of Him. I believe God is pleased because in doing so you have not reduced Him to your size. You are acknowledging his greatness, His omnipotence and omniscience. *I know thy works: behold, I have set before thee an open door, and no man can shut it: for thou hast a little strength, and hast kept my word, and hast not denied my name." (Rev.3.80)*

The Sky is the Limit: There is no limit to how much you can achieve if you are moving in a direction, which is consistent with God's design for your life. Your purpose! Your possibility then becomes endless as you nurture and develop your talent. Then you can say like David: *2 Bless the Lord, O my soul, and forget not all his benefits: Who forgiveth all thine iniquities; who healeth all thy diseases; Who redeemeth thy life from destruction; who crowneth thee with lovingkindness and tender mercies; Who satisfieth thy mouth with good things; so that thy youth is renewed like the eagle's. (Psalm 103:2-5).*

Europeans once believed that the Rock of Gibraltar was the end point beyond which you should not travel for fear you would fall off the earth. Explorers however did not limit themselves to this belief and in defying such, explored further and discovered a whole new world beyond, inhabited by a vast civilization of Arawak and other Indian tribes. You must not retire from your purpose in life. You may retire from a 9am to 5pm existence, but not from your purpose. Colonel Harland David Sanders became a chef at 40 and founded Kentucky fried chicken in his 60's. Michelangelo was 70 years old when he painted the frescoes in the Sistine Chapel. Verdi composed the opera Othello at 75. Neither age nor youth should be a hindrance or an excuse to pursuing your purpose in life. It is not true that you cannot teach "old dog new tricks." Dr. Irving Lorge, a Columbia University psychologist looked at aging and the mind and found that the body can get old, but the mind's ability to think and create, barring illness can stay with you until the age of 90 and beyond. I remember consulting with Sister Mary Paul Janchill, founder of The Center for Family Life -a child abuse prevention program in Brooklyn New York, on programmatic issues when I was first appointed as director of a similar type family center in the Bronx, New York. Sister Mary Paul was in her seventies when I met her and even then, she still had a passion for her work. At 88 years old, she had retired as director of the Center for Family Life, but not from child welfare circles. She maintained a quiet presence in child welfare circles - influencing policy decisions that affected the lives of vulnerable children and families in New York. Just a few weeks before her passing, she attended a policy meeting – with her walker in tow.

Dr. James Dumpson, another pioneer in human services, education, health, public policy and philanthropy did not allow age to stop him from promoting his philosophy of a caring society. I remember consulting with him on my doctoral dissertation proposal and was encouraged by his insight and wisdom. Even in his 90's Dr. Dumpson was still lecturing. He extended himself to helping the less fortunate in as far afield as Africa. In 2009, Dr. Dumpson celebrated his 100th birthday and was recognized as a familiar, popular, and pioneering leader in New York and in the African American community. Even at 100 years old, his body was frail, but his mind was still intact. The National Association of Social Workers (NASW) saluted him for his pioneering work in the fields of health, education, social justice, and academia; serving as advisor to Presidents Kennedy and Johnson, and on various advisory commissions, including the Presidents Commission on Narcotics and Drug Abuse. He was also appointed U.N. advisor to the government of Pakistan, to help the new government set up schools of social work after its partition from India.

An Oprah Winfrey show on people in the Blue Zone (meaning people who live a long and healthy life) showed heart surgeon Ellsworth Wareham of Loma Linda, who at 94 years old could still be found in the operating room performing surgeries. Dan Buettner and Dr. Dan Oz who studied people in the Blue Zone, said people in most Blue Zones don't even have a word for retirement because they have a sense of purpose. Buettner advised that before you retire knowing what your values and gifts are and where to share those gifts is a great investment.

CONSTRUCTIVE ACTION PLAN:

To help you grow into your purpose, ask yourself these questions:

1. If I had no money worries, what would I do for a livelihood?
2. Is my favorite subject/hobby a career or business possibility?
3. If I had five years left to live, how would I spend my time?

Your 5th Gem

STRUGGLE AGAINST THE ODDS

If you fall, fall on your back. If you can look up, you can get up (Les Brown). Success is to be measured not so much by the position that one has reached in life as by the obstacles which he has overcome while trying to succeed (Booker T. Washington). Christ paid an infinite price for us and according to the price he paid he expects us to value ourselves. We are not what we might be, or what it is God's will that we should be. God has given us reasoning powers, not to remain inactive or to be perverted to earthly and sordid pursuits...God has given us ability to think and to act. Stand in your God given personality. Be no other person's shadow. Expect that the Lord will work in and by and through you (E. G. White, Ministry of Healing, p.343).

Your 5th GEM encourages you to struggle against the odds, even when obstacles like brick walls are stacked against you and gate keepers like iron bars block your pathway. Booker T. Washington's autobiography *"Up from Slavery"* chronicles all the challenges he had to overcome in order to obtain an education. What is most striking about Booker T's story is his insatiable desire to get an education and improve himself.

Although he was a son of freed slaves, he did not have a slave like mentality. He had a goal in life and saw no task as too menial for him. His experience as a janitor served as his test of entry to Hampton University. The interviewer was not impressed with his shabby appearance or his promise as a student and told him to clean a classroom. This was her test to see his devotion to receiving an education. Booker T. had worked previously as a housekeeper for an exacting employer who paid attention to details, so he knew how to be thorough in cleaning a house. When he was through, the interviewer was so impressed with his janitorial skills that he was granted entry to Hampton. In the words of Theodore Roosevelt: "Do what you can with what you have, where you are." Col 3:23 and Ecc.9:10, remind us to do all task – whatever your hands find to do, you must do it well.

Self-fulfilling Prophecy: Many people are like eagles shuffling around like chickens with no sense of purpose or direction. Maybe as children they were told they would never amount to anything good or they were "good for nothing" so they walk around believing it. You cannot reach a higher standard than the one you set or perceive for yourself. Psychologists refer to this as the self-fulfilling prophecy or the Pygmalion effect. In other words, you believe and live what others say or expect of you. There is convincing research by Harvard professor of social psychology, Robert Rosenthal to suggest that a person behaves in a manner that is expected of him. Rosenthal described a classic experiment, with elementary school children from 18 classrooms. They randomly chose 20 percent of the children from each room and told the teachers they were very bright children with enormous potential. They explained that these children could be expected to show remarkable gains during the year. The experimental children showed average IQ gains of two points in verbal ability, seven points in reasoning and four points in overall IQ. The result is that the original expectation really becomes true. What you believe about yourself will determine how much you achieve in life. You must believe that you were created with enormous potential and that you can succeed, once you set your mind to do so. I remember a young lady from Jamaica who was disabled as a result of polio. She had a desire to go to college but did not have the funds or the means. I was able to share with her some information on a scholarship program offered at the local community college and without hesitation she jumped at the opportunity. She had visions of becoming

G.E.M.S. 87

an elementary school teacher and applied herself and eventually made it to the Dean's list. She did not limit herself based on her physical disability but succeeded despite it. You must not limit your possibility based on your present circumstances. Flip it and think of how you would like things to be instead. Fix that image in your mind. Remember the words of Jesus: "As a man thinketh so is he." Stop thinking limiting thoughts. *"The distribution of talent in this world should not be our concern. Our responsibility is to take the talents we have and ardently parlay them to the highest possible achievement," says Alan Loy McGinnis.*

You Must Refuse to Accept Being Defined in Negative Terms Strive to succeed despite adversity. Psychologists refer to individuals who succeed against the odds as resilient; they are like eagles that soar with the wind and rise above the storm. They can thrive and fulfill their potential despite or perhaps even because of adverse circumstances. These individuals see problems as opportunities for growth. I cannot help but think of my own life experience and the life experience of many others that I have counseled over the years - individuals whose lives have been lifted out of the dunghill of life. They are individuals whose lives were mired in poverty, broken or interrupted by abuse, abandonment or neglect; individuals whose parents were on welfare or drug addicted; individuals who knew what it felt like to beg for food, prostitute themselves, recycle bottles or bag groceries in supermarkets to help put food on the family's table; individuals who bounced from one foster home to another. As a teacher, youth and community worker, social worker, and clinician that have lived in major cities and states -London, California and New York, I have had firsthand experience of living and working among many such individuals. I remember working in New York City with children whose mothers were addicted to heroin and crack-cocaine. These children recalled mornings when their mothers were so strung out on drugs that they had to see themselves off to school. Many of these children became what psychologists refer to as "parentified" children – meaning they parented themselves, their parents and their siblings; yet some of these individuals overcame the odds, defied social and psychological ills and rose to achieve extraordinary feats. These individuals do not see themselves as others see them. The psychologist John Dewey sees these individuals as an internal force that strives to continue in being by turning the energies, which act upon it into a means of helping to further its own existence. The psalmist David identifies this source of power within as the power of God who does not abandon the poor and needy or the down cast. He says: *"The Lord also will be a refuge for the oppressed, a refuge in times of trouble. (Ps. 9:9); Thou, which hast shewed me great and sore troubles, shalt quicken me again, and shalt bring me up again from the depths of the earth." (Ps. 71:20,).*

I admire the perseverance, determination, resilience and drive of tennis stars, Serena and Venus Williams. They are examples of two sisters from economically distressed Compton California, whose father coached them in tennis as beginners and all the way to tennis stardom. The sisters trained hard and became world tennis champions - together winning Wimbledon multiple times, and multiple grand-slams and gold medals. They persisted despite their many adversities, unfavorable press reviews, and the limp applause they often received when they first started entering competitions. At one point when their sister died tragically, they lost focus for a while and were not playing well. They could easily have given up in discouragement, but they faced adversity head on, persevered and have been seeded among the very top tennis players of the world. You must have a determination never to give up come what may. When determination is combined with faith in God you will accomplish amazing feats. It was the Psalmist David who said: *"Thou through thy commandments hast made me wiser than mine enemies: for they are ever with me. I have more understanding than all my teachers: for thy testimonies are my meditation. (Ps 119:97-99).*

The Apostle Paul said, "I can do all things through Christ who strengthens me." If you believe in yourself as a part of God's creation and that he created you to rise above mediocrity, your possibilities will become endless. Through God's power, Elisha made an axe-head swim and you too can-do amazing things through the power of God within you. I like the comment made by Pastor J. Norton. He said, "It was God that gave power to Elisha to befriend the disconsolate young man, when he lamented the loss of the axe-head and in every generation since, God has enabled other faithful ones to do Elisha's work, and make the iron to swim. Charles the Second, (Norton continued) was trifling and licentious and locked up John Bunyan in Bedford jail and kept him there with his Bible for twelve long years, but it was during those years that Bunyan wrote the *Pilgrim's Progress* (a classic spiritual allegory about life's struggles) and that iron has continued to swim for many ages yet to come."

Struggle Against the Tide of Adversity: The question to you is - are you willing to struggle against the tide of adversity to be the best you that you can be? Are you willing to delay self-gratification to cultivate your talents? Are you willing to give up addictions that are destroying your life? Are you willing to give up associations that are pulling you down instead of lifting you up? The Psalmist David (in Psalm 1) said if you want to receive blessings don't seek counsel from those who themselves refuse to take counsel or don't find pleasure in being among those who are God fearing. Often those who are not God fearing go with their feelings rather than what is right in principle. For example, a person who is not God fearing or have strong morals will not counsel you against doing something that is wrong, if you can get away with it. I saw a young man with promise lose out on a promising medical career because he chose to link himself up with someone who was criminally involved; although he was not the perpetrator of the crime, he was guilty by association. To associate or take counsel from those who do not have your best interest at heart is to impede your own growth. You do not need to sit with individuals who scorn your efforts to improve yourself. These individuals are like crabs in a barrel, pulling you down or pouring acid contempt on anything you do, or the efforts you make to improve yourself. You will never soar like an eagle if you keep scratching around with chickens. Delight yourself in reading the Bible, meditating on God's words and in spending time with like-minded individuals. *Nothing is apparently more helpless, yet really more invincible, than the soul that feels its nothingness and relies wholly on God. (E.G. White, Prophets & King P. 175-176)*

Lay Hold on God's Promises: To lay hold on God's promises is to rely on His counsels; in so doing, your faith will be strengthened as you grow and whatever you do will prosper (Psalms 1). Even apparent failure will work for your good. You will be like a tree with deep roots that is planted by a river. Think about the patriarch Joseph for example, his life was not exactly "plain sailing." He experienced some despairing tsunamis in his life —he grew up in a highly dysfunctional and blended family, with some mean and vicious half siblings who did not care for him. On one occasion when he brought food for his brothers who were working in the field, his own brothers beat him almost to death before deciding to dump him in a pit. Pits are used for refuse and feces, but on this occasion the pit was dry. I imagine like David, Joseph cried out to God from that pit. David said in Psalm 40:1-2: *"I waited patiently for the Lord; and he inclined unto me, and heard my cry.He brought me up also out of an horrible pit, out of the miry clay, and set my feet upon a rock, and established my goings."*. When your situation seems like you are in a pit and there is no way out, you must cry out to God so that He can bring deliverance. In crying out to God, you are acknowledging His power to change - wonderfully change the most difficult of circumstances and bring deliverance; then, when deliverance comes, you will have no doubt who delivered you from your pit. God can work upon the heart of your very enemy to bring about changes in your favor. After having a change of heart, the brothers took Joseph out of the pit and sold him into slavery. While a slave, Joseph was sent to jail for a crime he did not commit, but through it all - struggles and triumphs - he maintained a constant relationship with God and God honored his faith and commitment. Joseph was an amazing counselor who was skilled at interpreting dreams and although he was in prison and was not obligated to share his skills, he used his skills nevertheless to be a blessing to the down-trodden. His blessings came as a result of two things: The first is that he was a problem solver, even in prison. When Pharaoh had a dream, and no one could interpret the dream, Joseph was able to do so and his skill as a problem solver made room for him. Second, it was through the act of helping the down-trodden while in prison that his blessing came. Joseph is what Adam Grant, author of *Give and Take* would call a "giver" and not a "me first taker." As a giver, takers will not always appreciate you or your efforts. The very ones you are giving aid to may be the very ones to turn against you; as in the case of Joseph's brothers but give anyway. Joseph did not become revengeful or mean spirited. Even in prison, he injected light to others and from the prison cell he was promoted to the palace. The Lord says, *"Because he hath set his love upon me, therefore will I deliver him: I will set him on high, because he hath known my name. (Ps 91:14); That I may cause those that love me to inherit substance; and I will fill their treasures.." (Prov.8: 21).*

The story of Jabez is that of a man who struggled against adversity and God blessed him simply because he asked. Although not much is known about Jabez, there is much more to his story. Jabez's mother bore him in pain and gave him a prophetic name, which meant pain and sorrow. Considering names in Bible times were supposed to be prophetic, his name wasn't the best choice for a child. Jabez could easily have lived out his name in a negative way. He could have seen himself as nothing more than a pain and cause pain to others, but he chose instead to live an honorable life. Jabez saw himself as a part of God's creation and conducted himself accordingly. It is said he was more honorable than his brothers. In other words, his piety and his life style were a cut above the rest. Living an honorable life however doesn't mean things will always work out for you.

In Jabez's case, things were not working out favorably for him, but in his sorrow, he cried out to God. In other words, he prayed, *"Oh that you would bless me and enlarge my borders and keep me from pain,"* and we are told that God answered his request. Jabez asked God for a blessing. People with a low sense of self -worth often do not like to ask for help, a promotion or advice because of the underlying feeling of shame and the fear of being rebuffed or turned down, leading to even more shame, but Jesus said: *"Ask, and it shall be given you; seek, and ye shall find; knock, and it shall be opened unto you." (Matt. 7:7).* James, the brother of Jesus in writing to his brothers and sisters in Jerusalem said, *"Ye lust, and have not: ye kill, and desire to have, and cannot obtain: ye fight and war, yet ye have not, because ye ask not. (James 4:2).* Don't be afraid to not only ask God for help but also ask people in influential positions for help. I have found that people who are hugely successful are quite humble about their success and are willing to share their knowledge and skills to help uplift others, but some will only give help if asked. Billionaire Warren Buffet, for example is reported to only give advice if he is asked. I will never forget one of my doctoral mentors, a Harvard graduate and author who took time out of his busy schedule to travel to New York and help me with my dissertation, yet he did not know me. When I offered to pay him, he dismissed the offer and said laughingly, "When you make your millions buy me a new car." In Jabez's case, he asked God for a blessing and God answered his prayer. According to Jewish writers, Jabez became an eminent writer and doctor in the law who was well respected for his piety; so much so that a town was named in his honor.

It was David who said *(Psalms 50:15): "And call upon me in the day of trouble: I will deliver thee, and thou shalt glorify me."* Don't be afraid to call upon God and ask for his favor in your life. When I struggled financially as a foreign student in the United States, I took courage from the Bible promises: Fear not, for I am with thee; be not dismayed, for I am thy God. I will strengthen thee, yea, I will help thee; yea I will uphold thee with the right hand of my righteousness… *Fear thou not; for I am with thee: be not dismayed; for I am thy God: I will strengthen thee; yea, I will help thee; yea, I will uphold thee with the right hand of my righteousness. Behold, all they that were incensed against thee shall be ashamed and confounded: they shall be as nothing; and they that strive with thee shall perish. Thou shalt seek them, and shalt not find them, even them that contended with thee: they that war against thee shall be as nothing, and as a thing of nought. For I the Lord thy God will hold thy right hand, saying unto thee, Fear not; I will help thee. Fear not, thou worm Jacob, and ye men of Israel; I will help thee, saith the Lord, and thy redeemer, the Holy One of Israel. Behold, I will make thee a new sharp threshing instrument having teeth: thou shalt thresh the mountains, and beat them small, and shalt make the hills as chaff. Thou shalt fan them, and the wind shall carry them away, and the whirlwind shall scatter them: and thou shalt rejoice in the Lord, and shalt glory in the Holy One of Israel. When the poor and needy seek water, and there is none, and their tongue faileth for thirst, I the Lord will hear them, I the God of Israel will not forsake them. I will open rivers in high places, and fountains in the midst of the valleys: I will make the wilderness a pool of water, and the dry land springs of water. I will plant in the wilderness the cedar, the shittah tree, and the myrtle, and the oil tree; I will set in the desert the fir tree, and the pine, and the box tree together: That they may see, and know, and consider, and understand together, that the hand of the Lord hath done this, and the Holy One of Israel hath created it. (Is 41:* 8-20)*. God heard my cry and did not disappoint me because I graduated from college almost debt free. I would have been debt free had I not gone on a spending spree for clothes I did not need.

God Cares for Your Every Need: I remember a point in my life when I was exhausted from over extending myself in too many different directions. Someone said, "you need to rest;" I said in response "I need a cruise." My daughter added, "I will pray for you mom, that God will give you a cruise." Within a month of this prayer Dr. Elliston Rhaming, the Bahamian ambassador to the United Nations wanted to reciprocate our kindness to him as guest in our home while in the United States and gifted my family with a cruise to the Bahamas. *Prayer is a heaven-ordained means of success…prayer moves heaven…. Prayer, faith confidence in God, bring a divine power that sets human calculations at their real worth – nothingness…He who places himself where God can enlighten him advances, as it were, from partial obscurity of dawn to the full radiance of noonday. E. G. White – Reflecting Christ. P159.*

Conditions for Answered Prayers: If you are praying and your prayers have not been answered, you should first look within yourself and see if there are things that you are doing or failing to do that are preventing answers to your prayers. Ask yourself these 10 questions: Am I asking with the wrong motives (James 4:3)? Do I really believe that God will answer my prayers (James 1:6)? Am I arrogant in thinking that God owes me an answer or owes me favors (Job 35:12)? Am I engaging in sins or behaviors and practices that are not in line with God's moral code of conduct (His Ten commandments) and am I willing to give them up (Psalm 66:18)? Do I have unconfessed Sins (Is 59:2)? Am I holding grudges and not willing to forgive (Mark 11:24)? Am I just blatantly wayward and disobedient (Prov. 28:9)? Am I abusive in my relationships with my spouse, my children, my coworkers or do I mistreat others (1 Peter 3:7)? Am I asking but not according to God's will (1John 5:14); or, am I so selfish that I don't even think of others (Eph. 4:32)?

If you have answered "yes" to any of these questions, you can make a change through self-surrender. Like Jacob who wrestled for his life and pleaded for a blessing, you too must seek for a transformation of character and a willingness to bring your will into conformity to God's will. It was through self-surrender and a steadfast faith that a change occurred in Jacob's life. He said, "I will not let thee go, except Thou bless me" (Gen 32:26). Jacob pleaded with a determined spirit and his name was changed from Jacob meaning-one that cheated to Israel, meaning: "Ruled by God's will; *And he said, Thy name shall be called no more Jacob, but Israel: for as a prince hast thou power with God and with men, and hast prevailed.*" (Gen 32:28). When God has blessed you, do not take the glory for yourself. He has blessed you for <u>His</u> glory. Jesus delayed in performing many miracles for people to see the manifestation of God's power and bring glory to God's name. This does not mean that you must hide or dismiss your achievements or your accomplishments, thinking it is humility. God created you to shine. There was a time in my life that I was afraid to shine and worried that people would perceive me negatively, so I often down played or dismissed my accomplishments, or I would simply hide in the shadows of others. The following statement by Ellen White served as encouragement for me to shine:

The Lord is disappointed when His people place a low estimate upon themselves. He desires His chosen heritage to value themselves according to the price He has placed upon them...He has use for them and He is well pleased when they make the very highest demands upon Him, that they may glorify His name. They may expect large things, if they have faith in His promises. E. G. White. Desire of Ages, p.668

Your 6th Gem

TAP INTO THE SOURCE OF YOUR STRENGTH

Praise ye the Lord. Blessed is the man that feareth the Lord, that delighteth greatly in his commandments. His seed shall be mighty upon earth: the generation of the upright shall be blessed. Wealth and riches shall be in his house: and his righteousness endureth for ever (Psalm 112:1-3)

Children are naturally dependent on their parents and caregivers for their basic needs, but as adults, there is a tendency to transfer that dependency to what is more tangible like – money, job, family and material things. God wants you to exercise faith and transfer your dependence from the tangibles around you to Him and what He can do in and through you, for His glory. This can be a challenge for those who have never had a father who was dependable, reliable or available; maybe he was abusive or an alcoholic who was one day loving and next a monster. Without an earthly father who provided support and care, it is hard to imagine a God who can genuinely care for you. Telling you that God loves you may even sound trite and meaningless if you have had to struggle in life, on your own. You may even project your anger towards your earthly father unto God - feeling anger towards God for abandoning you in times of despair and fearing that you must go through your struggles alone.

God's Big Picture Plan: The interesting thing about God's plan for you is that it is bigger than any plan that you could think of or imagine. The problem is that we often short circuit His master plan through lack of trust. The patriarch Job had every reason for distrusting God and giving up on God. He had lost everything, so what was there to live for? However, Job did not give up on God. A disappointment is an opportunity to not only build faith, but to also build your character. Job was a man of character. He said, "Although they slay me, I will still trust in Him." He trusted in God implicitly and God, his heavenly father came through for him even bigger than before. Daniel landed unjustly in a furnace and in a den of lions, but in each scenario, Daniel maintained his faith in God and God came through for him miraculously; he ended up receiving a big promotion. Joseph was thrown into a pit by his brothers and then in prison by Potiphar, but God came through for him big time! Because of his skills in interpreting dreams (problem solving), Joseph landed an unexpected and big-time promotion in Pharaoh's palace as the chief executive officer. These are just a few examples of God-fearing individuals who experienced the power of God to come through big time for them and in a remarkable way. If God could do it then, why can't He do it now? He has not changed. He was the same God yesterday; He is the same God today and will be the same God tomorrow. *Not because we see or feel that God hears us are we to believe. We are to trust in His promises. When we come to Him in faith, every petition enters the heart of God. When we have asked His blessing, we should believe that we receive it, and thank Him that we have received it. Then we are to go about our duties, assured that the blessing will be realized when we need it most. When we have learned to do this, we shall know that our prayers are answered. God will do for us, "exceedingly abundantly", "according to the riches of His glory", and "the working of His mighty power" (Eph.3:20, 16: 1:19. E. G. White, Desire of Ages. p. 166).*

God's Unconditional Love: Children who grow up in homes deprived of parental love or have "refrigerator mothers" who are cold and indifferent often experience clinical depression, which leaves them questioning why anyone should love them –even God. They see love as conditional; they don't think anyone can love them for themselves, so they over-achieve, enter co-dependent relationships, or look for love in all the wrong places. They are ambitious to win favors instead of being ambitious as a normal trait. Without that inner source of self-worth, they work hard to please others. They even work hard in church to win God's favor and the favor of others. If this profile fits you, what I can say to you is that God has not abandoned you or forgotten you. His love for you is unconditional, so you do not have to earn His favor or His love. He says draw nigh to Him and He will draw nigh to you. Jesus told the story of the prodigal son who left his father and squandered his substance on those whose affections he sought to earn. Even after making this foolish decision, and eventually "wising up" to his wasted life and coming to his senses, his father did not abandon him, or use it as an opportunity to make an example of him. When the son eventually realized his need of a father and in humility he returned to his father and asked for forgiveness, his father accepted him unconditionally. In fact, his father was always on the lookout for him and before anyone could see how low his son had fallen and before the household could make fun of him, his father ran to meet him, hugged him and covered him in his best robe. It has been said that in the Jewish custom a man should not run because he would have to lift his robe and show his legs, which would be considered shameful but, in this case, the father not only bore his son's shame by lifting his robe and running to him, he also quickly covered his son's shame and treated him as royalty. Only the unconditional love of a father could do that. After Adam and Eve sinned, they tried to cover their shame with fig leaves, but the fig leaves were not adequate, so God provided them with covering that was adequate. God loves and cares for you because you are His own creation. He loves you unconditionally, so you don't need to earn His favor or stay away from Him in shame.

If you have distanced yourself from God or you are working to earn His favor, it is time that you tell God how you really feel and let Him tell you how He feels about you. Don't rush. Wait for His response. You may need to go for a prayer walk or grab your Bible and read a psalm; listen to some praise and worship songs alone, spend time with nature, or just remain silent right where you are in meditation and God will surely speak to you. Sometimes God will impress someone to speak to you as in the case of Oprah Winfrey. Oprah related in her May 2010 Oprah magazine that Wintley Phipps, a Seventh day Adventist Pastor and gospel singer was performing in Baltimore (at which time she was a local news anchor). Phipps was impressed to go back stage and tell

Oprah that God had impressed him to tell her that God holds her in His hand, that He has shown great favor to her and that she will speak to millions of people in the world, in and through His name." Oprah noted, they did not know each other, but she had always believed those things herself, even before that conversation. "In the time just before I left Nashville for Baltimore," Oprah stated, "I was speaking in churches a lot. I remember speaking at a women's day service—I had my red Cutlass outside, packed and ready to drive to Baltimore. And my sermon was, *"I don't know what the future holds, but I know who holds the future."* I have no fear about the future. I have no fear about anything, because I really do understand that I am God's child and that He has guided me through everything and will continue to until the end."

You must believe that you are God's child: God cares for you implicitly as though you were the only child in the world. The story was told of two boys playing in the field; one rich and the other poor. The rich boy bragged: "You see that big house on the hill, my dad owns it. You see that airplane flying in the air my dad owns it." The poor boy looked up assuredly at the house and said: "You see the hill on which your daddy's house rest, my daddy owns it; you see the airspace in which your dad's plane fly, my daddy owns it and you see this ground on which we stand, my daddy owns it. My daddy owns the whole world." You must rest in the assurance that you are God's child and that God loves you; He has your best interests at heart, but first you must believe it. Claim now the promises of Isaiah 54:11-17: *O thou afflicted, tossed with tempest, and not comforted, behold, I will lay thy stones with fair colours, and lay thy foundations with sapphires. And I will make thy windows of agates, and thy gates of carbuncles, and all thy borders of pleasant stones. And all thy children shall be taught of the Lord; and great shall be the peace of thy children. In righteousness shalt thou be established: thou shalt be far from oppression; for thou shalt not fear: and from terror; for it shall not come near thee. Behold, they shall surely gather together, but not by me: whosoever shall gather together against thee shall fall for thy sake. Behold, I have created the smith that bloweth the coals in the fire, and that bringeth forth an instrument for his work; and I have created the waster to destroy. No weapon that is formed against thee shall prosper; and every tongue that shall rise against thee in judgment thou shalt condemn. This is the heritage of the servants of the Lord, and their righteousness is of me, saith the Lord.*

Don't Give Up or Give In: My friend Ena sent me the following email story called "Scars of Life," the author is unknown, but I like it because it embodies God's love for us. The story goes, some years ago, on a hot summer day in South Florida, a little boy decided to go for a swim in the old swimming hole behind his house. In a hurry to dive into the cool water, he ran out the back door, leaving behind shoes, socks, and shirt as he went. He dived into the water, not realizing that as he swam toward the middle of the lake, an alligator was swimming toward the shore. His father, working in the yard, saw the two as they got closer and closer together. In utter fear, he ran toward the water, yelling to his son as loudly as he could. Hearing his voice, the little boy became alarmed and made a U-turn to swim to his father. It was too late. Just as he reached his father, the alligator reached him. From the dock, the father grabbed his little boy by the arms just as the alligator snatched his legs. That began an incredible tug-of-war between the two. The alligator was much stronger than the father, but the father was much too passionate to let go. A farmer happened to drive by, heard the screams, raced from his truck, took aim and shot the alligator. Remarkably, after weeks and weeks in the hospital, the little boy survived. His legs were extremely scarred by the vicious attack of the animal. And, on his arms, were deep scratches where his father's fingernails dug into his flesh in his effort to hang on to the son he loved. The newspaper reporter who interviewed the boy after the trauma asked if he would show him his scars. The boy lifted his pant legs. And then, with obvious pride, he said to the reporter, "But look at my arms. I have great scars on my arms, too. I have them because my Dad wouldn't let go." This story stresses the father's hold unto his son, but I can imagine that boy was also clinging to his father for his dear life and would not let go. Jesus experienced what medical science call "hematidrosis," which is a rare, but very real, medical condition where one's sweat will contain blood. It results from *extreme* anguish. "My soul is overwhelmed with sorrow to the point of death" (Matthew 26:38; cf. Mark 14:34) said Jesus in the Garden of Gethsemane. He knew the torture that he was about to experience, yet he did not give up. He prayed fervently, and he relied on his father for strength to see him through. God can see you through whatever struggles you face, or you are about to face.

You may have done some regrettable things in your life or some regrettable things have happened to you, but God has not let go of you. During your struggle, He has been there holding on to you. Sometimes we give up too soon and stop praying; We let go just when deliverance is near and lose precious blessings. Judas could have witnessed the greatest miracle ever, but he was impatient; he compromised in doing wrong by selling Jesus for 30 pieces of silver and then committed suicide when his dream of being offered an exalted position was not realized. Sadly, for Judas, he sold his soul to evil desires and as a result he missed out on resurrection morning. Don't compromise with wrong. Just don't give up. Don't miss out on resurrection morning, in three days, Jesus rose again and in three days things could change dramatically for you. In three days, you could go from rags to riches. In three days, your desires could be granted. In three days, amazing things could happen. Don't give up on God, for He won't give up on you. He is ever faithful and will come through for you. A loving father wants to protect his child from harm and as a child of God, you can rest assure that He wants to protect you and provide for you in every way possible. Sometimes we foolishly enter dangerous situations - oblivious to what perils are ahead; the journey of life is filled with challenges, but God does not leave you to struggle alone. You must move over sometimes and let God take the driver's seat. Surrender to Him and He will come through for you.

Take assurance from Habakkuk 3:17-19: *although the fig tree shall not blossom, neither shall fruit be in the vines; the labour of the olive shall fail, and the fields shall yield no meat; the flock shall be cut off from the fold, and there shall be no herd in the stalls: Yet I will rejoice in the Lord, I will joy in the God of my salvation. The Lord God is my strength, and he will make my feet like hinds' feet, and he will make me to walk upon mine high places. To the chief singer on my stringed instruments.*

Feeling Abandoned by God: At times in your life you may feel abandoned by God - especially if you have worked hard all your life and you just can't see anything good happening. You might have lost everything that you have worked hard for through no fault of your own. I often see raccoons in my backyard, and they are there because property developers have destroyed their natural habitat. Similarly, in life you may find yourself displaced and having to struggle to survive through no fault of your own, or through poor decisions and poor choices. Moses lived in Pharaoh's palace, so you could say he grew up privileged. He attended the equivalent of an ivy-league college, the best in Egypt. He was self-confident with a strong sense of social justice, to the point of taking the life of an Egyptian who was treating a Hebrew slave unjustly. After his misdeed was exposed, he escaped for his life and ended up caring for sheep for an extended length of time – 40 years. At the end of 40 years, his self–confidence was so shaken that he doubted his own ability to even speak, but God knew his heart and chose him to lead the children of Israel out of Egyptian bondage.

The beautiful story of Ruth and Naomi is a reassuring reminder that when you are down to nothing God is up to something. Naomi went to live in Moab with her husband and her sons because their crops had failed. You could say their business went belly-up during a recession and they moved to another place to improve their situation, but things got even worse there. Naomi's husband and sons died while in Moab and she was left a pauper. Overwhelmed with depression, Naomi decided to go back home. She instructed her daughters-in-law to return to their family, but while Orpah decided to return, Ruth resolved to stick by Naomi's side, assuring her that they are going to see the tough times through together. To paraphrase Ruth: "I am not going to let you go through this alone. Regardless of what you say I am not going to leave you or return home, for your people shall be my people and your God my God; I'll be there for you Naomi, through thick and thin and God will see us through this." It was Ruth's faith in God that helped Naomi get through those difficult times and Ruth's faith was not disappointed. While gathering scraps to survive, she met Boaz, a wealthy man and they fell in love and got married. Together they had a son, through whose lineage came several kings – David, Solomon and the King of Kings himself, Jesus Christ. You just don't know how God is going to move in your life. I know many young people whose parents brought them to the United States as children and they lost their legal immigration status because their visa expired, and their parents never returned to their home country. Without proper immigration documentation many could not move forward, but President Barack Obama introduced the Deferred Action for Childhood Arrivals (DACA) Program, which made it possible for them to remain in the country without fear of deportation and apply for work permits, to increase their opportunities. When your faith is growing weak, God will send someone to encourage you or help make a way for you. Don't turn away the help that he sends. Just trust God and trust His word to guide you through your situation or your challenges. Be assured that God can remove any burden or yoke: *And it shall come to pass in that day, that his burden shall be taken away from off thy shoulder, and his yoke from off thy neck, and the yoke shall be destroyed because of the anointing. (Isaiah 10:27).*

<u>Dealing with Prejudice:</u> I remember arriving from London, England to Loma Linda University in California and feeling like "a fish out of water;" being a new foreign student, I knew no one on campus and didn't know my way around. I felt alone and friendless and decided to go for a long walk on the grounds of the beautiful campus. I said, "Lord you speak to us through nature; speak to me now Lord. Show me what to do." I had no idea how God would respond. I circled the grounds of the campus hoping for an answer, but there was nothing. As I walked back to the dormitory, I was struck by the presence of two squirrels facing each other as though frozen in time. I stood and watched them for a while and neither one would budge. I watched to see their next move, but neither one moved. As I observed the squirrel, Solomon's proverb came to mind "to have friends you must make yourself friendly" (Prov. 3:6). I returned to the dorm determined to be the first to be friendly; as I entered the elevator, I said hello to another student, Janice who also happened to be a foreign student. We became friends and through our friendship, I met other friends. By being friendly, I made life time friends with people from all over the world and learned a great deal about different cultures in the process. I also saw that prejudice is simply pre-judging people negatively without knowing them and that Jesus came to break down the walls of prejudices. Prejudice is a destructive force that limits one's growth, development and world view. God also hates prejudice as he demonstrated in the life of Miriam, the sister of Moses who disparaged Moses' wife Zipporah, an Ethiopian, because of her skin color. Miriam had a leadership role among the women of Israel and God was so displeased with her behavior - creating division along color line, that he made an example of her. She became leprous – white as snow. It is as though God said, "if you think she is too black, I will show you what white looks like." The interesting thing about color differences is that after death, if you dig up the grave of a white person and of a black person the color of their bones would be calcified the same. Melanin is what makes the difference in skin pigmentation.

My experience of working among families of different cultures, ethnicities and social class has led me to realize that families, regardless of their ethnicity are all plagued with the same life (sin) problems – youth alienation from parents, dishonesty, domestic violence and child abuse; substance abuse, alcoholism, and mental illness – problems that destroy lives, cause trauma and tear relationships and families apart. Years have passed since my years at Loma Linda, but the people I met there have remained etched in my memory as my blessings and my teachers when I needed them the most. Certainly, my life has been enriched as a result of my relationship with them.

It's Time to Pray: I find that oftentimes we are so busy that we never sit still to hear what God has to say to us. We live in an electronic age with high speed Internet. Speed is the desired result. We want quick answers to everything, yet God says, "Come let us reason together" (Is 1:18). In other words, "sit down and talk to me" – put down the electronic gizmos, the social media or the cell phone and meditate on God. The e-mails will always be there. Postings on social media about your daily activities is like standing in the middle of busy Grand Central Station in New York City or Heathrow airport in London and telling everyone what you are doing. Who really cares? Take time out for prayer and meditation instead.

God counsels you to acknowledge him in all your ways and He will direct your path. God wants you to talk to Him. He wants you to cast your cares upon Him because He cares for you. He is interested in every aspect of your life. Jesus promised as He ascended to heaven that He would send us a comforter in the form of the Holy Spirit, so essentially, God has never left us alone. The Holy Spirit is the third person of the God head *that lives with you and will be in you" (John 14:16, 17)* and will prompt you to do what is right and pleasing to God. Unfortunately, you can grieve the Holy Spirit by your resistance to its promptings. When the Holy Spirit prompts you to do what is right you must respond to its biddings. If you do not know how to do so, or where to begin you may need to consult with your pastor, or a person who has had an experiential relationship with God. Of course, you could just get down on your knees and tell God you don't know where to begin. The Holy Spirit will guide you.

Pastor Jerome Barber, a frequent speaker at Wall Street Wednesday Worship service in Manhattan, New York City with founders Dr. Susan Johnson Cook and Brother Jason told the story of his down-syndrome son, Abraham *(and here repeated with his permission)*. His family took Abraham to a roller - skating rink and Abraham immediately began to skate. Seeing how well he could roller skate, his sister took him ice-skating, but she soon realized that learning to ice skate was more of a challenge than roller skating. As soon as he went on the ice he fell and could not get up. The instructor at the ice rink skated over to him and said, "you must get on your knees if you want to get up." Like Abraham, if you want to get up from where you are, you must get down on your knees. Humbly kneel in prayer. In kneeling or bowing before someone you are showing humility and submission. Humble yourself before the Lord today and watch him lift you up (James 4:10). Cast all your anxieties upon Him for he cares for you (1Peter 5:7).

A Diverted Path: I read of a young man who felt called by God to become a clergy, but at Bible College his professors told him that he was not cut out to be a pastor because he did not work well with people. Hearing this, the young man became devastated and quit school. He also gave up on God and never set his foot back in a church. He never prayed about the matter or asked God to redirect his path into another field since pastoral ministry was not his calling. He just gave up on the journey. Sometimes God leads you through a diverted path to help you get to your ultimate destination. I received a major county award for the prestigious Chelsea School of Art in London, but after a few months at art school, I realized art school was not the place for me. I didn't want to disappoint family, friends and teachers, and so I felt caught in a bind and was experiencing cognitive dissonance. I became depressed and stopped eating. I also had no desire to go back to college. While I was home in bed, people from the church came and prayed with me and the dean of the school visited me and asked what I wanted to do. I decided to go into teaching and the dean took me to several universities in London and told me to choose the one I wished to attend. I chose Whiteland's Teacher's College where I was able to pursue dual programs in teaching and youth and community studies–for which I received a distinction. These two courses of study combined helped me to meet influential people and opened amazing doors of opportunities for me.

Surrender to God's Leading: The path in which God is leading you is a safe one, despite the obstacles. Paul assures in 2 Cor. 12:9 that *"And he said unto me, My grace is sufficient for thee: for my strength is made perfect in weakness. Most gladly therefore will I rather glory in my infirmities, that the power of Christ may rest upon me..."* Pray earnestly about any matter that has you feeling defeated; pray when things do not work out as expected. God is a loving father who cares for you. Trust Him to direct your path and watch God come through for you in the most unbelievable way. Just *By humility and the fear of the Lord are riches, and honour, and life (Prov.22:*

4). The rich young ruler, a Pharisee and Zacchaeus, the tax collector and a Publican were both rich guys and both wanted a more fulfilled life, so they sought out Christ for the answer. Jesus told the rich young ruler: *If you would be perfect, go, sell what you possess and give to the poor and you will have treasure in heaven; and come, follow me." When the young man heard this, he went away sorrowful, for he had great possessions (Luke 18:18-30).* Zacchaeus on the other hand, after his encounter with Jesus voluntarily offered to give half of his goods to the poor. The interesting thing about Jesus' directive to the young ruler is that if the young man had sold his possessions they would have multiplied and if he had given to the poor, he would have ended up being even richer than before because his act of giving to the poor would have been an acknowledgment of God as the wealth giver. Often, we do not achieve all that God intends for us because our view of God is too small. Jesus was killed because the people saw him only as the king of the Jews. Jesus knew himself to be King of Kings and Lord of Lords. In His most trying moment in Gethsemane, at his weakest, he prayed for God's will to be done in his life. Don't give up on yourself if things have not turned out as expected, for through your weakness God can show His strength. Through your weakness God's name will be glorified. Through your weakness God's power will be manifested.

The song *All to Jesus I Surrender was* written in1896 by Judson W. Van DeVenter and remains one of my favorite hymns. Van DeVenter struggled between his desire to be an artist and an evangelist. He surrendered to God and he was led to become an evangelist and discovered a hidden and untapped talent. It was then that he penned the words of this song: *All to Jesus I surrender all to him I freely give.* The question for you today is: Have you surrendered your all to God? What is stopping you? Who or what are you choosing above God? God's ideal for you is to elevate you to become godlike in character. *Higher than the highest human thought can reach is God's ideal for his children – godliness and godlikeness,* says E.G. White. Just change the way you see yourself and you will start the process of change in your life. Take counsel from Paul's statement: *Rejoice evermore. Pray without ceasing. In every thing give thanks: for this is the will of God in Christ Jesus concerning you. Quench not the Spirit. Despise not prophesyings. Prove all things; hold fast that which is good. Abstain from all appearance of evil. 1 Thess. 5:16-22*

CONSTRUCTIVE ACTION

1. Lord today I surrender my _____
2. Lord, today I present my deepest desires to you believing that you
   will grant me the wisdom that I need to _____

Your 7th Gem

MOVE FROM FEAR TO FAITH

The secret of the Lord is with them that fear him; and he will shew them his covenant. (Psalm 25: 14). "Every failure on the part of the children of God is due to their lack of faith. When shadows encompass the soul, when we want light and guidance, we must look up. There is light beyond the darkness. Remove your mind from the distressing situation and think of God's power to help, sustain and guide." (E.G. White, Patriarchs & Prophets, p. 655).

Your 7th GEM is aimed at helping to strengthen your faith. We live in a world where evidence plays an important role in decision-making. In a United States court of law, a preponderance of evidence is needed to win a case. In both the public and private service industries, programs must be evidence based in order to get funding. It is not surprising therefore that people tend to want proof that God exists. The truth remains that a belief in God is a faith experience. It also takes faith to believe in evolution because scientist cannot prove how life began. They can simply hypothesize and support their hypothesis with scientific evidence. Faith in God requires believing in someone you cannot see and accepting the inspired words of those that have experienced God. I fly to Europe often, yet I do not know or even see the pilot. I just have faith that he or she is not a deranged lunatic. I trust he is sane and will take me to my destination safely. Essentially it takes faith to fly in an airplane and similarly it takes faith to believe in God.

You must have faith that whatever challenges you are facing, God will bring you through. My favorite Bible texts when I face life's challenges are: *For thus saith the Lord God, the Holy One of Israel; In returning and rest shall ye be saved; in quietness and in confidence shall be your strength: and ye would not. (Isaiah 30:15); I can do all things through Christ which strengtheneth me. (Phil.4: 13);* For God hath not given us the spirit of fear; but of power, and of love, and of a sound mind. *(2Tim 1:7).* This does not suggest that my confidence in God does not sag from time to time. Faith in God is a growing experience. During the process of writing this book, I was once again forced to look at my relationship with God as my heavenly father. Sometimes it seemed like he was just nowhere around, but a relationship with God is not based on feeling but on faith. If your relationship is based on feelings you will not experience a "walk with God" because when you are feeling down, or your feelings overwhelm you, you will give up on the journey. If you have confidence that the source of your strength lies in a supernatural power that is greater than you are, and it is on this power source that you rely, then even when the way seems dark and there seems to be no light at the end of the tunnel, your faith in God will sustain you for the journey, for His strength is made perfect in your weakness. I was encouraged by the words of Gabby Douglas, first African American gold medal gymnast. During the competition Gabby said she trusted in God and affirmed her faith in him by repeating scriptures and God honored her faith in a big way. *Likewise, ye younger, submit yourselves unto the elder. Yea, all of you be subject one to another, and be clothed with humility: for God resisteth the proud, and giveth grace to the humble.*

Humble yourselves therefore under the mighty hand of God, that he may exalt you in due time: (1Peter 5:5-6).

Reaching Life's Crossroad: My decision to migrate to the United States was a huge step for me in my journey of life; I recall reaching a crossroad in my life and feeling unsure of which road to take; I was not yet 30 years old and had already obtained my master's degree in Sociology and Social Policy and was receiving successive promotions with the Inner London Education Authorities. Doors of opportunity were certainly opening for me in England; I was also an elected community representative serving on the North Lewisham Law Center Management Committee, the Telegraph Hill Neighborhood Council and the Albany Alternative Education Council. There were individuals - king makers who were prepping and steering me in the direction of a political career. The future looked bright, but internally I felt unfulfilled. I felt a spiritual vacuum inside. Although I was attending church and participating, I felt a need to extend my usefulness, but I had no idea which direction to take. I mentioned my crossroad experience to my pastor at the time - Pastor David Hughes and I remember his comment because it registered with me. He said in his rich American accent: "Well, you remember what Jesus said to the rich young ruler." I retorted, "Well, I am not rich, and I am not a young ruler." I knew the story of the rich young ruler. The rich young ruler admired Jesus and wanted to be like him. He wanted a deeper spiritual experience, but he wasn't willing to make any life style changes or sacrifice anything. He wasn't willing to leave his comfort zone or his prestigious position. I knew that if I wanted to reach a higher standard of spiritual experience, I could not be like the rich young ruler that went to Jesus asking for direction in his life but left feeling sorrowful. I realized that I would have to make some life-style changes that would require much humility of spirit and a lot of faith. I would also have to surrender all my trappings of success and seek God in faith, believing His promises and trusting His words.

The Path to Faith: In sharing my feelings and my life goals with Pastor Hughes, he asked if I had considered attending Oakwood College (now University) in America. I had already obtained a master's degree from a university in London, so Oakwood did not seem like the right path for me. Coincidentally, I had developed an interest in Family Systems Theory and had written sometime earlier to Loma Linda University in California to enquire about their Marriage and Family Therapy program. Within a week or two of my conversation with Pastor Hughes, I received a personalized letter from Loma University saying: "If you are thinking of applying, now is the time to apply." Deciding which road to take was not easy because at about the same time, my job offered me a promotion and an executive leadership scholarship. Do I go to California or do I stay? Do I continue in the path that seemed sure or do I follow the path of uncertainty? As I struggled with my decision, I came across the devotional book, *This Day with God by Ellen G. White*; where in one devotional feature she noted that…. *"Frequently the absolute best evidence that we can have that we are in the right way is that the least advance costs us effort and that darkness shrouds our pathway. It has been my experience that the loftiest heights of faith we can only reach through darkness and clouds."* It is my presumption that Ellen White came to this conclusion because to follow the path of the unknown requires lots of faith and total reliance on God. Quite frankly, the only road that looked dark to me and required much faith was the path of the unknown – going to California. I took assurance from God's leading in the life of Abraham and trusted him to guide me. *By faith Abraham, when he was called to go out into a place which he should after receive for an inheritance, obeyed; and he went out, not knowing whither he went. By faith he sojourned in the land of promise, as in a strange country, dwelling in tabernacles with Isaac and Jacob, the heirs with him of the same promise: For he looked for a city which hath foundations, whose builder and maker is God. Through faith also Sara herself received strength to conceive seed, and was delivered of a child when she was past age, because she judged him faithful who had promised. (Heb. 11: 8-11).*

I had toured some of the northern and southern states of the United States a year prior, but I had never been to California; I knew no one there and I had no idea what to expect apart from what I had read in the school's prospectus and seen on a video. I struggled with tremendous fear as my anxiety heightened over which road to take. My anxiety and fears were not irrational because I knew the opportunities that were available to me in England, but I didn't know what opportunities were available to me in America. I knew I had to decide, but I wanted to be sure it was the right decision. I prayed about it, and sought counsel for… *Without counsel purposes are disappointed: but in the multitude of counsellors they are established. (Prov. 15:22).*

My Personal Journey of Faith: After weighing all my options, I made my decision to give up all my possessions and positions including my job in England and travel to the United States; and so, began my amazing journey of faith. I decided to go to Loma Linda University with a goal of returning to London to open my own clinical practice. I had property and savings and decided to liquidate all my assets to attend school in California. I did not know what the future would hold for me, but in the words of Oprah Winfrey, I knew who held my future. I thought I would be able to work and go to school, but upon arrival in the United States, I was told that all the paid internships were already taken, and I could only work on campus because I was a foreign student. I was filled with fear. I arrived a day before school started and all the available jobs on campus were also already taken. I feared I would not have enough money to survive the first semester furthermore two years. The thought of not accomplishing my goal filled me with even more fear and anxiety. In California, you need a car to get around. I worried about getting to my internship without a car. I was alone in California with no family or friends to advise or guide me. For the first time, I understood what the Psalmist David meant when he said *I feel like a lonely bird upon a roof-top.* Alone and feeling lonely, I found myself spending time in the study of God's word and the writings of Ellen G. White. More importantly, I spent time on my knees asking for guidance and direction every step of the way. From that experience, I came to realize that successful Christian living is a personal and individual relationship with God, guided by Biblical principles and lifestyle changes. It is not a set of do's and don'ts. The dos and don'ts are given out of love and are for our benefit. Take the Ten Commandments for example, only a loving God would say don't worship material things; love and respect your parents, don't kill anyone, don't steal or envy what is not yours. Take a day out to rest from your labor and don't cheat on your spouse. God's rules are meant as a guide for successful daily living and not to restrict you. *For this God is our God forever and ever: He will be our guide even unto death. Ps.48: 14.* From the assurances and promises in the Bible supported by the interpretive writings of Ellen White in her books such *as Desire of Ages, Patriarchs and Prophets, Prophets and Kings, Acts of the Apostles and Ministry of Healing,* I received reassurances that God would see me through.

<u>Surviving Adversity:</u> My first year at Loma Linda University was a humbling experience. As a foreign student, I heeded the Biblical counsel that "whatever your hands find to do, do it with all of your might." I survived financially by baby-sitting, making sandwiches for the vending machine in the men's dorm, working as a front desk receptionist in the girls' dorm and doing odd jobs on campus. I was also grateful for the welfare food from the Campus Hill church's food pantry. My Japanese classmate Diane, who interned at the same site, gave me a ride to my internship and in return I provided lunch for the both of us. The experience seemed like a lesson on how to survive hard times. I could easily have given up and returned to England, but I believed that even in this experience there were life lessons to be learned. *I waited patiently for the Lord; and he inclined unto me and heard my cry. He brought me up also out of a horrible pit, out of the miry clay, and set my feet upon a rock, and established my goings. And he hath put a new song in my mouth, even praise unto our God: many shall see it, and fear, and shall trust in the Lord (Ps.40: 1-3)*

In my second year at University, I was able to obtain a paid internship at the San Bernardino County Superior Court. I believe that in doing a job, I should not work to please my supervisor, but to please God, which means I do my best in the sight of God and allow God to do the rest. In so doing my supervisor and the judges were happy with my work and told me that I could work for as many hours as I was permitted. After two years, I graduated from Loma Linda University almost debt free. I could have graduated debt free, but I went clothes shopping for items of clothing that on reflection, I didn't need because I had good quality clothing from England that were European classics, which had not aged in style or become threadbare. As I reflect on this experience, it was truly a miracle that I managed to survive those two years almost debt free. All I know is that God provided for my every and need in remarkable ways.

Facing Roadblocks and Crushing Disappointments: The challenge of being a foreign student did not end there. After graduating, I tried to get employment to at least earn some money before going back to England, but I met only roadblocks because I did not have a Green Card. After applying for a few jobs and getting nowhere, I decided to return to England empty handed. On my way back to England, I stopped in New York to visit relatives. My relatives suggested getting some work experience in New York before going back to London. My cousin Joyce remarked, "If you can make it in New York, you can make it anywhere." Since I was not going back to a job in London, I had nothing to lose by trying. This same cousin took me to her attorney in Manhattan to process my immigration papers. Her attorney advised me to first get a job in my profession and he would process my H-I professional status visa. He also gave me a photocopied list of non-profit organizations to which I could apply for a job. I was hopeful that things would work out and sent my resume to all the agencies listed. A couple of weeks went by and there was no response. The weeks turned into months. I was staying with my sister who was happy for my company, but I was becoming increasingly anxious because I had just enough money left for my airfare back to London. All my hopes and dreams were crushed. I felt abandoned by God. As my prospects grew darker by the day, all the negative beliefs about me that I had absorbed over the years came flooding back. Assurance came from this statement by E.G. White. *"You may be perplexed in business; your prospects may grow darker and darker, and you may be threatened with loss. But do not become discouraged; cast your care upon God and remain calm and cheerful. Begin every day with earnest prayer, not omitting to offer praise and thanksgiving. Ask for wisdom to manage your affairs with discretion, and thus prevent loss and disaster. Do all you can on your part to bring about favorable results; Jesus has promised divine aid, but not aside from human efforts."*— *(The Review and Herald, February 3, 1885).* Every evening I would go jogging to release stress and tension. I remember while jogging one night crying out to God for help and in tears pouring out my heart to Him. I returned to my sister's apartment after regaining my composure and there waiting for me was my sister's neighbor, Serge. He said he had a job for me. I thought to myself "what kind of a job is he able to offer me when he is an employee himself." He clarified that the non-profit organization for which he worked was looking for someone with my qualifications. I was dubious about the possibility of obtaining employment after so many failed attempts but followed up, nonetheless. When I called about the job, I was already so dejected that I did not try to sell myself. I told Elizabeth Slane, the interviewer at the other end of the telephone line, all the qualifications they required, which made me ineligible for the job and then explained the qualifications and certifications I possessed. This is not what you do when you search for a job. You should sell yourself in the best possible light, but in my case, I was already feeling dejected and was so sure that they would not hire me that I decided to disqualify myself first. I just could not deal with another rejection. To my surprise, Elizabeth who became my supervisor said in her rich German accent: "You are exactly what we are looking for." I added that I did not have my green card, only a student visa. There was a chuckle in her voice. "No problem" was the response, "I understand, I've been there; we will sponsor you, come and see me tomorrow."

Puzzled by God's Leading: I could not believe the turn of events. I returned to the lawyer in my excitement with the paperwork to be processed for my green card. He told me it would cost $4,000 dollars. I did not have $400 furthermore $4,000. I offered to pay once

I had started working. He stood up, extending his right hand to indicate that the conversation was over, shook my hand and said, "Have a great day." This was such a shocking blow; I was dumbfounded. I had a job offer, but no money to process my paperwork. I felt like God was toying with my emotions. What was I supposed to do? I remember getting on the E-train at Lexington Avenue in Manhattan and sobbing all the way back to Hollis Queens. Nothing made any sense to me. I wondered about God's leading in my life and again like David cried out to him for help: *Unto thee O Lord, do I lift up my soul. O my God, I trust in thee: let me not be ashamed, let not mine enemies' triumph over me. Yea let none that wait on thee be ashamed. Shew me thy ways, O Lord; teach me thy paths. O keep my soul and deliver me: let me not be ashamed; for I put my trust in thee. Let integrity and uprightness preserve me; for I wait on thee. Redeem Israel O God, out of all his troubles (Psalm 25).*

My sister had not yet come home from work. I was alone in the house and tears just kept flooding. I resolved that maybe I should just go back to England and in making that decision, I felt more at peace; but I was still puzzled at God's leading in my life. Nothing made any sense. In the stillness of the moment, my left hand, as though guided by a gentle force went between the seat and arm of the couch, pulling out the paper with the list of agencies that the lawyer had given to me previously. I turned over the paper and on the backside was listed Catholic Charities Immigration Services and without any forethought, I dialed the number. I don't think I was very coherent, but somehow, I was put through to someone who could help me. A lady with a kind voice answered and asked me a few questions. I did not realize that my student visa was about to expire. She told me that since my visa would expire in three days, my professional status visa application had to be postmarked the day of my call. She advised me to come in and see her right away. I mustered up enough energy to take a dollar cab (commuter cab) and get back on the E train headed for Manhattan. I met the lady with the kind voice on the 16th floor. She was very warm, caring and reassuring. She must have seen my tear stained cheek. She told me I was lucky because she was scheduled to leave the job at the end of the week and had already delayed her leaving date because they had not yet found a replacement for her. It seemed God had delayed her leaving date just for my sake! She completed my application and told me the cost would be $90! And that I could pay after I had started working. God turned my sorrow into joy in the most remarkable way! *For the Lord will not cast off forever: But though he cause grief, yet will he have compassion according to the multitude of his mercies. For he doth not afflict willingly nor grieve the children of men (Lam. 3:31-33).*

God Knows How to Meet Your Need: I was assigned to work at the agency's two psychiatric group homes that were in my community – one was next door to my sister's house! God just knows how to meet our needs! I had no money or transportation to get around, so he provided a job for me - next door to my sister's house! Working with psychiatrically disabled teenagers in a group home would not have been my first choice of employment because I knew the challenges that I would have to face in working with that population, but that was God's choice for me. Sometimes we look for the easiest way out, when the hard way could be the very life experience that is needed to help us grow. This "bread and butter" work experience in "the trenches" became an important part of my lifelong learning and experience. I learned firsthand about mental illness, the impact of abuse and neglect on human behaviors and the bondage of addictions. The work was extremely challenging. The residents were mentally unstable, or gang involved. Some had been criminally involved and even drug addicted. Others displayed behaviors that were threatening and confrontational. I saw rage at its worse and violent confrontations involving weapons, but I was taught restraint techniques, which helped when I needed to subdue them. One young man who was a diagnosed paranoid schizophrenic even threatened to shoot me when he was in one of his paranoid episodes. Almost all the residents were emotionally volatile and were ready to fight at the "drop of a hat." Yet, working among these individuals taught me compassion for the downtrodden, setting boundaries and human relations skills needful for dealing with vulnerable individuals of varying temperaments and personalities. I also learned that given the right help and support; proper guidance, a wholesome environment and opportunity for advancement, people are able to change; like a wilting plant in the wrong sized pot that is repotted in good soil with some fertilizer, they are able to rise from the depths of despair and despondency – the dunghill of life and make something of themselves.

Stop Playing God: In working with the psychiatrically challenged population, through an education incentive program that our team developed, I saw young men and women gain mental stability, stop selling and using drugs; obtain a marketable skill and lead productive lives - even going on to college. I also witnessed those who refused to take counsel, continue their walk on a destructive path and ended up dead or in jail. The job required that I multitask and interface with many different systems and individuals of varying strata, all of which helped to broaden my professional and world-view. When I left England, I wanted to broaden my experience and certainly this job helped me along the way. From this experience, I gave up my "Pollyanna attitude" of wanting to "change the world." I recall one day returning from the psychiatric emergency room with a female resident who had been engaging in self-mutilating behavior (cutting); I was feeling exhausted from the activities of the day and trying to be responsive to the multiple needs of the residents, when a female resident who had recently returned from being hospitalized for psychosis looked at me and remarked, "You need to stop playing God; you cannot save the world you know." It was a wake-up call for me. I was putting a lot of effort into helping the residents, but I wasn't seeing rapid results at the rate I expected and was feeling dejected. I wanted to "fix" the residents quickly. Her statement reminded of Psalm 119:29 which says: *Remove from me the way of lying: and grant me thy law graciously..* I concluded that she was right. I decided then and there that God was in control and I was simply his instrument; As such, I can only do my part to the best of my ability. My interventions though small, would create the rippling effect necessary to ultimately influence change. It was after this epiphany that I received a promotion, which placed me in a position where I was able to influence policy and program design and improve overall conditions for the residents. I learned also that how you see yourself in relation to God is going to influence how well you cope with life's challenges. If you believe that you are a child of God, then you must believe that He is your heavenly father and that He has your best interest at heart. He will never fail you or forsake you. He will lead you in the path that will help you to become the best you that you can be because he wants the best for you. *3 John 2 says: Beloved, I wish above all things that thou mayest prosper and be in health, even as thy soul prospereth.*

Fear is Life's Biggest Faith Blocker: Fear is often a signal that danger is a head, so don't move forward blindly - be careful; but fear can also become so overwhelming that it immobilizes you and blocks your ability to come up with creative solutions to a problem or even try new endeavors. Fear can cripple success. It can arrest your ability to improve your situation or move you from an inferior position to a superior one. In abusive and oppressive relationships, fear is often used to keep people in a subordinate position. God sent Jonah to warn the people of Nineveh, to turn from their wicked ways, but Jonah did not want to visit Nineveh partly because of fear of the Ninevites. The Ninevites were a wicked and blood thirsty people. They were notorious for making examples of people by parading their blood thirsty actions of beheaded people on raised poles in the market square. The scourging and crucifixion of Christ was similarly a cruel act to instill fear in his disciples, so much so that the disciples hid after they saw how Jesus was scourged and tortured. Africans that were brought to America as slaves were likewise beaten and lynched to make examples of them and instill fear and submission in other slaves. Systems and institutions make example of individuals who dare to challenge the status quo through firing, character assassination or execution.

Fear can drive you to abandon your faith in God and resort to fables, psychics and get rich quick schemes. Is it any wonder that the Bible says "fear not" 74 times and "be not afraid" 29 times? The children of Israel expressed fear when they came to the Red Sea. The sea was in front, but there was no bridge to cross over and behind was the Egyptian army pursuing them. If Moses had cowered in fear when sandwiched between the Egyptian army and the Red Sea, the Israelites would have had to return to Egyptian bondage. If Jesus had cowered in fear in the Garden of Gethsemane and allowed his fear of his imminent death to overwhelm him, we would not have Christianity today and the blessed hope that it gives. If Rosa Parks and Dr. Martin Luther King had cowered in fear instead of protesting against the evils of segregation, we would not have had a civil rights movement in America; and if Nelson Mandela had cowered in fear, apartheid would not have ended in South Africa. *It was through faith and prayer that Jacob, from being a man of feebleness and sin, became a prince with God. It is thus that you may become men and women of high and holy purpose, of noble life, men and women who will not for any consideration be swayed from truth, right and justice (E.G. White Ministry of Healing, p. 511).*

If you have prayed for God to do something special in your life, but in moving forward you see a blockage, don't give up in despair. That spirit of fear is not from God. For God hath not given us the spirit of fear; but of power, and of love, and of a sound mind. (2 Timothy 1:7). "Always do what you are afraid to do" says Ralph Waldo Emerson. Do not allow fear to hold you back from achieving your desires in life. It is often more comfortable to stay with the familiar than to move into an uncharted course. You must be bold, and powerful forces will assist you. Do not fear what others might say. If Mary Magdalene, the woman with the alabaster box and a questionable past had been fearful of what those around her would say about her entering a home uninvited and anointing Jesus' feet and drying them with her hair – her crowning glory - she would not have been recorded in history for her act of submission and kindness. Mary had a reputation of being a sexually promiscuous sinner, but she did not let that stop her from achieving her goal. She could have avoided the crowd, but in this instance, she did not care what people had to say about her. Don't allow fear of what people might say about you stop you from achieving your goal or filling a void - living right and doing right. Jesus was an invited guest, but his host failed to treat him the way he ought to have been treated. It was the host responsibility to make sure that Jesus' feet were washed but it was Mary that moved forward and filled that void. In so doing, she took on the role of both a servant and a leader and was recorded in history for her bravery.

When Your Mind is Troubled: When your mind is troubled, you must look for opportunities to see where you can be of service. Stop focusing on yourself and your fears. Follow Jesus' commission. Feed the homeless, visit a nursing home or the sick. Help someone. The very act of helping someone will help you to put things into perspective and help to remove your difficulties. *You must live a twofold life – a life of thought and action, of silent prayer and earnest work. The strength received through communion with God, united with earnest effort in training the mind to thoughtfulness and caretaking, prepares one for daily duties and keeps the spirit in peace under all circumstances, however trying (E. G White. The Ministry of Healing). Be not therefore anxious for the morrow… sufficient unto the day is the evil* thereof. Matt 6:34, RV.

Facing Barriers: Have you ever noticed a paved sidewalk with a crack in it? Although it might be paved with concrete, if there is a crack in the concrete, weeds or tufts of grass will grow through that crack. Not even the force of the concrete can stop that tuft of grass from growing. The concrete pavement was designed to prevent the grass from growing; likewise, individuals will set up barriers that might block your progress, or vilify your character, but when you have faith in God, even though there might be powerful forces at work against you, God who is all powerful will make a way for you, but you must make every effort to struggle against adversity and not give up. The walls of Jericho were fortified with an inner wall and a retaining wall that were strong enough, thick enough, and high enough to protect the giants on the inside, yet with a simple act of marching around it and blowing a horn, God tore it down. The gates of hell cannot prevail against you if you have faith in God.

Abraham was a man of faith, but through a spirit of fear he compromised his faith when his life was threatened. Don't give up or give in when faced with challenges; just one small act of compromise can lead to a downward slide. Maintain your confidence in God. There are two root Latin words in the word confidence – con and fides. *Con* means *with* and *fide* means *trust*. If you maintain your trust in God, He will make the way clear. Your *Success* will come as you struggle against great mountains of difficulty. God allows obstacles as a test of faith. When you feel fenced in, this is the time to trust in God and in the power of his Spirit. Continue to climb the mountain of challenges that you face, one by one, until you reach the very top. Don't be afraid of the height, the view looks vastly different and much better from the top. The following poem was written by my husband and has been a source of encouragement to me:

Your Rugged Road ~by Serge Valcourt

Your road may be rugged, and your feet pained, and calloused
Elements of fear spread chaos in your path as struggles and hard
times hit you hard and discouragement and misery pile up high
in your back yard.
Child of God, do not torment your soul, nor lose hope in the fold,
isn't God capable of strengthening your stronghold?
He provides food for birds and shelter for ants certainly he can
take care of your desires and wants.
Your road may be rugged, and your feet may be sore, but keep
climbing the mountain and see Calvary afore.

See His arms outstretched wide, so no need to cry and sigh. Keep moving closer His promises are nigh. Your answer is waiting with blessings and more. Just stay the course, He will come through for you on time and for sure.

Your 8th Gem

HAVE A VISION

Where there is no vision, the people perish: but he that keepeth the law, happy is he. Proverbs 29:18 "And the LORD answered me, and said, write the vision, and make it plain upon tables, that he may run that readeth it. For the vision is yet for an appointed time, but at the end it shall speak, and not lie: though it tarry, wait for it; because it will surely come, it will not tarry." Hab. 2:2-3 (KJV).

Your 8th GEM counsels you to have a vision of what you would like to achieve in life. Jamaica is a tiny island in the Caribbean, which has a total area of 10,990 sq. km (4,243 sq. mi) and extends, at maximum, 235 km (146 mi) N – S and 82 km (51 mi) E – W. The total coastline is 1,022 km (634 mi), yet it always has representatives in the national Olympics. In the 2008 Olympics in Beijing, Jamaican athletes collectively gained a total of 11 medals outdoing countries that are larger in size and with more economic resources. In 1994, the first Jamaican bobsleigh team made history in the Calgary Olympic winter game. Jamaica does not have snow or winter; it is located in the tropics, but the competitors saw snow in their minds. The Jamaican bobsleigh team did not win but showed courage throughout. Indeed, the Jamaican athletes are from a small island in the Caribbean, but they do not see themselves as small people. They see themselves as being capable of competing among the best of the best. Although adverse conditions and inequities might limit your opportunities, how you think can influence how you respond to your circumstances.

Your beliefs about yourself and your capabilities will shape how high or how far you go in life. If a person believes he or she cannot do any better, he will settle into a comfortable state of existence. If you are comfortable with your existence why strive for anything better? Expand your thinking and you will expand your horizon. Do not allow theories that are based on fallacious reasoning to limit your thinking about your capabilities. It has been said that people of color are less intelligent than whites and that people from Asia are smarter in the sciences than other groups, but what is this based on? Just think for a moment, if I administer an intelligence test and one of the questions asks, "What would you find in Piccadilly Circus?" If you have never been to London or heard of Piccadilly Circus, you might respond "animals" based on your understanding of the word circus. Does that mean you are not intelligent? Of course not! It simply means your level of exposure is limited to what you know. Now, if I were to take you to London or you were to read a book about London, you would know that Piccadilly Circus is a place in London, and you would most likely see people and a whole lot of pigeons. People from Asia learn math in binaries of 10, which is a much easier way to start out learning math than counting from one to 100; it doesn't make people from Asia smarter, but it does give them an edge in math. From my experience of living among people from Asia, I find also that they are much better at pooling their knowledge and resources than other groups. When I was at University for example, I helped one student from Asia with a paper for which she received an "A" grade. She did not keep the source of her help to herself; she brought her fellow Asian students for me to also help them improve their grade.

<u>You Must Understand the Society in Which You Live and Function</u> Certain countries believe in social stratification, while others believe in individualism. Understanding this difference is important because in order to achieve your personal best you must understand how the society is structured in order to succeed in it. I grew up in London and was able to obtain the general certificates of education (GCE's) necessary to get into university. However, some of my peers did not pass their GCE's and therefore could not get into university to achieve their dreams of entering certain professions. Does it mean that they were not as smart as those students who obtained their GCE's? Absolutely not! Some of these same friends migrated to the United States and were able to become high powered professionals. My friends did not suddenly become intelligent because they moved to the United States. They knew they were intelligent, so they moved to a place that was structured differently and could accommodate their individual academic ability and learning style, in order to achieve their personal goals in life. Of course, there are levels of ability; not everyone will reach the same development or excel with equal efficiency in the same work. *God does not expect the hyssop to attain the proportions of the cedar, or the olive the height of the stately palm. But each should aim just as high as the union of human with divine power makes it possible for him to reach (E. G. White, Education p. 267, 1903).*

You Must Have a Vision of What You Want Out of Life: The wise man Solomon said that *"without vision the people perish."* A vision is not a goal. A vision is a plan, a definite road-map and a strategy with time frames to get to the goal. There are times however when your vision might not be clear, and you have no idea what to do. If you are an all-rounder who is good at quite a few things, visualizing the path to take can become blurry. If your self-esteem is at an all-time low and you are lacking in confidence in your abilities, you might also have difficulty visualizing anything better for yourself. If such is the case, you will need to pray and seek counsel from those who are knowledgeable about the field you wish to enter or the decision you wish to make. Finding a mentor was not always easy for me because of the limited circle of mentoring individuals to which I was exposed; much of my mentoring experience came through the college and continuing education classes I attended. If I had an interest in a particular skill area or field of study and had no one to mentor me, I would attend a class and seek guidance from the instructor.

Stop the Pity Party: Sitting around being self-absorb and moping about how terrible your life has turned out will not change anything or accomplish anything. If anything, you will simply attract like-minded disaffected individuals who will help you to nurse your bitterness. When Job had lost everything he owned, he was not short of miserable comforters who simply made him feel even worse about himself by pointing out his faults and short comings. Find a mentor who will help you identify your strengths and help you build on them. If you do not have a mentor, take personal inventory of your skills, competencies and your accomplishments. Have a vision of what you wish to accomplish in life and write it down. Ask yourself: "What would I like to accomplish in life, if I had only 24 hours in which to do it?" What would you do? In other words, think about your hopes, your dreams and your aspirations and develop an action plan for accomplishing your vision. Create a vision board with pictures from a magazine. Take small steps. What would you like to accomplish in the short term? What would you like to accomplish in the long term? What steps do you need to take to accomplish your goals? If you wish to accomplish a certain profession, you may need to go to college first. If you cannot afford to attend college fulltime, you could start by taking one or two classes at a time. I accomplished both of my doctoral degrees by taking three credits each semester. It took several years to accomplish – stopping and starting - but I was able to accomplish both - one step at a time. I have encouraged many individuals to do the same and those that have done so have accomplished their goals. A mother who decided to go back to school and took just one class at a time described it as "a bug"; once you start on the road to accomplishing your goals you will get hooked and an inner force – the Holy Spirit just propels you forward.

Barbara Corcoran, a successful Manhattan real estate dealer offers a useful road map for developing a mental picture of where you want to go in life. Corcoran suggests that you must first decide how much money you want to make and then work your plans backward. Visualize yourself as being phenomenally successful in the position that you desire. Make sure the details are clear. See your-self dressed in the actual outfit – even the colors. Think about how you are feeling. This vision will serve as your direction. Having developed a picture of yourself as a success, take time to plan how you are going to get there. Decide how you are going to earn the income you desire; what you need to do; people you need to reach out to, your strengths and weaknesses – areas of weakness that need shoring up and then, present your plans to God, realizing that *There are many devices in a man's heart; nevertheless the counsel of the Lord, that shall stand. A man's heart deviseth his way: but the Lord directeth his steps. (Prov. 19:21 & Prov. 16:9).* In other words, while this might be your plan, God may have something better in mind so allow him to work out His plan in your life.

Dealing with Disappointments: Don't force your way into situations through malicious scheming or give up because you are rejected or fired from a job. Paul Arden in his book: *'It's not how good you are, it's how good you want to be'* makes the following statement which resonates with me: He says that being fired often means you are at odds with your company and the job isn't right for you. I read about a young man, who was sure that God had led him into the ministry, but when his professors told him he was too controlling to be a minister he gave up on his dream and his belief in God, instead of simply switching courses and considering another profession that might be more suited for him. If you believe God cares for you, then you must accept that even disappointments will work for your good. The story was told of two tear drops meeting one day and introducing themselves. One said, "I am the tear drops of the one that was rejected;" the other said "and I am the tear drops of the one that was chosen." In other words, you may be crying over a lost love, only to meet the one chosen over you also in tears over the one you lost.

All Things Can Work Together for Your Good: I like the story that is told in the Talmud of the rabbi who went in search of mystery and took his three possessions with him - his lamp, his rooster and his donkey. On his journey he stopped in a village to rest, but they chased him out, so having no place to sleep he settled in the forest to spend the night. He did not complain, he said, "All that God does is done well." He lit his little lamp and was about to read the Torah before retiring to sleep when a fierce wind came and blew out the lamp. A wild beast then came and ate the rooster and thieves stole his donkey. In response to these losses the rabbi said, "All that God does is done well." The next morning the rabbi had to go back through the village. To his shock and horror, during the night, marauding soldiers came and killed everyone in the village and went looking in the forest for runaways, where he had slept. Reflecting on all the events of his life he said, "truly, all that God does is done well" for if the wind had not blown out the light the soldiers would have found him; if the rooster had crowed, the soldiers would have found him; if the donkey had brayed, the soldiers would have found him, and he would have been killed. I have had many similar experiences where my disappointments have worked out ultimately in my best interest.

I recall working at a company for almost two decades. During that time, I helped to bring in millions of dollars in grants and doubled the programs in size. I reached a point where I felt in order to grow, I needed to leave. After giving two month's notice, three days before leaving, the executive director asked me not to leave and offered me a promotion and a considerable salary increase. The company had been good to me, so I felt very disloyal in leaving. *Let not mercy and truth forsake thee: bind them about thy neck; write them upon the table of thine heart* (Prov. 3.3) says the wise man Solomon, so the decision to leave bothered me. After being away for two years, I saw an advertisement for the very position that had been offered to me before I left the company and I applied. I had a good track record and had acquired new knowledge and skills that would have been an asset to the company and thought they would be happy to hire me. By this time, the company was under new executive leadership. After going through multiple interviews with people I had either worked alongside or supervised, I met with the new executive director of the company and was asked about salary requirements. I told him the salary I was offered by his predecessor just prior to leaving and he grimaced in response and said I would be hearing from him. He called me a few days later and told me he had decided to hire someone else. I felt shocked and disappointed but resolved that "God knows best;" I also felt a sense of relief because I no longer felt disloyal since I made efforts to return and they had rejected me. A few months later, I heard devastating news about the company that had a crippling effect on its reputation and financial structure. I realized then that truly the Apostle Paul was right when he said in Romans 8:28 *And we know that all things work together for good to them that love God, to them who are the called according to his purpose.*

Owning Your Vision: You must be sure your vision is your own and not someone else's. It is quite common to be the vicarious emissary of someone else's vision. It is important to be clear as to whose vision you are living. Be sure it is your own. Living someone else's dream or vision can lead to unresolved anger, resentment and unfulfilled desires. I have seen individuals in therapy who are living their parents' dreams or expectations - only to find themselves stuck in a profession or a marriage that they simply hate; not wanting to disappoint their parents, they remain in it only to feel unfulfilled. Some get stuck with expenses and student loans only to burrow themselves into a deep hole and not able to find their way out. This does not suggest that you should not seek advice or accept counsel from your parents. Ironically, they have your best interest at heart and want the best for you. However, it is important to know if their counsel is an attempt to satisfy their own ego and live vicariously through you or they want you to be the best you that you can be. Noted physician Dr. David Viscott wrote: *"What is your life worth if it is ruled by anything other than the search for truth about your-self? If your parents haven't yet accepted themselves, how can they ever accept you? The purpose of your life is not to justify theirs."*

Jesus was able to help his mother come to terms with this fact when they attended a wedding together in Cana of Galilee. At the wedding, the host ran out of wine. Knowing her son's capabilities, his mother used her influence and parental pressure to try and get him to turn water into wine. Jesus pointed out to his mother that his time had not yet come; in other words, the purpose of his life is not to justify hers. In turning water into wine, she desired for Jesus to reveal himself as the Messiah and be hailed king of Israel. Can you imagine how proud she would have been to see her son as king of Israel! But her desire for him was not consistent with His vision or knowledge of God's will for His life. Jesus therefore responded to her faith in him when she said, *"Whatever He tells you to do, do it"* and not her desire for Jesus to reveal himself as king. Jesus had a clear sense of his vision and purpose and not even His love for his mother could divert him from that.

The Job You Hate: Maybe you are stuck in a job you hate, but the benefits are good, so you make a career of it. Whatever the reason, it is important to be honest with yourself. You owe yourself the truth. If you are not fulfilling your own purpose in life, then think about what you need to do to move towards your vision. Don't quit the job that you are doing now unless you see an open door. *Whatsoever thy hand findeth to do, do it with thy might; for there is no work, nor device, nor knowledge, nor wisdom, in the grave, whither thou goest. (Ecc. 9:10).* You may need to change your attitude towards the job you hate. In the words of Viktor Frankl: "When we are no longer able to change a situation - we are challenged to change ourselves."

Create a career plan of what you would like to become, the skills and steps you need to take to get there and how your current circumstances can become stepping-stones towards your goal. You can begin to take small steps towards accomplishing your vision for yourself and before long it will become clear enough for you to step into your future. In fact, God will bring people into your life to help you accomplish your vision. I remember wanting to start my own business, so I researched the business I wanted to pursue, obtained as much information as possible, and did my business plan, but felt the undertaking was too much to pursue on my own. I read somewhere that you can achieve your goal faster when you collaborate with someone who has the same vision. I looked around and shared my vision with two other individuals who were in my professional field and they were highly interested, but they sat back with folded arms and were waiting on me to do all the work. I felt somewhat discouraged, but never gave up on the idea. Then one day a new family joined our church. While in conversation with the wife she shared that her husband was in the same field and she introduced him to me. As we conversed, we found that we shared the exact same ideas for a business and had covered the same ground work. In fact, he was one-step ahead, but he had lost a lot of money and his collaborators had backed out on him. We were able to pool our information together and start the groundwork for a nonprofit organization. In the words of Vince Lombardi *"Leaders aren't born, they are made. And they are made just like anything else, through hard work. And that's the price we'll have to pay to achieve that goal, or any goal."*

My observation of successful leaders is that they have strong core values, clear vision of their mission and they live a balanced life –spiritually, emotionally and physically with the goal of bringing glory to God. Their vision is usually bigger than they themselves can carry and involves improving the lives of others. Jesus is our supreme example of a visionary leader which is reflected in the prophecy of Isaiah 61:1 & 2 and spoken of by Jesus in Luke 4:18 & 19 when he said: The Spirit of the Lord God is upon me; because the Lord hath anointed me to preach good tidings unto the meek; he hath sent me to bind up the brokenhearted, to proclaim liberty to the captives, and the opening of the prison to them that are bound; Jesus' life, ministry and teaching were a fulfilment of his vision and mission.

Despite having a vision, at times in life you might end up in a situation, which is totally unfavorable to you, as in the case of the patriarch Joseph. Joseph grew up in a highly dysfunctional family with paternal siblings that did not care for him. His attempts at building a relationship with them were met with scorn and mockery. But Joseph was God fearing so the favor of God was upon him. In other words, he lived by faith and God's grace was upon him. God had not forgotten Joseph and He has not forgotten you. Joseph had a vision of one day becoming great, but he did not know how God would order his steps for him to accomplish his vision. Joseph's brothers beat him to a pulp and threw him in a pit; it seemed things could not have gotten any worse, but they did. He got sold into slavery. As a slave, he served faithfully, yet he was accused falsely of raping his master's wife and landed in jail. Who would have expected him to rise from the pit to the palace? Amazing isn't it? *With He hath not dealt with us after our sins; nor rewarded us according to our iniquities. (Ps103: 10).* If Joseph had not been sold into slavery, he would not have ended up in Egypt. If Joseph had not been a slave he would not have ended up in Potiphar's house and if Joseph had not ended up in jail, he would not have had the opportunity to interpret the dreams of the butler and the baker and to finally experience the awesomeness of God by interpreting Pharaoh's dream and becoming the Prime minister of Egypt. Once you have a vision, God can allow even adverse circumstances to work for your good. *God's ideal for His children is higher than the highest human thought can reach (E.G. White, Desire of Ages p. 271).* I have a friend who was fired from his job with a major corporation in New York City for not being willing to compromise his principles. He could not get another job in his field because the "old boy network" worked against him. He left the city and went to another state where he met his wife and together, they opened a successful health food business. Psalm 31:20 reminds us Thou shalt hide them in the secret of thy presence from the pride of man: thou shalt keep them secretly in a pavilion from the strife of tongues.

God Is Able to Orchestrate Events to Your Benefit: On one occasion, I remember being invited to speak at short notice at a Women's Ministries event at a Manhattan church because the appointed speaker had cancelled. After my presentation, a young lady approached me. She said that she had graduated from one of the universities I attended, but she had not been able to obtain employment. Although she wasn't employed, she had been using her time wisely by becoming involved in the women's ministry program at her church. It was this same ministry that had invited me to speak. Coincidently, (or providentially) I had received a government grant for a demonstration project and was looking for someone with her qualifications to fill the position. My office had interviewed several people but none of them was the right fit. This young lady's qualifications, experience and personality was exactly the profile we were looking for, so she was hired for the job and excelled in it. It is said that God has over a thousand and one ways of working things out in your favor. His promise is that: *And they shall build houses, and inhabit them; and they shall plant vineyards, and eat the fruit of them. They shall not build, and another inhabit; they shall not plant, and another eat: for as the days of a tree are the days of my people, and mine elect shall long enjoy the work of their hands. They shall not labour in vain, nor bring forth for trouble; for they are the seed of the blessed of the Lord, and their offspring with them. And it shall come to pass, that before they call, I will answer; and while they are yet speaking, I will hear.Is. 65:21-24)*

If you have experienced financial loss or job loss, stop looking back at the door that is closed behind you and start looking forward at the open door in front of you. Lot's wife turned into a pillar of salt because she looked back at the door that was closed behind her. Her family did not look back and did not even realize her fate. Do not dwell on your past successes or failures. Look to the future instead. You will never move forward in life if you keep looking back at what you had or what could have been. "Action is the foundational key to all success," says the artist Pablo Picasso. Learn from the past and move forward in faith into the future. If you are at a place in your life when you are feeling hemmed in and cannot decide how to move forward, the following are questions that life coaches would have you ask yourself to help you get your life into perspective: If time and money were not an issue for me, what would I do with my life? What stops me from doing or having what I really want right now? What do I need to stop doing in order to move forward? What scares me the most about moving forward?

As you attempt to answer these questions you will begin to untangle yourself and work towards a vision for yourself. It is said that elephants in a circus will not move any further than the length of the rope to which they were attached when being trained. Similarly, your life experience may limit your thinking about your possibilities, but you must free yourself from limiting and self-defeating thinking and create a vision of the life you want for yourself for you to soar with wings as eagles. *Isaiah 40:29-31 says: He giveth power to the faint; and to them that have no might he increaseth strength. Even the youths shall faint and be weary, and the young men shall utterly fall: But they that wait upon the Lord shall renew their strength; they shall mount up with wings as eagles; they shall run, and not be weary; and they shall walk, and not faint.*

Dreams by Langston Hughes

Hold fast to dreams;
For if dreams die
Life is a broken-winged bird;
That cannot fly.
Hold fast to dreams;
For when dreams go
Life is a barren field;
Frozen with snow.

Your 9th Gem

STOP SINGING THE BLUES

Hope deferred maketh the heart sick: but when the desire cometh, it is a tree of life. (Proverbs 13:12). When we are encompassed with doubt, perplexed by circumstances, or afflicted by poverty or distress, Satan seeks to shake our confidence in Jehovah. It is then that he arrays before us our mistakes and tempts us to distrust God, to question His love. He hopes to discourage the soul and break our hold on God. (E.G. White Prophets and Kings, p.174-175)

Be careful about the things you spend time thinking and worrying about. It was Dr. Frank Crane, a Presbyterian minister who once said, "Our best friends and our worst enemies are our thoughts. A thought can do us more good than a doctor, or a banker or a faithful friend. It can also do us more harm than a brick." The song *"By the Rivers of Babylon"* by Bob Marley was based on the experience of the children of Judah who were enslaved and could not sing the lord's song because they were depressed. They were looking back on the past instead of looking to the future with hope of a better day. Job also experienced deep discouragement and despondency after losing everything he owned, (even his entire household) but in his despondency he turned to God in faith and confidence, declaring *"Though he slay me, yet will I trust in him: but I will maintain mine own ways before him. (Job 13:15).* In return, the Lord was able to bless him abundantly. Nicole C. Mullen captures Job's hope in God in her wonderful song *"Redeemer."* The words of this song are an assurance of God's omnipotence and omnipresence and his loving care for you. In Psalms 107: 20, David notes that there is healing in God's words. *He sent his word, and healed them, and delivered them from their destructions."* God's words are found in the Bible. When you are depressed and encompassed with doubt read the Bible – especially the Psalms and sing or listen to songs that reassure you of God's power to heal and strengthen. Donnie McClurkin's *Just Stand* and *Get back up again* are songs that encourage enduring trust in God after you have done everything that is in your power to do. Of course, there are the old-time favorites like *All to Jesus I Surrender* and *I Need Thee Every Hour.* An elderly lady at my church would often lift the spirit of every prayer meeting with choruses like *"What a mighty God We Serve"* and *"Oh it is Jesus, yes, it is Jesus, tis Jesus in my soul for I have touched the hem of his garment."* Joseph Scriven's: *What a friend we have in Jesus* remains an all-time favorite. Although written in the 1800's, the words are still relevant today. *What a friend we have in Jesus, all our sins and griefs to bear! What a privilege to carry everything to God in Prayer! O what peace we often forfeit, O what needless pain we bear, all because we do not carry everything to God in prayer!"* Scriven wrote these words from his own life experience based on the many personal tragedies that he suffered. It is said that his fiancée drowned accidentally the night before their wedding and his second bride to be contracted pneumonia and died before their wedding could take place; from these experiences, Scriven began to live Jesus' Sermon on the Mount (Matt 5:2-16) by caring for those in need and giving freely of his limited possessions.

I listened to a sermon by Pastor Dick Baron, former General Conference Official of the Seventh day Adventist Church at the Mount Pisgah Seventh day Adventist Church in Miami, Florida. His theme was: *"Stop singing the blues."* The statement struck a chord with me because music is known to affect cognition positively or negatively. I recalled that in working with clinically depressed and mentally ill teenaged girls, whenever they listened to sad love songs and internalized the words as though applying to themselves, they went into psychosis. Pastor Baron encouraged the listening congregation to take the Psalmist David's advice and sing a new song. In other words, stop dwelling on your depressed condition and look to God in hope. Read the Psalms and you will see that David was often depressed and "cried enough tears to fill a bottle," but he resolved that he would continue to trust in God and sing praises to Him. On one occasion the Amalekites attacked Ziklag, burned it with fire, and took captive every single person who was there, from small to great. When David and his men came to the city, and found it destroyed and their wives, their sons, and their daughters taken captive, David and the people who were with him lifted their voices and wept - they cried until they had no more power to weep. David was greatly distressed, not only because his wives had been taken captive, but also his own people had turned on him and spoke of stoning him. All that David could do was to strengthen and encourage himself in the LORD, his God. *Bless the Lord, O my soul: and all that is within me, bless his holy name. Bless the Lord, O my soul, and forget not all his benefits: Who forgiveth all thine iniquities; who healeth all thy diseases; Who redeemeth thy life from destruction; who crowneth thee with lovingkindness and tender mercies; Who satisfieth thy mouth with good things; so that thy youth is renewed like the eagle's. (Ps 103:1-5).*

When You Are Feeling Blue, Sing Praises to God: Encourage yourself with positive self-talk. Change the way you think, and you will change the way you feel. If you are already depressed, why feed your depression by doing things that will make you more depressed? Why listen to songs that will depress your spirit? *Finally, brethren, whatsoever things are true, whatsoever things are honest, whatsoever things are just, whatsoever things are pure, whatsoever things are lovely, whatsoever things are of good report; if there be any virtue, and if there be any praise, think on these things. (Phil. 4:8).* Your life should be one of continuous praise to God in appreciation for His goodness and care. In so doing you can expect even larger blessings.

Listening to positive and uplifting music can decrease anxiety and depression as in King Saul's case. He often called for David to play his instrument to soothe his troubled mind. However, the lyrics to which you listen when you are depressed can also seriously impact your mental status if you internalize the words and think the words apply to you. The Blues for example is a genre of music developed by African Americans, during the period of the Great Depression and the oppressive Jim Crow era. The Blues is reflective of a period when the country was experiencing food rationing. For African Americans it was a time of extreme hardship. There was insufficient food and children suffered from pellagra and other nutritionally deficient diseases. As the saying goes, when the rich sneezes, the poor gets pneumonia. There were increased suicides resulting from worry and despair. Faced with such desperate conditions, African Americans like the children of Israel who were in captivity and sang mournfully *"By the Rivers of Babylon,"* made up mournful songs that reflected their depressed condition and state of mind. Their songs expressed feelings of sadness and disappointment that things weren't going their way. Blues music therefore became a means for people of color to express their depressed feelings and conditions. Dwelling on your depressed condition however, regardless of the genre of music will not uplift your spirit or turn your mind to God as the infinite source of power to sustain you in time of need. Under chattel slavery, Black people sang songs of hope and courage - Negro spirituals that helped them maintain their sanity under difficult circumstances. A song is a weapon, says Ellen White that we can always use against discouragement. *As we thus open the heart to the sunlight of the Savior's presence, we shall have health and His blessing (E. G. White, Ministry of Healing, p169).*

Thomas Dorsey who is recognized as the "father of gospel music" realized the benefits of singing "good news" or gospel songs about the creator when he stopped singing the Blues and began singing gospel songs. It is said that Dorsey struggled with mental illness while singing the Blues. After his recovery, Dorsey committed himself to composing sacred music. In August 1932, his wife and son died during childbirth. In his grief, he did not lose hope or have another mental breakdown. He looked to God for strength and was inspired to write the song "Take My Hand, Precious Lord." He went on to become the co-founder of the National Convention of Gospel Choirs and Choruses. As a result of a change in his thinking and focus, Dorsey became known as the father of gospel music. Dr. Defora Lane, author of the book *Music as Medicine*, concurs that people of color have used music since the days of slavery to reinforce their faith and to focus on the positive instead of the negative. A timeless song of hope is the Negro National Anthem *"Lift Every Voice and Sing"* written by James Weldon Johnson and set to music by his brother, John, in 1905. The words to this song are as follows:

Lift ev'ry voice and sing, till earth and heaven ring, ring with the harmonies of Liberty; Let our rejoicing rise High as the list'ning skies, let it resound loud as the rolling sea. Sing a song full of the faith that the dark past has taught us; Sing a song full of the hope that the present has brought us; Facing the rising sun of our new day begun, let us march on till victory is won.

The words are not mournful to depress the spirit. The words provide a message of hope and optimism. It is a source of inspiration for many. It talks about the struggle of a people *"stony the road we trod"* but the words also point to a better future — *"facing the rising sun of our new day begun, let us march on till victory is won."* When you are depressed don't sing or listen to songs to depress your spirit; instead, sing songs of faith, hope and courage. Sing praises to God. David said: *O sing unto the Lord a new song: sing unto the Lord, all the earth. Sing unto the Lord, bless his name; shew forth his salvation from day to day. Declare his glory among the heathen, his wonders among all people. For the Lord is great, and greatly to be praised: he is to be feared above all gods.* (Ps 96:1-4). *Let us come before his presence with thanksgiving, and make a joyful noise unto him with psalms. O come, let us worship and bow down: let us kneel before the Lord our maker. (Ps 95:1-7).*

When you are feeling blue, sing songs of joy and ask God to show forth his praises in you. He will not leave you comfortless to wallow in your pain. He promises to be your rock and your shelter in your time of storm, and He promises to keep you safe if you abide under his wings. I was moved by a beautiful e-mail story a friend shared with me about a forest fire in Yellowstone National Park, which illustrates my point. According to the story, as forest rangers began their trek up a mountain to assess the inferno's damage, one ranger found a bird literally petrified in ashes, perched statuesquely on the ground at the base of a tree. Somewhat sickened by the eerie sight, he knocked over the bird with a stick. When he gently struck it, three tiny chicks scurried from under their dead mother's wings. The loving mother, being aware of the impending disaster carried her offspring to the base of the tree and had gathered them under her wings, instinctively knowing that the toxic smoke would rise. She could have flown to safety but had refused to abandon her babies. The heat had scorched her small body, but the mother remained steadfast. The mother was willing to die, so that those under the cover of her wings would live.

<u>God Will Not Abandon You:</u> If a bird would not abandon its young, why do you think that God would abandon you? Those who live in the shelter of the most High will find rest in the shadow of the Almighty. *He that dwelleth in the secret place of the most High shall abide under the shadow of the Almighty. I will say of the Lord, He is my refuge and my fortress: my God; in him will I trust. Surely he shall deliver thee from the snare of the fowler, and from the noisome pestilence. He shall cover thee with his feathers, and under his wings shalt thou trust: his truth shall be thy shield and buckler.* Ps.91: 1-4

When the September 11, terrorist attack hit the twin towers in Manhattan, I was living in Queens and working in the Bronx. The attack was the most horrific and terrifying moment for New York City. Everyone was in a state of panic after witnessing two planes in succession crash into the World Trade Center. People were falling out of buildings and fleeing the area; New York City was in a state of frenzy and panic as people scurried to get home. My main concern was to pick up my one-year old daughter from day care. The Throggs Neck and Whitestone bridges were closed to buses and the trains were not running. My husband was in Brooklyn and was having trouble getting home. I needed to get across the Whitestone Bridge to get to my child. I was so determined to get across the bridge to get to my child, that I paid a taxi driver $70 just to cross the bridge. Ordinarily, I would have paid $10 at most, but at that point, the price to get to my child was insignificant compared to my desire to be sure she was with me and protected. If as a mother, getting to my child was my main concern, how about God's care for you? God promises that even a mother may forget her child, but He will not forget you. God's word doesn't lie so rely on His promises that He will take care of you. He will not leave you or forsake you. When Jehoshaphat was surrounded by two opposing armies, the Israelites were overwhelmed with fear, so Jehoshaphat conducted a song service, which confused his enemy and the enemy turned on themselves. The Israelites did not have to fight the battle themselves. They praised God in song and God took over their battle for them. God is ready and willing to fight your battles for you.

<u>Pass the Test</u>: Whatever you are going through, praise God for what He can and will do for you. If He does not release you from the problem you are experiencing through the experience, He will give you the strength to see your way through to the end. There is always a worthy purpose or lesson to be learned from the experience of adversity.

I spent eight years in a job that grew less challenging over the years; during that time, I applied for several positions for which I was more than qualified, but none materialized. It was during those years that I began to spend more time writing articles. On reflection, the nature of the job freed me up to do what I enjoy; in my previous positions, even my leisure time was taken up with work, but in this position, my leisure time belonged to me. I gained this insight only after I began writing this book. Your steps as well as your stops are ordered by God. Jesus was distressed at the thought of his crucifixion and pleaded with his father to work some other way out if possible, but God did not "remove the cup" because there was a worthy purpose in his suffering and eventual death. If Jesus had not died, he would not have risen again, and mankind would have been without hope of eternal life. The apostle John was ordered boiled to death in oil, but he continued to preach from within the pot and lived. This same John wrote the prophetic book of Revelation that today provides hope of Jesus' return. Just rest assured that there is a worthy purpose even in your suffering and disappointments.

If you are going through a painful life experience and you have been through a similar experience before, it may be possible that there is a lesson you must learn from the experience and you are not getting it. It's like failing a class and having to repeat it before getting your diploma. The children of Israel did not have to wander in the wilderness for 40 years. The Promised Land was within reach. They could have completed the journey in four months, but there were old habits that they needed to get rid of and unlearn before they could go into the Promise Land. If you find that there are painful areas of your life that you seem to keep repeating, it means you have not learned the lesson that could be blocking your path to success. Reflect for a moment; what negative attitudes, behaviors or practices do you need to change?

Clinical Depression: If painful memories keep haunting you, it is possible that you may be clinically depressed, or you may be experiencing post-traumatic stress disorder and need to seek professional help. Clinical depression may manifest itself in the form of withdrawal from people, absent mindedness and a refusal to get out of bed and take care of your personal needs. Over eating or not eating are also signs of depression. Not all problems can be answered with songs of praise. Richard Smallwood, a famous gospel singer and song writer was able to admit suffering from clinical depression and sought mental health services to help cope with his depression. Your mood might be influenced by two important neurotransmitters called GABA and serotonin; when these levels are low you won't feel like yourself. Yan thoughts fill your mind

Whatever life-experience you are going through, remember that there is a lesson to be learned or a story to be told that will benefit others. Ask God to show you the lesson that you need to learn from the experience you are going through, so that you can grow into the person that you need to become and be a blessing to humanity.

> The fear of the Lord is the instruction of wisdom; and before honour is humility. *(Proverbs 15:33). The Lord can work most effectually through those who are most sensible of their own insufficiency, and who will rely upon Him as their leader and source of strength. He will make them strong by uniting their weakness to His might, and wise by connecting their ignorance with His wisdom. If they would cherish true humility, the Lord could do much more for His people; but there are few who can be trusted with any large measure of responsibility or success without becoming self-confident and forgetful of their dependence upon God. Therefore, in choosing the instruments for His work, the Lord passes by those whom the world honors as great, talented, and brilliant. They are too often proud and self-sufficient. They feel competent to act without counsel from God."* (E.G. White Patriarchs and Prophets. p.554).

CONSTRUCTIVE ACTION PLAN

Your answers to the following will help you identify your pain spots, harbored resentment or unresolved feelings.

1. If I had 24 hours left to live, what life story would I share?
2. Who do I need to make peace with before I die?
3. How can I be a blessing through my painful experience?

Your 10th Gem

THE BLESSING IN HELPING

And if thou draw out thy soul to the hungry, and satisfy the afflicted soul; then shall thy light rise in obscurity, and thy darkness be as the noon day (Is. 58:10). There is that scattereth, and yet increaseth; and there is that withholdeth more than is meet, but it tendeth to poverty. The liberal soul shall be made fat: and he that watereth shall be watered also himself. (Prov.11: 24-25).s

As a child growing up in Jamaica, my family was relatively poor, but I never felt poor because my grandmother always shared what little she had with those less fortunate and even those more fortunate; it seemed that whenever the smell of frying onions pervaded the air, our yard would attract children and the aged. The children would start skipping and jumping and the elderly would pull up a chair under the divvy tree and they would make themselves comfortable until the meal was ready. My grandmother would then share what little we had with those present. Sometimes all we had were some boiled dumplings, breadfruit and salted cod fish with callaloo (Caribbean spinach) and onions; yet, we never lacked for food, clothing or shelter. Instead of focusing on your depressed condition and your lack, seek to be a blessing instead. Don't live only for your selfish indulgences. The more you focus on your own needs the less you will have to give. Think of the less fortunate and be willing to give. Ezekiel 16:49-50 says: *"Behold, this was the iniquity of thy sister Sodom, pride, fulness of bread, and abundance of idleness was in her and in her daughters, neither did she strengthen the hand of the poor and needy. And they were haughty, and committed abomination before me: therefore I took them away as I saw good.."* God states clearly that he destroyed the people of Sodom not only because they engaged in sodomy but also because of their pride, and their excess of food while the poor and needy suffered.

There is a blessing in giving to others: The story of Cornelius found in Acts of the Apostles, Chapter 10 is that of an Italian military man who gained a knowledge of God through his association with the Jews. He was a wealthy man who cared for the poor and was known far and near, by both Jews and Gentiles for his kindness and his honest dealings. He was a blessing to those who knew him. He was God fearing, but not a Christian. According to the Bible he was a devout man, and "one that feared God with his household, which gave alms to the people and prayed to God always." In one of his personal prayer sessions an angel appeared to him and told him that his prayers and good deeds had come up for a memorial before God and that he should contact the Apostle Peter to learn about God's plan for his life. Dorcas is another example of an individual whose life was filled with acts of kindness to the poor and needy. When she died, the entire community mourned her loss. When Peter saw how they were impacted by her loss, he prayed fervently to God on their behalf and God saw it fit to restore her to life so that she could continue her good work in the community. When I think of Dorcas and Cornelius, I think of my husband who is a very generous man. When our church heard he had heart problems and had to undergo surgery, they were so concerned that they went down in prayer for him. They even came to our house the night before he was scheduled for surgery and prayed with him. The next morning, the hospital called and rescheduled his appointment. He continued with the prescribed aspirin therapy and when he eventually went to have surgery, they found no blockage. He was restored to health so that he could continue his good deeds.

During the Jim Crow era, when African Americans were left to fend for themselves in segregated communities, African American women and men with little resources of their own took the lead in providing for those less fortunate. Their motto was "Lifting as we climb." Harlem Dowling Children's Home in New York City started as the Colored Orphan Asylum because of racial prejudice against children of color. According to historical research, a woman of color was caring for some orphaned children in Harlem. Two Quaker women were moved with compassion and gave her a little money to help in caring for the children. When they returned to check on her, this woman had taken in more children. The Quaker women tried to get some of the children into the white orphanages at the time, but they were rejected. Righteous indignation led these Quakers to start the Colored Orphan asylum. Their effort created a rippling effect, resulting in more colored orphan asylums all over the country. Carrie Steele worked as a maid at the Atlanta Terminal rail road station founded the Carrie Steele orphanage to serve infants and children that she found abandoned in the Atlanta Terminal Rail Road station. She cared for these children in her own home at night and watched them play in the terminal by day; a successful community fund- raising event led to the opening of The Carrie Steele Orphan Home in 1888. Mother Hale is another African American in New York City who took into her home, babies born addicted to crack, which led to the opening of Hale House.

After the devastating Earthquake in Haiti, in 2009, and seeing pictures of children hungry and displaced, I felt impressed to start a fund-raising drive to help the children of Haiti. I encouraged members of my church to empty their pockets and handbags at the end of each day and place their pocket change in a large water jar at the church for the children of Haiti. At the end of the year, we were able to present the large jar of money and the additional funds collected to a member of our church who had been working with poor children in Haiti. This member shared heart-rending stories of children eating dirt cakes when hungry and yet we in the western world waste so much food. This simple act of kindness created a rippling effect where other members started their own projects to help the people of Haiti. Sometimes God allows hardships to come our way so that we might be more sensitive to those less fortunate. In times of hardship, don't be afraid to share what little you have with others for in giving to the poor you are lending your resources to God. God will use those same people to be a blessing to you. President Bill Clinton created Economic Empowerment Zones in blighted districts while he was president and upon leaving the office of the president, he began looking for office space to establish his base. After experiencing some challenges finding affordable office space, he ended up setting up his own office in one of the very same empowerment zones that he established. Truly, "He that hath pity upon the poor lendeth unto the Lord; and that which he hath given will he pay him again." (Prov.19:17). *Thou shalt surely give him, and thine heart shall not be grieved when thou givest unto him: because that for this thing the Lord thy God shall bless thee in all thy works, and in all that thou puttest thine hand unto. (Deut.15:10).* Ellen White notes in Ministry of Healing, page 256 that Isaiah 58:7-11 is a prescription for mental and physical health and that if we desire to enjoy the true joys of life, we must put into practice the rules given in this scripture. *The Lord says (KJV):*

Is not this the kind of fasting I have chosen:
to loosen the chains of injustice
and untie the cords of the yoke,
to set the oppressed free
and break every yoke?
[7] Is it not to deal thy bread to the hungry, and that thou bring the poor that are cast out to thy house? when thou seest the naked, that thou cover him; and that thou hide not thyself from thine own flesh?
Then shall thy light break forth as the morning, and thine health shall spring forth speedily: and thy righteousness shall go before thee; the glory of the Lord shall be thy reward.
Then shalt thou call, and the Lord shall answer; thou shalt cry, and he shall say, Here I am. If thou take away from the midst of thee the yoke, the putting forth of the finger, and speaking vanity;
And if thou draw out thy soul to the hungry, and satisfy the afflicted soul; then shall thy light rise in obscurity, and thy darkness be as the noon day:
And the Lord shall guide thee continually, and satisfy thy soul in drought, and make fat thy bones: and thou shalt be like a watered garden, and like a spring of water, whose waters fail not.

CONSTRUCTIVE ACTION PLAN

1. Take a look at your closet and consider giving to the poor all the shoes or clothing you have not used or worn in the past two years and make room for your blessing.
2. There are many children in developing countries that need help; consider sponsoring a child OR become a mentor to a child
3. Start a not for profit organization or a foundation to help the poor
4. Go on a Mission trip and help build schools and homes in developing countries
5. Volunteer your time at the nearest senior citizens home or local hospital
6. Reach out to family members and neighbors - especially the elderly who may need your help and support.
7. Sponsor a child in a developing country or pay a child's school fees in a developing country.
8. Adopt a child or become a foster parent

Your 11th Gem

GET UP FROM THE DUNGHILL

The Lord maketh poor, and maketh rich: he bringeth low, and lifteth up. He raiseth up the poor out of the dust, and lifteth up the beggar from the dunghill, to set them among princes, and to make them inherit the throne of glory: for the pillars of the earth are the Lord's, and he hath set the world upon them (1Sam2: 7&8He raiseth up the poor out of the dust, and lifteth the needy out of the dunghill; (Ps 113:7).

The Bible gives us the examples of David and Hannah; both characters experienced extreme depression. They described the feeling as being in a dunghill. A dunghill is a place piled high with animal refuse. Growing up in the rural part of Jamaica with horses, donkeys and cows, I am used to seeing and smelling animal dung and I recall that the smell or sight was not the most pleasant. In Lamentations 4:5, dunghill is considered the worse and most wretched condition that you can face or the worse state in which you could find your-self. It is contrasted to a time when you were used to eating the finest of food to now foraging for food in the street and at food pantries or growing up wearing expensive designer clothes and now looking through trash piles and thrift stores for someone's discarded clothes.

David in the book of Psalms also speaks of feeling like a lonely bird upon a rooftop and crying enough tears to fill a bottle. God did not leave David or Hannah in this depressed state and neither will he leave you. Both David and Hannah speak of God raising up the poor out of the dust and lifting the needy out of the dunghill. It is said He takes the poor man out of the dust, lifting him up from his low position. Hannah was very depressed about her infertility. She had prayed about her condition many times before but received no answer from God. Her rival Peninnah teased her constantly, "What's happening Hannah, no baby yet? What's happening girlfriend, God cursed your womb?" Peninnah means pearl or beautiful to look at so she was indeed a rival to contend with. Each year, Hannah went to the temple with her loving husband and prayed about her condition, but she received no answer.

A Time Like No Other: This time Hannah was determined to get an answer from God. *Psalm 77:13 says: Thy way, O God, is in the sanctuary: who is so great a God as our God?* 1 Samuel 1:9 states that *So Hannah rose up after they had eaten in Shiloh, and after they had drunk. Now Eli the priest sat upon a seat by a post of the temple of the Lord.* This time she went into the inner court of the sanctuary (the temple) and poured her heart out to God. According to Exodus chapters 25-30, the early sanctuary consisted of the outer court with the altar of burnt offering and the laver of water and the inner court. The first room in the inner court was the holy place with the table of shew-bread, the seven-branch candlestick and the altar of incense. And the second room was the most holy place with the Ark of the Covenant, which contained the Ten Commandments. Sacrifices were offered in the outer court. Only the priest would be found in the inner court; there in the inner court, Eli saw Hannah and assuming her to be one of the prostitutes who had been carousing in the temple with his wayward, irreverent and alcoholic sons, he reprimanded her. Like Moses, Hannah wanted to see that God is real and to experience being in the very presence of God. This time she went straight to the throne of grace. This time, Hannah moved from the Alter of sacrifice to the Alter of faith. This time, her prayer was a different prayer from all the other prayers she had prayed in the past. Perhaps in the past she had asked for a child to stop her rival from teasing her, but this time her prayer was selfless; she prayed specifically for a son and promised God to give back the child to Him. This time and in this prayer, unlike her other prayers, she promised God a sacrificial offering - the very gift she would receive from God and God answered her prayer. We will get favor from God when we seek to "do good" with the gifts we receive from Him, for *he that diligently seeketh good procureth favor: but he that seeketh mischief, it shall come unto him. A good man obtaineth favor of the Lord (Ps.11:2&7 & 12:2).*

Stop Asking Selfishly: Often when we ask God for things, we ask to lavish on our selfish desires or to show off on our neighbors. This may have been Hannah's intent initially, but she came to a point in her life when she realized that blessings are gifts from God, and we must return to him a portion as a token of our appreciation. Therefore, tithing is important. I remember a point in my life where my income did not meet my expenses. I tried to increase my income by starting my own side business, but my efforts did not yield the income I expected. I worried about robbing God. For three days I agonized over my financial situation. In desperation I spread out my case before God. To my surprise, after three days, I received a notice that I had been given an increase that was retroactive for over 18 months. In giving back to God a tenth of our earnings we are acknowledging that God is the giver of all good gifts and we return a portion in gratitude for his goodness and mercies. In the same way that God heard Hannah's prayer and granted her request, God will hear your cry. There is nothing that is too hard for him. *Jesus said: If ye have faith as a grain of mustard seed, ye shall say unto this mountain, remove hence to yonder place; and it shall remove, and nothing shall be impossible unto you. Howbeit this kind goeth not out but by prayer and fasting (Matt 27:20).*

Like Hannah, David speaks of being in the dunghill. There were many instances in his life when, as a musician, he played music to soothe his depressed mental state. He had defeated Goliath and the Philistine army to claim the girl of his dreams (a princess) to help his family gain status and recognition and help his people overcome their inferior status; however, Saul, a totally insane king was jealous of his success and pursued him relentlessly to kill him. David's sadness was also in part caused by his own misdeeds. David conspired and committed homicide against another man in order to steal the man's wife and witnessed the consequences of his sinful action. His own son revolted against him when he condoned the rape of his daughter. Sometimes our own misdeeds, compromise or mismanagement of our funds can drive us into a state of depression or feeling blue. Incredible success can also lead to depression. Elijah experienced the power of God bringing fire from heaven as he challenged the prophets of Baal to do the same. Yet when Jezebel threatened to take his life, Elijah became depressed and said, "It is enough: now O Lord, take away my life; for I am not better than my fathers." This man of faith lost faith when he needed to exercise it the most. He allowed his distorted perception of the situation to cloud his better judgement. Some would say that Elijah experienced clinical depression and a bout of psychomotor retardation, which involves the slowing down of thoughts and actions. Others might see it as a lapse of faith in God. Regardless of his diagnosis, God did not leave him alone in the dunghill or in a state of despair. He sent an angel to feed him and touch him. God in his mercies does not leave us to suffer alone if we have made poor choices or poor decisions. He comforts us through his word, through a person or even through a thing such as an animal.

Dealing with Depression: For some, knowing that God cares may not be enough to arrest the overwhelming feeling of discouragement, despair or depression. Empty financial coffers and a feeling of aloneness and worthlessness can lead to sleepless nights - be it difficulty in falling asleep, staying asleep or early morning awakening at three or four o'clock in the morning. F. Scott Fitzgerald said, "In a real dark night of the soul it is always three o'clock in the morning - day after day." This further leads to fatigue. Authors Dr. Harold Bloomfield and Peter McWilliams in their book *How to Deal with Depression* note that depression can be an "all pervasive emotional-mental-physical source of misery." It is hard to hurt so completely and for so long without seeking some relief. It is at this point that many individuals give up on God, turn to drugs and alcohol, food, sex, TV, gambling, work – romance and religion (yes religion as opposed to God) as a way of self–medicating. Self-medicating on drugs, food, sex or alcohol exacerbates the feeling of guilt and shame and this leads to a vicious and downward spiral of destructive behavior.

Get Up and Take Action: It was William James the psychologist and philosopher that said: "Success or failure depends more upon attitude than upon capacity; successful men act as though they have accomplished or are enjoying something. Soon it becomes a reality."

Are you feeling down? Get up, get dressed, brush your teeth; put on clean clothes, put on perfume, comb your hair. Solomon says in Proverbs 27:9 that *Ointment and perfume rejoice the heart: so doth the sweetness of a man's friend by hearty counsel.* The simple physiological change in your posture is a powerful step towards change in behavior. Now look in the mirror and tell yourself that you are a worthy person; you are royalty, you are a child of God. Act, look, and feel successful. Appreciate that you are a part of God's creation; go for a walk and look around you at God's creation. Observe nature and the intricate details. Now recognize that you are created for God's glory and conduct yourself accordingly. You will be amazed at the positive results. Your thoughts will influence your actions, so stop dwelling on your depressed condition. Negative thoughts will only lead to further depression and depression to destructive behavior such as over eating, anorexia or bulimia; sexual passions, drugs or alcohol dependency. If a change of attitude doesn't help, stop the madness, seek God for guidance and get help from a qualified mental health professional. Like diabetes and high blood pressure, you may need medication to help the neurotransmitter of your brain function the way it should.

Take therefore no thought for the morrow: for the morrow shall take thought for the things of itself. Sufficient unto the day is the evil thereof. (Matt 6:34). Charles Allen in his book *All things are possible through prayer* notes that one reason people get tense and nervous is because they think they do not have the resources necessary for their lives. We are driven into an attitude of defeat and fear. We shrink back from life in a cowardly fashion. But "however long the night the day will break; it is always darkest before dawn. The road must become rough before it becomes smooth" and figuratively speaking, "the boat must go under the bridge to get to the other side" (African proverbs). When you know there is a God who truly is God, and that He is your God, you will feel as confident and relaxed as a child in the presence of a caring parent. In fact, anytime you have a lot on your mind and cannot sleep, write down everything that is bothering you in the form of a prayer or letter to God. Just talk to him. Keep a prayer journal. You will find after journaling your thoughts you will sleep much better because you have given all your cares and worries to one greater than you. You will also be able to look back at your many answered prayers. It is said that nine tenths of a person's worries are over things, which never come to pass, and the other tenth is over things of little or no consequence. That being the case, it would be wise to change your thinking and focus instead on God's promises found in the Bible. Worry is blind. Isn't today's trouble enough? Why take on tomorrow's trouble today? Furthermore, what can you change if you keep doing the same thing and thinking the same thoughts over and over? Can you expect different results?

Take assurance from God's promises that: *When the poor and needy seek water and there is none, and their tongue faileth for thirst, I the Lord will hear them. I the God of Israel will not forsake them I will open rivers in high places, and fountains in the midst of the valleys: I will make the wilderness a pool of water, and the dry land springs of water. I will plant in the wilderness the cedar, the shittah tree, and the myrtle, and the oil tree; I will set in the desert the fir tree, and the pine, and the box tree together: That they may see, and know, and consider, and understand together, that the hand of the Lord hath done this, and the Holy One of Israel hath created it. (Is. 41:18-20)*

<u>Do Something Different:</u> Zacchaeus was a dishonest man who wanted to change his life style. He had gained considerable wealth through his dishonest dealings, but he was not happy. It was as though he had climbed the ladder of success only to find that the ladder was leaned against a wall that was too short to reach the top. He was frustrated and wanted to make a lifestyle change; he wanted to be a better person and his only hope was to have an encounter with Christ. He had heard that Jesus was in town and he was determined to see him. As a successful businessman, he knew the importance of seizing an opportunity when it came his way, so he joined the crowd. However, being a short man got in the way of his encounter with Jesus. His height was a hindrance. The crowd dwarfed him. He could not see Jesus from the ground, so he decided to leave the crowd, climb the tree and go out on a limb.

Sometimes in life in order to accomplish your goal, you must make a change, seize an opportunity or just go out on a limb. You may have to uproot and go to another place, change jobs or leave familiar circumstances to get to a wealthy place or experience your breakthrough. I recall a young man who complained of feeling stuck in life. He acknowledged needing to go back to school to pursue higher education to improve his income but did not feel he could afford it. I was privy to a scholarship program in his field and encouraged him to apply. He did not do so. He decided instead to engage in multiple get rich quick schemes - none of which yielded any returns. Ten years later he was no better off than before. He happened to visit his hometown and saw that his cohorts in the same field had achieved considerable success, so he returned and asked me for the scholarship information that I had given him ten years ago; of course, it was too late. The funds had dried up and now he would have to pay out of pocket for the same program that he would have gotten for free. To get out of the dunghill you must be willing to experience change, but at the same time recognize that positive change comes with a price. It takes effort, determination and a decided mind to move from where you are to where you want to be. You will get out of the dunghill if you are willing to do what it takes to get out. *When in faith we take hold of His (God's) strength, He will change, wonderfully change, the most hopeless, discouraging outlook. He will do this for the glory of his name (E. G. White, The Story of Prophets and King, p. 260).*

Handel's Dunghill: Handel's famous *"Messiah"* was born out of a dunghill experience. According to historians, the famous musician George Frederic Handel lost much of his fortune when his genre of music decreased in popularity. He also suffered a stroke and was in recovery when Charles Jennens, an ardent fan and supporter of Handel's music, who himself was feeling greatly distressed over the death of his younger brother by suicide approached Handel with a compilation of scriptures to put to music. The scriptures prophesied of the Messiah's birth, suffering, triumph and redemption. Handel embraced the project and completed the composition in just three weeks. Handel then reached out to his favorite contralto, Susannah Cibber, who at the time was embroiled in a scandalous divorce from an abusive husband and whose children were removed from her care because she was considered an "unfit mother," to sing the part "despised and rejected." The collaboration was a huge success. The first performance was held in Dublin as a charitable event and the proceeds went to pay for the release of men who were in debtors' prison, a symbolic gesture of the Messiah's life as a debt for sinners. Since then the Messiah has been sung all over the world and in many different languages. Indeed, Handel was a brilliant musician, Jennens a wealthy man and Cibber a talented contralto, but it was their collaboration on the "Messiah" and their willingness to give back to the less fortunate to glorify God that helped change the downward trajectory of their lives.

Do What You can to Bring About a Positive Outcome: In the same way that Jennens turned to God in his distress over his brother's suicide and turned a negative experience into a positive, you too must cry out to God when you are in distress, but you must also do whatever is in your power to do to bring about the desired result. I recall working in the Bronx, New York for a non-profit organization that provided supportive services to children and families who were abused and neglected. The city had proposed budget cuts and service providers alike were all anxious about what would happen to their programs. Experience had taught me that when the storms of life are raging you must cry out for help to a power that is greater than you are and do what is necessary to bring about the result you want to see. We did not sit back in complacency. Those of us who were God fearing not only prayed for God's favor, but also, we started a letter writing campaign and lobbied legislators and those that had power and influence in Albany. Our efforts were not in vain because the funds were restored. Many times, in life when trouble overwhelms, we fail to cry out to God and suffer great loss. The disciples of Jesus were caught up in a storm on the sea. They tried in their own effort to row their way out, but without success; it was only when the boat was about to capsize that they remembered that Jesus was in the boat all along. It was then that they called out to him for help and Jesus did not disappoint them. He stilled the storm. Whatever storm is raging in your life you must cry out to God and watch Him work for you. There is no problem that is too big or too small for him to solve.

I misplaced one of my master's diplomas when we were renovating our home and I needed it urgently for employment purposes. I spent a week looking in every conceivable place but could not find it. I cried to God for help, but still no immediate answer. I needed to produce the certificate by the following Monday. On the Sunday prior, my daughter was in the backyard playing with a ball, while my husband was trimming the hedges and had the garage door open. I went outside to join them, when suddenly the ball fell from my daughter's hand, rolled into the garage and stopped right in front of an open box of papers with a brown manila envelope. I walked over to the garage to pick up the ball and curiously opened the box; there in the large manila envelope was my certificate. What made me decide to be outside at that time? Why did my daughter decide to play with a ball instead of her bike and why did the ball roll and stop in front of the box? I don't believe this to be a coincidence. I believe God cares about every aspect of our lives and the more in tune we are with him the more he will reveal his power to us. *All heaven awaits our demand upon its wisdom and strength. God is able to do exceedingly abundantly above all that we ask or think (Eph. 3:20; E. G. White,*

Patriarchs and Prophets, p. 515). And I say unto you, Ask, and it shall be given you; seek, and ye shall find; knock, and it shall be opened unto you. For every one that asketh receiveth; and he that seeketh findeth; and to him that knocketh it shall be opened. (Luke 11:9&10).

CONSTRUCTIVE ACTION PLAN:

Identify the problem that you face currently_____

_____

State in one concise statement what you would like God to do for you:

_____

_____

State what you will do in return for Him as an act of gratitude:

_____

_____

Your 12th Gem

YOUR CHANGE WILL COME

Therefore also now, saith the Lord, turn ye even to me with all your heart, and with fasting, and with weeping, and with mourning Therefore also now, saith the Lord, turn ye even to me with all your heart, and with fasting, and with weeping, and with mourning: And rend your heart, and not your garments, and turn unto the Lord your God: for he is gracious and merciful, slow to anger, and of great kindness, and repenteth him of the evil. Who knoweth if he will return and repent, and leave a blessing behind him; even a meat offering and a drink offering unto the Lord your God? Blow the trumpet in Zion, sanctify a fast, call a solemn assembly Joel 2:2 15-17, 12-14

Whatever you are going through, you must believe that a change will come. It may not come when you expect, or how you expect, but it will come when you come to terms with your state of being or the behavior or situation that you continue or resist facing. It is said the teacher will arrive when the student is ready. Look at where you are now and picture where you would like to be. Develop a clear mental picture of what that place in your life should look like. Write it down and ask God to bring it to pass according to his will. In other words, you do not know how, if or when God will bring it to pass, but when it comes you will know because you had a clear vision of it.

Think of the caterpillar and how it metamorphoses into a beautiful butterfly. It goes through a remarkable process of change. In fact, throughout its life span it goes through a series of changes, taking on different forms before it becomes that beautiful butterfly that everyone admires. First it starts as a tiny egg, which produces a larva, that we call a caterpillar. During this stage of being a caterpillar, it grows considerably - eating and shedding its skin about five times as it grows. When it stops growing, it forms a pupa (chrysalis) from the outside. The pupa appears to be just hanging there; but it is during this phase that change is taking place. Most of its organs and body parts dissolve and re-form into organs, tissues, limbs and wings. When the pupa has finished changing, it sheds its skin one last time and emerges as a butterfly. The butterfly is not able to fly right away. Its wings are folded up against its body so there is still more work to be done. The butterfly must pump blood into the wings to expand them so that it can fly. What an amazing process!

I read a story of a boy who tried to help a caterpillar by releasing it from its cocoon, but the poor butterfly could not fly because it did not have the opportunity to pump its wings. You too must go through a series of remarkable changes in your life if you expect to become the best you that God intends that you should be. There is a period in your life when you must spend time gaining knowledge or learning a skill. Once you gain a skill, new knowledge or new experience, you must think about how to apply it. This is often the most challenging part of your life because the process may seem slow or that nothing is changing, but you must not give up. You must keep trying. Like the folded wings of a butterfly you must put effort into what you do. Pump your wings. It was Patience Strong that wrote: *Keep going; keep showing you are not beaten yet. Keep moving keep proving though things are upset. It is all coming right as in time you will see. It is all for the best and the best is to be. Keep praying keep saying the dream is coming true; a wonderful future is waiting for you.*

Baffled by Circumstances. There have been times in my life when I have felt baffled by circumstances; times when I would pray, and nothing would change; times when I have been agnostic, times when I almost lost hope in God, yet each experience has come to strengthen my faith in God and His power to sustain, heal and deliver. If God is for you, who can be against you? I love the story of Joshua and the children of Israel marching around the walls of Jericho. The Israelites followed God's instructions, which must not have made much sense to the people of Jericho as they watched these insignificant, wayfaring wanderers march around their walls with horns in their hands. Yet as a result of this simple act of faith, the walls surrounding the city just tumbled down. They didn't have to hammer it down or use force. They simply had to follow God's command and trust Him to come through for them. The irony is that the people inside the walled city of Jericho were terrified of the people of Israel on the outside. In fact, they were so afraid that they kept the gates of the city tightly shut, with giants at each gate so that no one could come in or go out (Joshua 6:1). Just remember, giants, walls and gates cannot prevent the manifestation of God's power on your behalf. God had told Joshua, "And the Lord said unto Joshua, See, I have given into thine hand Jericho, and the king thereof, and the mighty men of valour." (Joshua 6:2) and Joshua acted on that promise.

Sometimes You Might Meet Walls of Prejudice in Your Life
People might pre-judge you because of your color, your age, your size, your gender or your nationality. They may set up walls of discrimination against you to prevent you from moving forward, but God can tear down those walls of partition and prejudice. Large corporations like giants may do you injustice, but God can bring them to their knees. I remember applying for a promotional position during my early years of employment with an established organization in England and the assistant executive director did not wish for me to get the position. She said I was too young and inexperienced, but when God's favor is upon you, the gates of hell cannot prevail against you. The chief executive director told me she was advised by the assistant executive director against hiring me for the position, but she had received good word from my direct supervisor and would like to give me a try. I was not about to disappoint her. After two years in the position and receiving rave reviews, commendations and awards, I was offered *Secondment*, which is a full scholarship with full salary and all expenses paid to go back to school and pursue higher education, with the commitment that I would return to the organization upon graduating. You do not need to fear manmade prejudices, obstacles or gate keepers. God is able and will do for you more than you can ask or thing. He can make the impossible

possible. Just trust Him. I agree with the statement by John Ortberg, which says: *"I strongly believe that the way we live is a consequence of the size of our God. The problem many of us have is that our God is too small. We are not convinced that we are absolutely safe in the hands of a fully competent, all-knowing, ever-present God."*

Single Versus Married: When I look at the population of Christian churches, women outnumber men. Many of these women are looking for partners, but God seems silent or the partners they meet are unsuitable. Many, because they are feeling lonely enter unequally yoked relationships. The term unequally yoked came from farming where a farmer might yoke a horse and a donkey together. Similarly, in relationships, you can become unequally yoked. In moments of loneliness, you may become emotionally entangled in a relationship that is not right for you and you end up being unequally yoked.

There was a time when I was confusing loneliness with being alone. Loneliness is a feeling – a need that is not being fulfilled where as being alone is being without companionship. Social neuroscientist John Cacioppo describes loneliness as the cousin to depression. He suggests it is contagious and increases the chance of early death by 20%. When I was lonely, I prayed for a companion, but God had to show me that I was confusing the noun alone with the adjective lonely. I needed to first realize that it is God that shall supply all my needs when I am feeling lonely and not a companion. Sometimes individuals get into a relationship or a marriage expecting the partner to become everything to them - even their therapist and then they wonder why the relationship doesn't work. It seemed God saw that I was not ready for such a commitment. I also knew there was much more that I wanted to accomplish before settling into a marriage. Quite honestly, I really enjoyed my freedom to travel and pursue my own desires and interests and feared the commitment of a marriage; I would joke about being the fun-loving aunt who could return my nieces and nephews to their parents and meant it. My loneliness was due to selfishness. I was way too selfish to enter a marriage. You cannot make a successful marriage if you are selfish. Marriage is a social connection that requires total commitment and lifestyle changes. You cannot be married and live as though you are single or commit to just 50%.

The LAW of Marriage: In marriage you must be able to give love, you must be able to affirm your partner and not be in competition. Your partner must know that he/she is wanted or needed by you. Remember this acronym- LAW: L=love, A=Affirmation, W=wanted. It was only when I became more at peace with myself and felt ready to share the LAW that I was ready for marriage. I recall that I was attending one of my annual Christian Home & School Retreats at a resort in Florida and was enjoying the beauty of the place when, for the first time, I had a strong desire to share the moment with someone; but there was no one there. It was the first time I truly felt alone as opposed to being lonely and saw myself being married. I was with a large group of people, but in the words of the poet Bacon, *faces were but a gallery of pictures*. It was at that moment that I began to give serious thought to marriage as companionship and decided that I was ready to commit to a marriage. As I reflected on the direction that I wanted my life to take I prayed, "Lord, I don't want to be single anymore. I would like a Christian husband and a child, preferably a daughter." I asked for a God-fearing husband with whom I could share my life and my blessings. It was not long after that I was introduced to two potential partners, both of whom were introduced by two pastors' wives. One gentleman was carrying a torch for his ex-wife and the other was looking for a wife. I choose the latter after much praying and getting to know him and his family; before long we were married. Because I was already 40 years old, my doctor had told me that I should not have a child because of the risk associated with age and with midlife pregnancies such as – placenta praevia, congenital deformities and Down's syndrome – these were also a concern for me. Since I was already working with abused and in some cases abandoned children, I had decided to devote myself to be a mother to the abused and motherless. My husband however was not convinced, and he prayed earnestly for a child. Each Sabbath that we went to church, he would put a prayer request in the prayer box believing he *"And he spake a parable unto them to this end, that men ought always to pray, and not to faint" (Luke 18:1)*. When I became pregnant, I was not aware that I was pregnant. I thought I had the flu. My husband suggested that I take a pregnancy test and sure enough I was pregnant.

Family and friends were excited to hear of my pregnancy. We began to make plans for the baby, but I had a fibroid tumor the size of a grapefruit, which outgrew the fetus resulting in a miscarriage. The miscarriage came as a huge disappointment to us. Our hopes were dashed. After the miscarriage, I had the tumor removed and God in his awesomeness did the most remarkable thing. A short while after the surgery, I became pregnant again and had a most beautiful baby girl. My beautiful daughter is a living testimony that there is nothing that is too hard for God. *Commit thy way unto the Lord; trust also in him; and he shall bring it to pass. (Ps. 37:5).* God will do great things for those who trust in Him. *The reason why His professed people have no greater strength is that they trust so much to their own wisdom, and do not give the Lord an opportunity to reveal His power in their behalf. He will help His believing children in every emergency if they will place their entire confidence in Him and faithfully obey him (Patriarchs & Prophets, E. G. White).*

YOUR CONSTRUCTIVE ACTION PLAN:

Now write your hopes, desires, dreams and aspiration to God in a prayer and leave the results to Him.

Your 13th Gem

KNOW WHO ARE YOU

I love them that love me; and those that seek me early shall find me. Riches and honour are with me; yea, durable riches and righteousness. My fruit is better than gold, yea, than fine gold; and my revenue than choice silver. I lead in the way of righteousness, in the midst of the paths of judgment: That I may cause those that love me to inherit substance; and I will fill their treasures. Prov.8: 17-21.

There are few who realize how far-reaching is the influence of their words and acts. How often the errors of parents produce the most disastrous effects upon their children and children's children, long after the actors themselves have been laid in the grave. Everyone is exerting an influence upon others and will be held accountable for the result of that influence. Words and actions have a telling power, and the long hereafter will show the effect of our life here. The impression made by our words and deeds will surely react upon ourselves in blessing or in cursing. This thought gives an awful solemnity to life and should draw us to God in humble prayer that He will guide us by His wisdom. E. G. White, Patriarchs & Prophets p. 554).

William Somerset Maughan said: "It is a very funny thing about life; if you refuse to accept anything but the best you can very soon get it." Knowing who you are in relation to the creator of the universe will determine how you see yourself and how you relate to life's challenges. God created man in his own image, but sin has since marred his creation. We don't know what God looks like, but we know that we are products of his creation. (*Even every one that is called by my name: for I have created him for my glory, I have formed him; yea, I have made him. Is. 43:7*). Look at yourself in the mirror. Breathe in and breathe out. You are a living organism made up of numerous cells that are intricately designed. The nucleus of your cells holds the chromosomes that direct all the cells activities. Each chromosome is made up of genes and each gene is composed of proteins and a material called DNA. DNA contains the instructions that direct the cell's growth, development, reproduction, and other processes; from the single fertilized cell came all the nerve, muscle, blood, bone, and other cells that make up your body. Each zygote contains the information that makes all of this happen. The body composition is the same for all humans regardless of their place of origin or whether they are black, brown or white. For people of color, years of psychological harm - starting with over 300 years of Slavery, and reinforced by economist, politicians, scientist, the media and sadly also religion promoted an erroneous belief system about blacks being less than human. As a result, the inhumane treatment of people who were not considered white (those with one drop of black blood) was condoned. The church reinforced this by saying that slavery is God ordained.

The Creation of Race and Racism is not of God: In the late 1800s, the terms race and racism were elevated to scientific status in order to justify the inhumane treatment of people of color. Social Darwinism, anthropology and anthropometry created a racial hierarchy with Caucasians as the superior race. A beginning scientist by the name of Johann Blumenbach introduced craniometry - a hierarchical pyramid of the five human racial types based on skull size to support the notion of Blacks being inferior. Blumenbach placed Caucasians or white people at the top because he believed that a skull found in the Caucasian Mountains "is the most beautiful form of the skull, from which the others diverge." This unscientific conjecture supported the illusion of white superiority. The result was a successful psychological racial divide, which has existed for hundreds of years, and has promoted a belief system that white people are superior and Blacks inferior. The interesting thing about this belief was that not all Blacks were foolish enough to accept it or all Whites naive enough to embrace it. God-fearing individuals realized they were being manipulated and that science and the Bible were being used as justification for treating their fellowmen as chattels. California News Reel conducted a biological study of students from different ethnicities and found no biological differences to identify their race. The study concluded that racial differences cannot be found in nature but in politics, economics and culture. The study further revealed how our social institutions "make" or constructed race by disproportionately channeling resources, power, status and wealth to white people. Eighteenth century, anthropologists therefore classified people into various racial groups to keep Black people who were an economic asset in a subordinate position.

God Deals with Nations not Racial Groups: The term race is a political creation and essentially a devious (satanic) illusion created to divide nations and to deceive and subjugate black people. Even the United States Pledge of Allegiance refers to "**one Nation under God**." There is only one human race but different nations. From Genesis to Revelation, the bible refers only to nations –Acts10:35 is a reminder that God deals with individuals and nations not race: *But in every nation he that feareth him, and worketh righteousness, is accepted with him.* Likewise, there is one animal kingdom but there are different species of animals; there are vertebrates and invertebrates; mammals and monotremes; some are warm blooded, and some are cold-blooded. In the plant kingdom, there are different types of plants. There are taproots, fibrous roots and coniferous roots. Even their leaves are different – There are simple leaves and compound leaves. There is variety in God's creation. God is a God of variety and He sees beauty in all His creation. Whatever your skin tone, ethnicity or country of origin, you must see yourself as a part of God's amazing creation and like the Psalmist David you must say to yourself, *"I am fearfully and wonderfully made."* Do not allow psychological put-downs or distortions of the truth to destroy your sense of personhood. You are a product of God's creation. This is what the LORD says— *But now thus saith the Lord that created thee, O Jacob, and he that formed thee, O Israel, Fear not: for I have redeemed thee, I have called thee by thy name; thou art mine." (Is 43:1).*

Nations in the Bible: You must believe and accept that God did not create you inferior to anyone. He created only one race, which is the humans. Nowhere in the Bible will you find reference to race except the one that you run. People were named according to their place of origin, for example, Jesus of Nazareth, Simon of Cyrene, and Paul of Tarsus. God does not condone prejudice based on skin color. Miriam was prejudiced against Moses' wife who was from Ethiopia – East Africa and as a result, God in an ironic twist struck her with leprosy – her whole body became as white as snow.

I recall as a child in Jamaica hearing Rastafarians, although a disparaged group at the time because of their rugged appearance and remote life style educate people of the Caribbean about their place in history as kings and queens. They pointed to His Imperial Majesty, Emperor Haile Selassie of Ethiopia as a direct descendant of King Solomon and the Queen of Sheba. The Rastafarian influence was so strong that in 1966, the Emperor of Ethiopia visited Jamaica, and received a tumultuous welcome. Rastafarians sang songs about Africa and the rivers of Babylon and spoke of the kings of Ethiopia and Africa and made Jamaicans aware that we did not descend from apes and savages as portrayed in the media, but from a royal Nubian lineage – King Solomon, the son of King David and the tribe of Judah.

History speaks of White individuals like Thaddeus Stevens, who was a radical Republican (when Republicans were abolitionists) that had a righteous abhorrence of slavery and the inhumane treatment of Blacks. Stevens advocated for the ratification of the 14th amendment of the United States constitution. This amendment grants citizenship to "all persons born or naturalized in the United States," which included former slaves who had just been freed after the Civil War. Another white individual who helped to change the course of history was Harriet Beecher Stowe, daughter of an abolitionist and the author of Uncle Tom's Cabin. Today, to be called an "Uncle Tom" is considered an insulting remark, but when Harriet Beecher Stowe wrote Uncle Tom's Cabin, she wrote it as a satire to expose the hypocrisy of slavery. The author pointed out that the character "Uncle Tom" was in fact morally superior in his behavior to his White slave master who was hailed as God fearing. Stowe's book was widely read and helped to influence societal change. Legend has it that when Abraham Lincoln met Beecher-Stowe he said: "So you are the little woman who wrote the book that started this Great War."

Race and the Power of the Media: The media – be it press, photography, advertising, cinema, broadcasting (radio and television) is a powerful tool that can be used to promote good or evil and to influence a whole nation of people. Harriet Beecher-Stowe's book, Uncle Tom's Cabin helped to influence positive change in society during slavery, but the media was also being used in a destructive manner to demonize individuals and groups and destroy their sense of self-worth. The movie the *Birth of a Nation* is a destructive film, which instilled fear of Blacks in the minds of Whites released just after emancipation. Certain newspapers and media outlets have continued to promote negative stereo-types of Blacks to reinforce a negative perception, especially of young black boys. You must become a critical thinker and consider if what is stated about you or your national group is fact or propaganda. Not everything you see on television is representative of the truth. Stock photos and news reel footages are often used to illustrate a point. I recall watching the news one morning and observing a colleague walking with a prominent politician who was running for office. I was surprised at seeing her on television because we were scheduled to meet within an hour. Surprisingly, she showed up for the meeting, but dressed differently and with a different hairstyle. She explained that the news clip was taken over two years prior at a walk for breast cancer but shown as though it was current and campaigning for a politician. Jeremy Lin, an Asian point guard who at one time played for the New York Knicks and emerged as a great basketball story after helping the Knicks win three games straight, became an overnight sensation with the help of the media. It seemed people could not get enough of him. The headlines said: "Linn Mania" and "Linn Sanity." Then his team, the Knicks played against Miami Heat and lost and the same media which hailed him as a phenomenon headlined that "Linn could not take the heat" and "Linn has a long way to go." Suddenly the halo was gone, and Linn was no longer headline news. Fortunately, Linn was centered in God and had a proper perspective on his success, so much so that when he was enjoying the lime light, he called his pastor and said: *"I'm just . . . so thankful. To even have a shot in the NBA, that's a blessing from God. To even be sitting on the bench to play garbage minutes, that's a blessing. To be playing that much! That's truly a blessing." (Ebenezer Samuel, NY Daily News, Feb 19, 2012).*

You do not have to give merit to, accept or condone society's negative definition of you; negative statements made about you, or condone acts of injustice to you or to minority groups. Jacobed and Miriam are remarkable women of the Bible. Pharaoh decided to kill all the male children born to the Israelites, but Jacobed decided that this was an unjust edict and kept her son alive. Later she strategized with Miriam, her daughter to place him in a basket in the Nile River, but close enough to Pharaoh's daughter, who was childless to notice him. As a result of this one wise act against injustice she saved the entire nation of Israel. Remember, as a person of color, your history does not start with slavery; you are created in the image of God. You are royalty, from a royal priesthood. Think and conduct yourself becoming of royalty.

In ancient traditions, treasures were hidden in earthen vessels or clay pots for safe keeping. The Dead Sea Scrolls were found hidden in some clay pots. The worth of the scrolls is priceless. You must see yourself as a treasure in an earthen vessel (2 Cor. 4:1-7). What is within you is far more precious than what is on the outside. It is like putting a Rolex watch in a clay pot. The color of clay varies in shade, so the color of the pot doesn't matter. The fact also that the pot is made of clay doesn't matter either. The clay pot doesn't change the value of the watch on the inside. Your skin color is just the outer vessel. Within you are the priceless treasures – your mind, your character and your personality - three essential features of the self that you must nurture. Make the most of your appearance, but you do not need to bleach your skin, chemically straighten your hair or disfigure your body through plastic surgery to look like someone the media presents as the feminine or masculine ideal of beauty. It's just someone's image of beauty, which will change overtime. The media can have a powerful influence over how you see and perceive yourself. Make the most of your appearance without trying to change into someone you are not. A leopard cannot change its spot. You are not ordinary or insignificant. God sees you as His beautiful creation, a person of inestimable value, a truly priceless treasure who was created for his glory.

Your capabilities will influence your position in life. Alice Coachman became the first black woman and the only woman of any nationality to receive an Olympic gold medal in the 1948 London Games from King George VI, during a time when Blacks were treated as inferior beings. Coachman lived in the segregated South under Jim Crow and had not been allowed to train at athletic fields with whites. Coachman trained in fields where she said: "There was a lot of grass and no track. No nothing." Upon her return from the London games, she sat in a segregated auditorium and the mayor would not shake her hand; she also had to leave by a side door. The unjust treatment Coachman experienced did not deter her however from seeing herself as a priceless gem. She used the experience to pave the way for other blacks by establishing the Alice Coachman Track and field Foundation to aid young athletes in financial need.

At the Core You Must Know Who You Are and Whose You Are: Rice is rice! It might be basmati, long grain rice, natural brown rice, or white rice, but it is still rice. You may cook it any way you like, but it is still rice. Don't digest every negative thing people say about you, your family or your place of origin. You must press the delete button on the computer of your mind. Social Darwinism, which supports the notion of the survival of the fittest, is another belief system that reinforces the notion of racial inferiority. By implication, black slaves functioned at a lower evolutionary state than whites; this belief system gives no consideration to years of being in a disadvantaged status. Again, those slaves that used the Bible to teach themselves to read saw that "in the beginning" God created animals, but He created man in His own image. If an individual is created in the image of God, how could he be less than human? His characteristics must also be Godlike. The curse of Ham has been used to suggest that people of color are cursed, but the Bible does not say that Ham was cursed. Noah said, "Cursed be Canaan a servant of servants shall he be unto his brethren." This was not a perpetual curse otherwise Jesus himself who came from the lineage of the Canaanites would also have been cursed. Knowing these facts are important to liberate your mind from mental slavery, shame, an inferior status, or seeing yourself as less than equal in the sight of God. You must see yourself as a son or daughter of God, for how you see yourself will influence how you respond to your life circumstances. Under slavery, there were many slaves who resisted the badge of slavery. Harriet Tubman, Sojourner Truth, Sam Sharpe and Nat Turner refused to be enslaved mentally and physically. Despite mistreatment, they helped to change the course of history.

If you see yourself as a child of God, then you cannot be an inferior being. God-fearing slaves saw themselves as children of God, with

Jesus as their king and deliverer; they believed that one-day God would deliver them from chattel slavery, and they held firmly to that hope until it was realized. They made up songs about a better day coming when they would be liberated from the chattel slavery system. They sang *Swing low sweet chariot coming forth to carry me home; I am going to lay down my burdens* and *Steel Away*. They had a profound faith in God as their heavenly father and God honored their faith as his children. *For those who lay hold of the divine assurances of God's word, there are wonderful possibilities. Before them lie vast fields of truth, vast resources of power. Glorious things are revealed. Privileges and duties, which they do not even suspect to be in the Bible, will be made manifest. All who walk in the path of humble obedience, fulfilling his purpose, will know more and more of the oracles of God (E. G. White, Ministry of Healing, p.319).*

How you see yourself in relation to God's creation will determine how you interact with others and how far you will go in life. It was Frederick Douglas who said: "Whatever you persistently allow to occupy your thoughts will magnify in your life." Jesus said, "as a man thinketh so is he." If you think of yourself as a slave, you will act like one. If you see yourself as inferior, you will act like someone who is inferior. Your self-worth is proportionate to the estimation you place on yourself. If you do not put limits on yourself and what God can do in and through you, it is impossible for you not to be an achiever. Eleanor Roosevelt, a woman with a liberated mind and obviously not influenced by stereotypes, was a strong opponent of Jim Crow laws and racists acts against people of color. One day she attended a segregated meeting and instead of sitting on the side with the whites she pulled a chair and placed it in the middle of the isle. Now that's a woman with gumption! Is it any wonder that she said: "No one can make you feel inferior without your consent?"

You do not need to consent to negative stereotypes. If you honestly believe that you are a part of God's creation, then you must develop confidence in who you are and whose you are. God desires to restore you to himself and see his beauty and his character reflected in you and for this you must strive. Have confidence in what God can do in and through you. There is ample research to suggest that there is a greater correlation between self-confidence and achievement than between IQ and achievement. Have confidence in God as your heavenly father for, *"In quietness and in confidence shall be your strength."* By seeing yourself as a child of God and believing that *"with God all things are possible"* (Matt 19:26) and *"You can do all things through Christ who strengthens you,"* you can accomplish more than you have ever dreamed possible. You must not be satisfied with reaching a low standard or avoid responsibility for fear of failure or feeling less than. You must work to ascend the entire rung of the ladder of your potential. *"Education makes a people easy to lead, but difficult to drive; easy to govern, but impossible to enslave"* says Lord Brougham, a supporter of the abolition of slavery. *There is nothing more calculated to energize the mind, and strengthen the intellect, than the study of the Word of God. No other book is so potent to elevate the thoughts, to give vigor to the faculties, as the broad, ennobling truths of the Bible. If God's words were studied as it should be, men would have a breath of mind, a nobility of character, and stability of purpose, that is rarely seen in these times. E. G. White, FCE 126 (R&H, 7/17/1888).* Daniel and his companions are examples of individuals who were slaves in a foreign country, who enjoyed certain privileges in the king's court - not only because of their brilliance, but also, they knew who they were and whose they were and did not allow their privileged position to change their allegiance to God. Even in the face of adversity, they maintained their profound faith and confidence in God and God honored their faith. He showed up for them in a furnace that was so hot it killed the men who threw them in; yet, only the fetters that were used to tie them up and prevent them from escaping were singed. Strict compliance with the requirements of Heaven brings temporal as well as spiritual blessings (*E. G. White, Prophets & Kings, p.545-546*).

CONSTRUCTIVE ACTION PLAN:

I will make it a habit to spend at least 15 minutes each day in reading the Bible or a bible inspired book to help maintain my relationship with God.

Your 14th Gem

BUILD YOUR CHARACTER

"Watch your thoughts; they become words. Watch your words; they become actions. Watch your actions; they become habits. Watch your habits; they become character. Watch your character; it becomes your destiny" (Frank Outlaw).

God has given us intellectual and moral powers, but to a great extent every person is the architect of his own character. Every day the structure is going up. Strength of character consists of two things – power of will and power of self-control. The real greatness and nobility of the man is measured by the power and of the feelings that he subdues, not by the power of the feelings that subdue him. The strongest man is he, who while sensitive to abuse, will yet restrain passion and forgive his enemies. Such men are true heroes. (E. G. White, Testimony Treasures p.602)

Over the past 30 years, I have had the good fortune of living in London, California and New York. This experience has afforded me the opportunity of working among individuals and families from both low and high-income communities. Disproportionately, many of the individuals in low-income communities are poor or people of color. Young people often refer to some of these communities as the "hood" or the ghetto. By the hood they mean graffiti ridden housing projects infested with drugs, escalating crime statistic and gang activity. Many of these individuals with whom I worked were written off as failures – yet, today they are leading productive lives. Today, some have become successful entrepreneurs, doctors, bankers, mental health professionals, and writers. They have achieved more than they had ever dreamed possible. The question is what made the difference between those who succeeded and those that didn't. From my experience of working with these individuals, and my own life experience, coupled with an understanding of the slave experience, I have come to realize that there are distinct behaviors, actions and beliefs that influence whether you move on from the ordinary to the extraordinary or remain stuck in a state of constant struggle. To get out of the dunghill of life, you must think, believe and do things in a certain way.

Becoming Your Best, you; Becoming Self-actualized: The famous Brooklyn born psychologist, Abraham Maslow notes that only two percent of people achieve their full potential or reach what he calls self-actualization. He looked at the lives of famous individuals recorded in history books such as Jane Adams, Abraham Lincoln, Thomas Jefferson, Albert Einstein, Eleanor Roosevelt and other individuals that he knew personally and pointed out certain qualities that were common to these individuals but are not seen in most people. He observed that these individuals are independent thinkers, who rely on their own experiences and judgment. They do not allow culture or environment to shape their opinions and views; they are creative, original, spontaneous, lacking in prejudice and are problem solvers. They accept others unconditionally without trying to change them; they do things that result in the greatest good to themselves and their fellow men. These individuals take on challenges that are seen by others as "impossible." It is as though they are one with life, nature or God - the finite man connecting with the infinite God.

Interestingly enough, Maslow's pyramid starts with man's need to fulfill his basic physiological needs before he can reach a state of self-actualization, whereas Jesus turns the pyramid upside down and counsels us to first seek the kingdom of God and God's righteousness – right doing – to become self-actualized; Jesus reverses the order and starts with the need to first become self-actualized. Jesus assures that by ordering your life in this manner – seeking God first and being the best you that you can be; becoming a problem solver, seeking to uplift humanity, and not being prejudiced, all your needs will be met. *It is the glory of God to give his virtue to his children. He desires to see men and women reaching the highest standard; and when by faith they lay hold of the power of Christ, when they plead His unfailing promises, and claim them as their own, when with an importunity that will not be denied they seek for the power of the Holy Spirit, they will be made complete in Him (E.G. White, Acts of the Apostles, p530).*

George Washington Carver is an example of an individual who became self-actualized. His primary focus was on helping his people, which resulted in his becoming one of the nation's greatest educators and agricultural researchers. Carver was born the son of slaves in 1864 on the Moses Carver plantation, hence the name Carver. He was not a strong child, so he was given work around the yard taking care of the flowers instead of being put to work in the field. Through this chore of caring for flowers, he developed an interest in the use of plants and herbs to help those who were sick. He had an extraordinary knowledge of plants and was given the nickname "The plant doctor." His art teacher noticed his extensive knowledge of plants and encouraged him to attend college and pursue a course in horticulture. He was the first African American to attend Iowa State College. According to historians, Carver developed scientific skills in plant pathology and mycology-a branch of botany and encouraged his students to see nature as a great teacher. He believed that education should be "made common"—used for the betterment of the people in the community and he lived by his word. It is documented that he created 325 products from peanuts, more than 100 products from sweet potatoes and hundreds more from a dozen other plants native to the South. These products helped to improve the economic conditions of rural communities by offering alternative crops to cotton that were beneficial for the farmers and for the land. Carver could be seen as functioning at the highest level of self-actualization; only a small percentage of people get to that top level. It is said that the majority functions at a lower level. Not because they are incapable, but because they are anxious about survival issues. They worry about job security, paying the mortgage, self-esteem issues such as getting recognition, being influential, driving the right car, and living in the right neighborhood. When you ask these individuals how they are doing, they might say "surviving" yet God wants you to move beyond this low level of functioning. He doesn't want you to survive. He wants you to become self-actualized – free from fear and worry and being the best you that you can be. It is by first becoming self-actualized that all your needs will be supplied. The Apostle Paul said: *I have written unto you, fathers, because ye have known him that is from the beginning. I have written unto you, young men, because ye are strong, and the word of God abideth in you, and ye have overcome the wicked one. Love not the world, neither the things that are in the world. If any man love the world, the love of the Father is not in him. For all that is in the world, the lust of the flesh, and the lust of the eyes, and the pride of life, is not of the Father, but is of the world. And the world passeth away, and the lust thereof: but he that doeth the will of God abideth for ever. (1John 2:15 & 16).*

The Act of Surrender: The act of surrender is the uplifted outstretched palms. Lift your hands in surrender and tell God your cares, your hopes, your dreams and your aspirations. He will not fail you. Whatever stage of need you are in at this point in your life, God wants you to be free from worry. God gives the assurance that He knows the plans He has for you; plans for our welfare and not for evil to give you a future and a hope. He says you must call upon Him, seek Him with all our heart and come and pray to Him and He will listen (Jer. 29: 11-14). Job was a God-fearing man who stayed away from evil. He had a large family of seven sons and three daughters and was immensely wealthy. He was perhaps the largest cattle herder in the region, but he lost everything. After losing everything he was angry that God had dealt so unfairly with him and thought death was preferable to life. He was a God-fearing man and yet he was suffering. Job questioned God and even argued with Him, but he did not give up on God. It was not until he humbled himself and admitted his ignorance of the creative power of God and prayed for his friends that the Lord blessed him with twice as much as he had before. *And I will make them and the places round about my hill a blessing; and I will cause the shower to come down in his season; there shall be showers of blessing. (Ez.34: 26). For a just man falleth seven times, and riseth up again: but the wicked shall fall into mischief. (Prov. 24:16).* Higher than the highest human thought can reach is God's ideal for His children. Godliness-godlikeness – is the goal to be reached (E. G White, Edu. P18). Every human being, created in the image of God is endowed with a power akin to that of the creator – individuality, power to think and do. The men and women in whom this power is developed are the men who bear responsibilities, who are leaders in enterprise, and who influence character (E. G. White, Education, p.17).

CONSTRUCTIVE ACTION PLAN:

- What goals would I like to achieve that could solve a human problem?
- What prevents me from moving forward in achieving that goal?
- If I don't have the resources, with whom can I collaborate to achieve this goal?

Your 15th Gem

THE SKY IS THE LIMIT

*By humility and the fear of the Lord are riches, and honour, and life.
(Prov. 22:4).* The Cultivated Mind Measures the Man.--Never
think that you have learned enough and that you may now
relax your efforts. The cultivated mind is the measure of the
man. Your education should continue during your lifetime;
every day you should be learning and putting to practical use
the knowledge gained. --MH 499 (1905).

Although the Bible was written over two thousand years ago, it is still
a relevant book today. It is an inspired book, which chronicles the
history of mankind and predicts the future. It is filled with stories of
individuals and the workings of God in their lives. It is the book that
still transforms and sustains lives today. Indeed, the Bible is all about
life, and God's power to transform lives. From reading the Bible, it is
possible to obtain practical wisdom and guidance for life decisions.
From an understanding of Divine leading in the lives of individuals, it
is possible to learn how to live at peace with ones' self, with others and
with God. If you have an e-mail buddy, the only way you would get to

know that person is by reading his e-mail. The Bible is your direct way to get to know God. You get to know God by studying and digesting His words, studying nature and through daily prayer and meditation. *"Acquaint now thyself with him, and be at peace: thereby good shall come unto thee." s(Job 22:21). "There is nothing more calculated to strengthen the intellect than the study of the scriptures. No other book is so potent to elevate the thoughts, to give vigor to the faculties, as the broad, ennobling truths of the bible. If God's word were studied as it should be, men would have a breath of mind, a nobility of character, and a stability of purpose rarely seen in these times" (E. G. White. Steps to Christ, p. 91).*

We are here in this world to become like God in character and through our lives we reveal him to the world. Of course, no man has ever seen God. All around us nature speaks of his creative power, but nature is not God. What we do know is that God is both a spirit and a personal being. As a personal being He sits in His high and holy place surrounded by a retinue of angels. It is through His Spirit and these angels that He responds or ministers to us. Since no one has ever seen God, it is by faith we accept that He is our creator and that mankind – the crowning act of His creative power was created by Him to express His glory! Therefore, in order to express His glory, you must take on His character; but you cannot reveal His character if you do not know Him nor have a relationship with Him. E.G. White counsels: *Let the student take the Bible as his guide and stand firm for principle, and he may aspire to any height of attainment. All the philosophies of human nature have led to confusion and shame when God has not been recognized as all in all. But the precious faith inspired of God imparts strength and nobility of character (E.G. White, Ministry of Healing, p.319).*

Moses grew up in Egypt where he was used to seeing many gods. He was surrounded with awesome splendor and enormous symbolic images of Egyptian deities. As a member of the household of Pharaoh he himself was considered a god and was raised to assume leadership of Egypt. After fleeing from Pharaoh's palace, he had to face himself. Stripped of the splendor and images of stardom, he was surrounded only by nature. It was then that Moses asked God to reveal himself to him. He wanted to see God for himself. It is easier to believe what you can see rather than what you cannot see. That is why media advertising is so powerful. People tend to believe what they can see. Moses wanted to see God, but he could not see God and live because the brightness of God's glory would have overwhelmed him. Instead, God permitted

His goodness to pass before him. He revealed to Moses that He is a God full of mercy, longsuffering, loving and forgiving and that as His representative, Moses was to reflect His character to the children of Israel.

A Desire to Know God: Like the patriarchs of old, if you have a strong desire to know God, He will not disappoint you. It was David who said: *"As the hart panteth after the water brooks, so panteth my soul after thee, O God." Ps. 42:1.* Like Moses, you must spend time considering God's creative power revealed through nature. As you study nature, you cannot help but acknowledge God as the creator. Solomon studied nature. The book of Proverbs provides illustrations of his observations. Job saw the power of God in nature and Jesus used nature to illustrate his points. Many of the parables Jesus told are replete with examples from nature. Joseph studied the workings of nature, which helped him interpret Pharaoh's dream. A study of nature reveals the power and workings of God while the Bible reveals the character of God. In 1969, when the lunar module landed on the moon, astronaut Neil Armstrong could not help but acknowledge the awesomeness of God as he stepped out into space; I was only a child at the time, but I will never forget his declaration that: *"the heavens declare the glory of God and his firmament showeth his handy work."* Nature reveals the love, awesomeness and power of God. *Whatsoever the Lord pleased, that did he in heaven, and in earth, in the seas, and all deep places. He giveth snow like wool: he scattereth the hoarfrost like ashes. He hath also established them forever and ever; He giveth snow like wool…He causeth the vapors to ascend from the ends of the earth; He maketh lightenings with rain (Ps 135:6, 7; 147:16, 148:5, 6; s).*

Your Daily Food, Bible Reading & Eating Disorder: There are many inspirational books written by individuals who have developed a personal relationship with God that can lead to insight and strengthen your faith in God; none of these books however can replace the Bible. A daily study of the Bible helps to keep you connected with God and transform your character to become more like him. Try going a few months without eating a healthy meal and watch what happens to your mind and body. You will become emaciated, have mood swings and may even begin to hallucinate as in the case of individuals that suffer from anorexia nervosa, bulimia or malnutrition. The lack of nutrients upsets the body chemistry and neurotransmitters of the brain. Without food, the body begins to feed on itself and may eventually result in death. I will never forget my favorite country and western singer Karen Carpenter or my beautiful school mate Lois; both died untimely deaths as a result of their battles with anorexia nervosa. They restricted their food intake to cope with painful feelings such as anger, shame and self-loathing, or even fear of growing up. By saying no to food, they felt more powerful and in control, but this is a temporary feeling and their focus becomes self-absorbing and eventually self-destructive. Similarly, not staying connected with God and not studying the Bible can result in spiritual anorexia and even spiritual death. *The fear of the Lord is the beginning of wisdom: and the knowledge of the holy is understanding. (Prov. 9:10). The great work of life is character building, and a knowledge of God is the foundation of all true education. The teaching of the Bible has a vital bearing upon man's prosperity in all the relations of this life…Studied and obeyed, the word of God would give to the world men of stronger and more active intellect than will the closest application to all the subjects that human philosophy embraces. It would give men of strength and solidity of character, of keen perception and sound judgment- men who would be an honor to God and a blessing to the world (E.G. White, Patriarchs and Prophets, p.559).*

I remember at one point in my life questioning the existence of God and his reason for allowing some people to live their lives mired in abject poverty while a few have more than enough. I wondered how a loving God could allow death to steal away a loved one, or the reason that one person works hard and someone else gets the promotion. If there is a God, why does he not do something? With meditation and a study of the Bible, I came to realize that the answers to these questions rested in my understanding of God and the quality of my relationship with Him. The story was told of a god-fearing man in a barbershop and an atheist barber having a conversation about God; the atheist barber said there was no God. The God-fearing man listened and said nothing. Upon leaving the barbershop, he saw a man with straggly looking unkempt hair. The God-fearing man returned to the barbershop and said to the barber "there is no barber." The barber was puzzled by his comment. "Of course, there is," the barber replied; "I just cut your hair." The god-fearing man said "No, there isn't; if there was a barber, there would be no one with straggly hair." This story illustrates the point that God has given men faculties and capabilities along with freedom of choice. You may choose to serve him if you wish. There is no pressure, but if you do choose to serve God, he will not disappoint you. *But as it is written, Eye hath not seen, nor ear heard, neither have entered into the heart of man, the things which God hath prepared for them that love him. 1 Cor. 2:9).* God will work with the gifts he has given to you. Divine power when combined with human effort will result in success, for in Christ righteousness you can accomplish everything.

When Cares Overwhelm You: There will be times when you may feel overwhelmed by the cares of this life. You have given just about everything you have got. Your energy is sapped. You have prayed, and you have fasted, but nothing happens. Anxiety may set in. You may even doubt God's existence, as did John the Baptist, after King Herod locked him up in a dungeon for speaking up and speaking out about Herod's licentious behavior. This same John laid the coast for Jesus, yet under depressed condition he asked if Jesus was the Messiah or if he should expect another. Your situation may be depressing, but don't give up. At your lowest point God will send messages of hope and comfort as he did with David, Elijah, Hezekiah and the woman at the well. Remember the good shepherd goes looking for his sheep and God will come looking for you. You don't have to get into a tizzy and go chasing after Him. Sometimes you just must stand still and wait for His Salvation. It may come in the form of someone giving you a book, a tract, a message from a preacher or a perfect stranger. Ironically, it may come through nature or even an animal as with Elijah. I remember visiting Jamaica at a time in my life when I was feeling totally exhausted physically, emotionally and financially. I was successful in credentials, but the financial returns were not equal to my professional qualifications. I wanted to spend time pursuing my own passion and had spent time and money investing in my interests but working full time and pursuing my own interest left me feeling like I was chasing rabbits. I prayed continually and had done everything in my power to bring about the desired results, but it seemed like nothing was working out for me. I felt stuck and going nowhere fast. I began questioning my relationship with God and then that "ah, ha" moment came. I was traveling from Falmouth to Montego Bay in a Jutha bus and was struck by the sight of a black bird (a raven) sitting alone on a fence among the plush greenery of banana and breadfruit trees. There were no other birds around. The black bird seemed so majestic, yet so alone. The scene left an indelible impression on my mind. The image of that black bird on a stump, just sitting there waiting kept coming back to me. I was reminded of Matt 6: 25-27, which says:

Therefore I say unto you, Take no thought for your life, what ye shall eat, or what ye shall drink; nor yet for your body, what ye shall put on. Is not the life more than meat, and the body than raiment? Behold the fowls of the air: for they sow not, neither do they reap, nor gather into barns; yet your heavenly Father feedeth them. Are ye not much better than they? Which of you by taking thought can add one cubit unto his stature? This text was reassuring but not the answer I was looking for. Then I found the answer in the story of Elijah and Ahab (1Kings 18:41-46 and 19:1-8). Elijah did not see any sign of rain, but he told Ahab to get up, eat and drink for there is a sound of abundance of rain. Elijah had done everything that God had told him to do and having done everything that was in his power to do, he had faith that Heaven would outpour the blessings.

A Token of God's Favor: The same God who had sent the drought had promised an abundance of rain as the reward for right doing and now Elijah waited for the promised blessing. In an attitude of humility, he prayed to God for rain. Elijah sent his servant six times and six times the servant returned saying there is nothing. Elijah could have given up hope, but he did not give up in despair. On the seventh trip, the servant saw a little cloud appear out of the sea like a man's hand and that was enough for Elijah. He saw a small token of God's favor. It was then that I realized I had done everything in my power to improve my situation, so I simply needed to stop chasing rabbits and like the black bird, just wait in God's "presence" for a while in order to eventually enjoy his "presents."

Like seasons, it doesn't matter what you do. You cannot force summer to come in winter. You must wait for summer to come. A mango tree will not produce mangoes when it is not in season. Whatever you are going through don't give up on God; He won't give up on you. God sent a raven in the morning and in the evening to feed Elijah. The raven is a scavenger, which according to Leviticus 11 is an unclean bird yet God used it to feed Elijah. My mother pointed out to me that there was a famine in the land and food was scarce so the only bird that could safely take food to Elijah would have been a raven; no one would consider killing a raven or taking food from it.

If you are going through hard times or a financial down turn, God can use anything or anyone to help you out of your situation. Don't focus on your lack. Focus in faith on what you want God to do for you instead and trust him to come through for you in the most amazing way. Mephibosheth, prince Jonathan's son and the grandson of King Saul was crippled; he had lost his heritage and was living in Lo Debar – a place of nothing or no bread, meaning he was living in abject poverty; yet when Mephibosheth least expected, God worked through King David to move him out of Lo Debar to the palace -a place of opulence and opportunity. William Cowper, the English author who was a trained lawyer who never practiced law wrote the hymn *God Moves in Mysterious Ways* was known to often struggle with depression and doubt. The story is told that one night he decided to commit suicide by drowning himself. It is said that he called a cab and told the driver to take him to the Thames River in London. However, thick fog came down and prevented them from finding the river (another version of the story has the driver getting lost deliberately). After driving around lost for a while, the cab driver finally stopped and let Cowper out. To Cowper's surprise, he found himself on his own doorstep: God had sent the fog to keep him from killing himself. Even in our blackest moments, God watches over us. I remember when I first came to New York after graduating from university and was job hunting; several months went by and I did not get a job offer or even an interview; then one evening a young neighbor, Serge came to my sister's house and said he had a job for me. I remember thinking "what kind of job could he have for me" since he was an employee himself, but God used this young man to speak to a superior at his job about an opening that met my qualifications and through his influence I was hired.

Whatever trials you are going through, just believe that God is working in your best interest for *"Being confident of this very thing, that he which hath begun a good work in you will perform it until the day of Jesus Christ:" (Philippians 1:6).* Like precious metal you may have to go through a purifying process before you can be put on display or be put to good use. My grandmother was a potter and I remember the amazing process – the much kneading, and spinning, shaping and firing that the clay had to go through before it could become that beautiful vessel ready for display. Don't give in to feelings of despair and hopelessness. There is a way out. Ask God to work with you as he did with David. Ask him to fill your cup as he did the woman at the well; ask him to feed you as he did Elijah and ask him to bless you and enlarge your coast as he did Jabez. God will bring you into a wealthy place. Take courage from Ps.66:8-13: *Let everyone bless God and sing praises for he holds our lives in His hands. And He holds our feet to the path. You have purified us with fire, O Lord, like silver in a crucible. You captured us in your net and laid great burdens on our backs. You sent troops to ride across our broken bodies. We went through fire and flood. But in the end, you brought us into wealth and great abundance* (Living Bible).

Your 16th Gem

CULTIVATING FAITH THAT WORKS

We must cherish and cultivate the faith of which prophets and apostles have testified – the faith that lays hold on the promises of God and waits for deliverance in his appointed time and way (E.G. White, Prophets and Kings p. 387-388). Ask, and it shall be given you; seek, and ye shall find; knock, and it shall be opened unto you: For every one that asketh receiveth; and he that seeketh findeth; and to him that knocketh it shall be opened. Or what man is there of you, whom if his son ask bread, will he give him a stone? Or if he ask a fish, will he give him a serpent? If ye then, being evil, know how to give good gifts unto your children, how much more shall your Father which is in heaven give good things to them that ask him? (Matt7:7-11).

Faith is not emotionalism or whimsical feelings. It is hoping and believing that you will get the result you want even when you cannot see it. It is having a relationship with God based on knowing him as your creator, redeemer and provider. Without faith it is impossible to please God; *for he that cometh to God must believe that He is, and that He is a rewarder of them that diligently seek him (Hebrews 11:6).* I was fascinated by the observations of Dr. Viktor Frankl, an Austrian psychiatrist who survived the Nazi concentration camps in World War II. Dr. Frankl noticed that when prisoners stopped believing in the future, they suddenly stopped functioning and could not be helped. Many would die between Christmas and New Year, conceivably because of dashed hopes that they would be released by Christmas. One man dreamed that they would be liberated by March thirtieth, but when this did not happen on the 29th day of March he started running a high fever; on the thirtieth he became delirious and by March 31st he was dead. He died because his belief, his faith and his hope had died. Solomon says *Hope deferred maketh the heart sick: but when the desire cometh, it is a tree of life. (Prov.13:12).* Faith is being sure of what we hope for and certain of what we do not see. This is what the ancients were commended for (Hebrew 11:1).

Faith Requires that You Trust God: Hold on tightly for dear life and rely totally on God. I remember attending a World Business Forum at Radio City Music Hall in New York City. The featured speakers included some noted civic and business leaders such as Rudy Giuliani, Jack Welch, Anne M. Mulcahy and former president of the United States, William (Bill) Jefferson Clinton. Bill Clinton was the most popular of all the speakers and many people signed up for his seminar on philanthropy. Those that signed up for his seminar were invited to have cocktails with him in the Green Room at the end of the day. I was among those that had signed up for his seminar, but when I entered the Green room it was elbowroom only. People were pressing against each other just to get a photo opportunity, shake his hand or to compliment the former president. For me, it was the end of a long day; I was tired, and I was not prepared to edge my way over for a handshake, so I stood and observed the interactions. As I watched the crowd elbowing their way to get close to Mr. Clinton and his ease in moving among the crowd - making eye contact with each individual as though that person was the only person in the room, I could not help but reflect on the faith of the woman that had been hemorrhaging for 12 years and her desire to touch the hem of Jesus' garment. My mother had fibroid tumors and had hemorrhaged for many years; so much so that she became weak and anemic and eventually had to have blood transfusion and a hysterectomy. Standing in the corner feeling listless, I visualized the plight of the woman. This woman had heard of Jesus and desperately wanted to see him to obtain healing. Jesus was her only hope, but her emaciated body could not keep up with the jostling crowd; her only recourse was to touch the hem of Jesus' garment. Falling to the ground and dragging her listless body with an outstretched arm, she reached out and touched the hem of Jesus' garment. As she touched his hem, her answer came. She received instant healing, acknowledgement and a blessing from Jesus. Standing alone in the corner of the Green room, the former president looked across and nodded in acknowledgement of my presence. And in the same way that the former president of the United States did not ignore this sole black woman in the corner but nodded in acknowledgement as though I was more important than all those jostling for a photo opportunity, Jesus, King of Kings, has not ignored you. He did not ignore the woman in her pain and suffering and he certainly won't ignore you either. He sees you and He can do for you more than you can ask or think.

Your Faith Must Be Specific and Not Just a Thought: Faith must be a strong desire to see result. This sick woman was clear in her mind what she wanted and knew what she needed to do in order to accomplish her goal. So too, when you set a goal, it must be SMART. Sean Doran, who is said to have developed the SMART acronym in November 1981, says goals must be Specific, Measurable, Achievable, Realistic, and Time specific. It must be a SMART move. If you want to lose weight for example, you might say: I want to lose 15 pounds. I will lose 1 pound per week for 15 weeks and in 5 months' time, I will weigh 150 lbs. I will eat one less slice of bread and walk for one mile two evenings a week, from 7 – 9pm. This goal is achievable because it is specific, measurable and has time frames.

The prophet Elijah showed amazing faith in God. Elijah prayed six times earnestly for rain and even at the sixth time his prayer was not answered. He could easily have given up in defeat, but he persevered in pleading to God and God honored his faith. Elijah's servant observed a small cloud out of the sea, like a man's hand and this small sign was enough to strengthen his faith that God would send rain. You must be able to visualize what you hope for and be certain that although you cannot see it, you have confidence that God will bring it to pass. When you board an aircraft, your goal is to get to your destination. You know where you are going; you can even visualize the place; you do not always see the pilot, but you have faith that he will get you there safely. It takes faith; It takes surrender, and it takes a willingness to accept that the pilot has skills and competencies and knows how best to navigate the plane. You would not go into the cockpit and offer to take over. You must have a similar faith in God. Do not give your troubles to him and take them back. He said cast all your cares upon him for he cares for you. You may not know how, when or where God will bring about your desired result, but you can be assured that God will come through for you in his time and in his way... *If he sees it best not to grant your desires, He will counterbalance the refusal by giving you tokens of His love and entrusting to you another service...often our plans fail that God's plans for us may succeed (E.G White, Min. of Healing p.473)*

I remember my husband deciding to do a major upgrade on our home. The upgrade required that we move out and rent an apartment in the interim. According to the contractor the job was supposed to take three months, but the three months turned into seven months. I became fearful that we would lose our home because we were depleting all our cash reserves by paying rent and mortgage. I did a lot of praying for God to intervene and intervene he did! The contractor was arrested for his dishonest practices and his company went bankrupt, which freed us to hire someone else to complete the job. In the end, the job cost a lot less than we had anticipated. You must not only know about faith, you must talk faith, and act faith. Faith is taking the first step even when you don't see the whole staircase, says Dr. Martin Luther King Jnr. Of course, you cannot believe in God and disobey or defy him at the same time. You must pray for "His will to be done" in your life. The first line of the Lord's Prayer requires that you acknowledge God as your heavenly father. Tell him your deepest desires. He does not need a scripted prayer. Tell him what you might be afraid of or ashamed of telling even your closest friend. Tell him your joys, your sorrows and your pains. If you doubt His existence tell him that too. Job had a real heart to heart with God after he lost his wealth and his family. This is not about wallowing in emotionalism – one day trusting and next day doubting or behaving like greedy children with a list of "gimmes" – give me this and give me that. It is a personal relationship with God.

Enoch walked with God. In other words, he did nothing without consulting with God. Get into the habit of having such a close relationship with God that you consult him in every aspect of your life. The prophet Daniel prayed three times a day so when his coworkers conspired against him, he did not fear for his life because he had enough faith that **his** God would deliver him. In faith he went down on his knees and prayed, giving thanks to God, which was his norm (Daniel 6:10). You must ask and believe that God will answer, but you must also ask God for His will to be done in your life instead of telling him what His will ought to be.

The Lord's Prayer is a reminder that it is important to pray for God's will to be done. By praying for God's will to be done you free yourself from fear and worry because you have surrendered your will to him, believing that he will act in your best interest at the right time and in a way that will work to your favor. As you build your relationship with God, like Job, when things go wrong, as they sometimes will, you will be able to say, "Though they slay me, yet will I trust in Him." Job was a righteous man, but his faith in God was not a perfected faith until after he lost everything. He had fears that one day he would wake up and lose everything and when disaster struck, he confessed that what he feared had come upon him. Satan was able to attack him on this one weak spot; when you start expressing fear instead of faith Satan will attack you too. Fear is not of God for God has not given you a spirit of fear. Faith in God cannot be analyzed scientifically, but when it is combined with prayer it becomes the basis for all miracles.

Jesus said if you have faith the size of a mustard seed – the smallest seed, you can move mountains. My mother told me a story of a lady who was testing to see if a literal mountain could be moved through prayer, so she prayed for the mountain close to her house to be removed. She did it for a week, but nothing happened; then one day a work crew came to the area with crane and bulldozers and started moving the mountain to build a highway. God can move mountains, but it takes faith. Having faith in God alone is not enough. You must also have faith in yourself and what you can accomplish in life. I have often wondered why there are so many religious people who shuffle along on a low plain when there are so many mountains they could climb. Many are highly skilled and intelligent, but it is apparent that they do not have faith in themselves and in God to move beyond a certain level. Some are overwhelmed with fear - fear of failure, fear of being criticized, fear of being incompetent or fear of feeling foolish. Through learned negative life scripts – things they were told they could not do or become - whether by parents, teachers or people they respect, they internalize these life scripts and limit their own achievement. Like a stunted plant they never grow to their full potential. They repeat the cycle of madness by doing the same thing every day and expect a different result. God wants you to exercise faith in what He can do in and through you. You must replace fear with faith. *Be strong and of a good courage, fear not, nor be afraid of them: for the Lord thy God, he it is that doth go with thee; he will not fail thee, nor forsake thee. (Deuteronomy 31:6).*

CONSTRUCTIVE ACTION PLAN:

Today I place my fears of _____ and anxieties over _____ before the Lord knowing that He can do for me more than I can ask or think.

Your 17th Gem

OBTAINING GOD'S GIFTS AND FAVORS

The earth is the Lord's, and all its fullness, the world and those who dwell therein. (Psalms 24:1 NKJ); For every beast of the forest is MINE, and the cattle on a thousand hills. (PSALMS 50:10 NKJ); I know all the birds of the mountains, And the wild beasts of the field are MINE. (PSALMS 50:11, NKJ). The silver is MINE, and the gold is MINE,' says the Lord of hosts. (HAGGAI 2:8 NKJ). Yet ye have not, because ye ask not. (James 4:2, 1 John 3:22, 23).

First, we must decide what we want and be specific about it. It must be quantifiable or definite, but it must be consistent with God's will. In Genesis 28:20-22, it is noted that Jacob made a vow, saying: *"If God will be with me, and will keep me in this way that I go, and will give me bread to eat, and raiment to put on, So that I come again to my father's house in peace; then shall the Lord be my God: And this stone, which I have set for a pillar, shall be God's house: and of all that thou shalt give me I will surely give the tenth unto thee.."* I remember after graduating from college and was jobless, I pledged that if God provided me with a job consistent with my skills and qualifications, I would return one tenth of my earnings in tithe.

Having confidence in God's words, based on Malachi 3, I claimed God's promise. Prior to being jobless (when I was employed) I did not fail to return a faithful tithe and I did not squander my funds thoughtlessly, and therefore I made the request believing that God would answer my prayer and answer he certainly did. Within a relatively short time after making this vow, God blessed me with a job, which was consistent with my qualifications. *We reap whatever we sow, and we speak whatever we believe (1 Corinthians 4:13).*

God owns everything. Like a loving parent who sets up a trust fund for his children long before they are ready for college, God made provision for man long before he created man; He created everything needful for his survival. He created oxygen, he created light, he created vegetation for food, and he created an Edenic home. God has already made provision for you. His resources are limitless. That is why you never ever need to worry about your needs, especially money. Money is a manmade commodity based on a credit system. When you use up your credit and your debt to income ratio is too high you will not get any more credit, but God's resources are tangible and limitless. They are his gifts to us. Whatever we have or think we own are God's gifts to us during our lifetime existence on earth so don't hold on to earthly possessions too tightly and selfishly. Like a wet bar of soap that is held too tightly, it can easily slip away from you. At the same time, you do not want to be so slack with the gifts that God has given to you that they slip away from you. "A slack hand leads to poverty" counsels the wise man Solomon. Be mindful of your incoming and your outgoing. Keep a budget and watch your spending. Be sure to return a portion of God's gifts to him. This is often referred to as tithes and offerings. *Bring ye all the tithes into the storehouse, that there may be meat in mine house, and prove me now herewith, saith the Lord of hosts, if I will not open you the windows of heaven, and pour you out a blessing, that there shall not be room enough to receive it. (Mal. 3:10).*

I have often seen television evangelists appeal to viewers to give a certain percentage of their income, promising that God would give them twice as much as before. I recall one television evangelist sending me a letter with a prophetic message of abundance, but on condition that I send a fixed amount of money. With each letter came a request for an even larger sum of money. The letters kept coming even though I did not respond. After a year, I was asked to send fifty times as much as the first request. The letter suggested that I borrow the money if I did not have it to avoid forfeiting my blessing. This obviously is exploitation of the vulnerable in the name of Jesus. The motivation to give on the part of the vulnerable is prompted out of a desire for a guaranteed return. It is not prompted out of a love relationship with God. This is called a quid pro quo relationship. In legal terms, *quid pro quo* means trading an item or service in return for something of value, usually when the propriety or equity of the transaction is in question. God is not involved in a quid pro quo relationship with us because He does not force the will. However, you do reap what you sow: *But this I say, He which soweth sparingly shall reap also sparingly; and he which soweth bountifully shall reap also bountifully. Every man according as he purposeth in his heart, so let him give; not grudgingly, or of necessity: for God loveth a cheerful giver.. (2 Cor. 9:6-7)*

Tithes and offerings are expressions of gratitude to God for all the provisions he has made for us. Since we take nothing with us when we die, tithing is an acknowledgement that ownership of all that we have belongs to God. The tithe ensures that there are funds in God's house to spread messages of God's goodness, do acts of justice and mercy and to replicate His character throughout the world. The story of Elijah and the widow is a good example of tithing. The widow had only a little oil and a little meal left, and Elijah said, "bring it to me." She could have said it was not enough to share, but she acted in faith. Her faith in bringing the meal to Elijah resulted in the woman witnessing a marvelous miracle. God blessed her as well. He opened endless possibilities for her.

When God promises to open the windows of heaven, you can be sure that he will open windows of opportunity for you. It is up to you to respond in faith, act in faith and receive the blessing that the faith action will bring. "God gives us opportunities, our success depends on the use we make of them," Says E.G. White *(Prophets and Kings, p. 486)*. Make use of the opportunities that come your way, and your blessings will multiply. There are times when you may not see the blessings right away. I remember a point in my life, after doing a budget and taking out my tithe first, my income did not meet my expenses. I began to take stock of my spending and came to realize that like an ocean with tributaries, I needed to look at the tributaries –frivolous spending habits that were causing a leakage in my income and take steps to close them. After closing some of the tributaries, my income was still not enough so I spread out my case before the Lord and asked for his help. A short while after I received a generous pay increase, which was backdated for eighteen months. On another occasion, my bank account was low and unexpectedly I received an inheritance. When my mortgage was under water, over a period of three years, I was able to reduce the interest rates from seven percent to three and a half percent. Your beliefs about what God can do for you should not be limited to what you can see but also what you can conceive and believe.

At times it is through difficult financial challenges that your faith will be tried. It is then that you can exercise the passive graces, as you return to God a portion of His own in tithes and offerings. As you exercise faith and submission, like Job you will say, "'though he slays me, yet will I trust in him." When withholding tithes because your funds are low, you may experience guilt at not being able to return a faithful tithe. Guilt then leads to depression, which can also be a warning to take stock of your spending and turn away from behaviors or spending habits that might be destructive such as the excessive or unnecessary spending on stuff that you want but do not need. The feeling of guilt could also be an opportunity for God to bring you back into a healthy relationship with him and to cleanse and make you entirely guilt-free (_Romans 3:23_).

Ironically, tithing does not lead to lack, if anything tithing will help you to get out of debt, for when you tithe you are forced to budget and when you budget you are more likely to live within your means. Tithing comes from the principles of agriculture. Tithe means a tenth. Farmers did not use up all the land; they left a tenth of the land to follow so that the harvest can be greater the next year. In Bible time, the people being primarily agricultural would also bring a tithe of their produce - grain, fruits, vegetables, or cattle, fowl etc. to the local priests who were responsible for its distribution. The priests had a storehouse for storing the grain, meal, cattle, etc. It is for this reason that God said you are to bring all the tithes into the storehouse that there may be meat in His house. The patriarch Joseph introduced the storehouse concept to Pharaoh where one fifth of the harvest was stored in store-houses, and as a result the people of Egypt prospered under his leadership - so much so that during a terrible famine, his brothers who sold him into slavery came to Egypt to purchase grain from him.

Today the local church would be considered the storehouse - the place where people are able to receive their ministry and care. The purpose of returning a tithe therefore is to support your church's ministry and spread God's goodness on earth through his ministers. A tithe is given out of love and appreciation to God and not to reap a reward or urge God's favor. Returning a faithful tithe encourages you to live by faith and in living by faith you will develop even greater faith! You will trust God more because of your walk of faith. You will stop worrying because you have confidence that God is your father and that he will not fail you: *"Therefore take no thought, saying, What shall we eat? or, What shall we drink? or, Wherewithal shall we be clothed? For after all these things do the Gentiles seek:) for your heavenly Father knoweth that ye have need of all these things. But seek ye first the kingdom of God, and his righteousness; and all these things shall be added unto you. Take therefore no thought for the morrow: for the morrow shall take thought for the things of itself. Sufficient unto the day is the evil thereof."* (Matthew 6:31–34). You will experience wonderful peace of mind when you come to fully trust in God (Philippians 4:6–7). After regularly setting aside the tithe of my income, I have learned to allocate the remaining portion. With careful budgeting and financial discipline, God has often surprised me with unexpected income, discounts, price reductions and gifts that I call "blessings." If after returning your tithe your income does not meet your expenses, you may need to look at your current employment position to see if you are "settling" rather than reaching to improve your condition. Maybe you need to question if you are really maximizing your potential. I obtained part-time teaching opportunity at a local University after I needed more income and realizing that I was not maximizing my potentials. There are rungs of success that you must climb. Look around you, there problems that need solving. Ask God for wisdom and move forward in faith as He reveals His will to you.

Be careful about addictive behaviors: Addictive behaviors can eat away at your finances as you use up your resources to support your habit. Alcohol, cigarettes, substances or impulsive shopping and purchases may give you a "high" because your brain is releasing endorphins and dopamine, but over time, your desires for these feelings will grow and can become addictive. Your addiction to shop for example can result from a compulsion to get bargains or match items, impress others, or in most cases obtain emotional release. Regardless of the reason, it is important to acknowledge your compulsive behavior and address it through cognitive restructuring – changing the way you think. I was struck by this statement, which has helped to shape my thinking: *He [God] has entrusted to men and women an abundance of means for the carrying forward of His plan of mercy and benevolence. He bids His stewards of* *means invest their money in the work of feeding the hungry, clothing the naked, and preaching the gospel to the poor. Perfection of character cannot possibly be attained without self-sacrifice (E. G. White, Testimonies for the Church, Vol 9. P11).*

CONSTRUCTIVE ACTION PLAN

Write your own budget plan. A basic budget requires that you look at your income and your expenses. Your budget may be divided as follows: Tithe/Charitable giving (10%); Savings (10%); and living expenses (80%). Check that your expenses are in line with your income. If your expenses and income are not in line, consider how you might adjust your expenses or seek ways to increase or supplement your income.

Your 18th Gem

YOU CAN REACH HIGHER

Seest thou a man diligent in his business? he shall stand before kings;
he shall not stand before mean men. Prov. 22:29.

I was watching a television documentary on the bush tribe in the
Philippines. This tribe lived like cavemen. They were pounding corn
with a mortar and some of the men wore loincloth. They lived in thatched
roof huts and had little to eat. Such primitive existence in the 21 Century
is a contrast to the Western world where there is an ample supply of food,
clothing and adequate shelter. If this bush tribe does not desire anything
better than what they know, or if they are not exposed to anything better
and are not connected with a source greater than themselves how can
they achieve more than what they have? If the bush tribe's life does not
extend beyond this tribe, then there is no need to change. If one member
of the tribe leaves and gets an education in improved ways of doing,
but does not return to the tribe, the tribe will remain unchanged. Cults
similarly remain static if no one invades or attempts to change their
practices. Communities and churches lose their vigor when individuals
who desire better for themselves move away and there is no one to replace

them. Urban blight is an example of this. People who can afford to live elsewhere move away and carry their know-how and economic resources with them resulting in the neglect of those communities.

Mary McLeod Bethune was the fifteenth child of a poor family in the South. Coming up from poverty and ignorance she was determined to help her people. As a student of color with potential, she was selected from her community to attend Scotia College. It is said when she returned home from college, she brought a pair of slippers for her father to cover his bare feet when he returned from work, forks for her mother and toothbrushes for everyone. These simple gifts may seem insignificant but at that time, they were the beginning of a life changing experience for a poor family. Mary McLeod Bethune decided after graduating that learning for life's sake was important and in 1904, she founded and developed the Bethune-Cookman College to further help her people. Napoleon Hill, author of Think and Grow Rich notes that as knowledge is acquired, it must be organized and put into use, for a definite purpose. Through practical plans...Successful men in all callings never stop acquiring specialized knowledge related to their major purpose, business, or profession. Those who are not successful usually make the mistake of believing that the knowledge-acquiring period ends when one finishes school... The order of the day is specialization! (Napoleon Hill Think and Grow Rich p.87)

A reservoir is manmade, but it plays an important role in preserving life. As it releases water, the water flows through downstream waterways to be used for drinking water lower down the system - sometimes hundreds of miles further downstream. It can also be used for irrigation where water is released into canals for use in farmlands or in homes. I grew up in Jamaica near a reservoir, which served us water for drinking and water for irrigation; when there was water shortage, as children everyone would take their little buckets and go to the reservoir for water. As I reflect on those days, a thought from St Bernard of Clairvaux comes to mind: "........we should seek to become reservoirs rather than canals. For a canal just allows the water to flow through it, but a reservoir waits until it is filled before overflowing then it can communicate without loss to itself. In the church today (i.e. twelfth century), we have many canals but few reservoirs."

When we consider God's creative process there is nothing static about it. God's creation expresses his glory. It is new every morning. "New every morning is His love." Each day nature reveals His glory and as His created beings, we too must reveal His glory. As we acquaint ourselves with God a transformation takes place in our character. I have seen many drug addicts and criminals develop a relationship with God and their lives become totally transformed. The founders of Alcohol Anonymous (AA) experienced a life- changing transformation after they admitted to personal powerlessness over alcohol and that their lives had become unmanageable. In humility they came to believe that a power greater than themselves could restore them to sanity. They acquainted themselves with God. The basic principles of AA were borrowed mainly from the fields of religion and medicine.

It is impossible to acquaint yourself with the character of God and not begin to experience a transformation. As you spend time meditating on the character of God the more like him you will become. We are told that Enoch walked with God. In other words, he included God into every aspect of his life. It is for this reason that you must not simply own a Bible, but you must spend time reading it. Spend at least15 minutes each day, preferably first thing in the morning reading the Bible. It is *"The"* book- like a road map that will direct your life into the right channel. God's power is absolute so if you rely on his strength you will discern more clearly the path your life must take. Your aspirations will be unselfish, and your motives and purpose will rise above the inferior. You will truly reach the level of self-actualization. *"God fixes no limit to the advancement of those who desire to be filled with the knowledge of His will in all wisdom and spiritual understanding. Through prayer, through watchfulness, through growth in knowledge and understanding, they are to be strengthened with all might according to His glorious power." (The Acts of the Apostles, P. 478).*

I have always tried to bring out the best in others and encourage them to reach higher; as a result, there are many individuals that I have helped and mentored over the years that are today leading productive lives. I remember encouraging one young lady who was an excellent typist to go back to school and upgrade her computer skills. This seemed like a reasonable suggestion, but she responded, "Why should I? I am happy just the way I am." As the years went by, she was unable to meet the increasing demands of the job because she simply did not have the necessary technical and computer skills to get the job done. Eventually it became necessary to hire someone else to do her job and ultimately replace her. Life is not static, and we do not live in isolation of others; unless one continues to upgrade his/her skills or knowledge, in the scheme of things, he/she will be left behind. Similarly, whole groups of people or communities can be left behind if certain beliefs, practices and conditions are not improved relative to time and progress. It is said that a law of the mind is that whatever we focus on we become. Sitting down and watching soap operas or movies all day will not improve your mind or your intellect. Pick up a book, go back to school, or do an on-line course if you do not have time to go to school. Improve yourself. Mentor someone. Invent something that will improve your life and the lives of others. Do not become a couch potato. *Yet a little sleep, a little slumber, a little folding of the hands to sleep Prov. 24:33&34 (NIV)*

Author Jim Collins identifies five levels of leadership. The first is becoming a highly capable individual. The next is being a contributing team member, the third a competent member, the fourth is an effective leader and the fifth is becoming the executive. The point here is that even leadership is not static. There are stages of growth and development that must be mastered; however, very few people ever get to the executive level because they fail to improve their skills in order to prepare themselves for the next level or through lack of confidence, they put a low estimate on themselves and resign to a position. *The mind as well as the muscles should be trained to the most diligent and persevering efforts.* If you do not stretch your mind, *it will remain small in thinking. The mind must grapple with difficult problems to avoid losing the power of growth. The elements of character that make a man successful and honored among men – the irrepressible desire for some greater good, the indomitable will, the strenuous exertion, the untiring perseverance- are not to be crushed out. By the grace of God, they are to be directed to objects as much higher than mere selfish and temporal interests as the heavens are higher than the earth. In the Bible, we learn of the power that created the world. Through a study of the Bible the mind of man is brought in connection with the infinite mind (E. G. White, Ministry of Healing).*

CONSTRUCTIVE ACTION PLAN

List three personal goals you would like to achieve in the next year. Your goals must be specific, measurable, realistic, and have time frames:

1. _____

2. _____

3. _____

Your 19th Gem

YOUR POWER TO GET WEALTH

But thou shalt remember the Lord thy God for it is he that give thee the power to get wealth, that he may establish his covenant which he swore unto thy fathers, as it is this day (Deut.8:16-18). Spiritual prosperity is closely bound up with Christian liberality.... Would that men make their prosperity secure? Let them place it in the hands that bear the marks of the crucifixion. Would they enjoy their substance? Let them use it to bless the needy and suffering. Would they increase their possessions? Let them heed the divine injunction, Honor the Lord with thy substance, and with the first fruits of all thine increase: so, shall thy barns be filled with plenty, and thy presses shall burst out with new wine." Proverbs 3:9,10. Let them seek to retain their possessions for selfish purposes, and it will be to their eternal loss. But let their treasure be given to God and from that moment it bears His inscription. It is sealed with His immutability – E. G. White –The Acts of the Apostles, pp, 344, 345

It is estimated that there are 10 million millionaires around the world. Of that number, the United States has the most with 2.87 million, out of a population of 305 million. In 2009, despite an economic down turn, these millionaires saw their wealth soar to 18.9 percent (to 39 trillion dollars). This means the rich got richer while the poor became poorer. Is it any wonder that the poor desires to become rich? Growing up in a religious community, I often heard sermons about the dangers of getting rich, but not the benefits of being rich. Virtue in living a life of poverty was stressed, where as being rich was condemned. I knew from memory the Bible text, "It is easier for a camel to go through the eye of a needle than for a rich man to enter the kingdom of God" (Mark 10:25). Being rich was not something to desire. It took some personal research on getting rich and living among the rich to get a proper perspective on riches. From my research, I came to realize that riches in the hands of the right person can be a tremendous blessing. I also saw that God wants us to prosper and be in health. There are numerous positive references between the books of Genesis and Proverbs about prosperity. David begged God to send prosperity. He said: *Save now, I beseech thee, O Lord: O Lord, I beseech thee, send now prosperity. (PS 118:25).* However, I believe that as a Christian, the desire should not be for riches but rather for creative opportunities in order to be a blessing and from which will flow enough financial blessings to supply your every need. If you are creative, you will create new opportunities, but if you are simply rich you can lose it all. Similarly, if you inherit a large sum of money and don't invest it wisely it will soon disappear. The wise man Solomon says: *Wilt thou set thine eyes upon that which is not? for riches certainly make themselves wings; they fly away as an eagle toward heaven. Prov. 23:5.* It is pointless being rich if your riches are not touching lives. The purpose of having riches is to be a blessing. I like the statement made by Dennis Hawthorne from Jamaica who owns a shipping company in Brooklyn, New York: He says, *"It is not the amount of money or the level of education that makes you successful, but rather the people that benefit, beyond your families and friends, as a result of your accomplishments."*

There are enough texts in the Bible to show that poverty is not God ordained. There should be no poor among you, for in the land the Lord your God is giving you to possess as your inheritance, he will richly bless you (Deut 15:4); wealth and honor come from you (God); you are the ruler of all things. In your hands are strength and power to exalt and give strength to all (1 Chron. 29:12). The Lord brings death and makes alive; He brings down to the grave and raises up. The Lord sends poverty and wealth; he humbles, and he exalts. He raises the poor from the dust and lifts the needy from the ash heap; he seats them with princes and has them inherit a throne of honor (1Sam 2:6). He built villages and acquired great numbers of flocks and herds, for God had given him very great riches (2 Chr. 32:29); The blessing of the Lord brings wealth, and he adds no trouble to it (Prov. 10:22). There are examples in the Bible of people like Isaac, Naomi and Job who became poor and were restored to even greater wealth. In Naomi's case she had lost everything – her husband, her sons and her possessions. She had become so angry and depressed over her situation that she even took on the name Mara, meaning bitter. The bitter person may feel cheated or short-changed by life in general because of how much they feel they've been denied their due. Naomi's restoration came after she decided to leave Moab, a heathen land, and return to being among her god-fearing kin; in Job's case he had lost everything – his wealth, his health and his family; it was after he reflected and acknowledged God as omnipotent and omnipresent that God restored his wealth and a new family. In Isaac's case he had dug some wells multiple times, which his enemies sabotaged; it was also after God appeared to him in a dream saying "I am the God of your father Abraham: do not fear, for I am with you. I will bless you and multiply your descendants for my servant Abraham's sake" that Isaac then built an altar and called on the name of the Lord. David saw that even in affliction, God can change your circumstances; *For thou, O God has proved us: thou have tried us, as silver is tried. Thou broughtest us into the net; thou laidst affliction upon our loins. Thou hast caused men to ride over our heads; we went through fire and through water: but thou broughtest us out into a wealthy place (Ps. 66:10-12).*

Biblical Reasons for Poverty In my observations of people who are poor, I see that poverty can result from many factors. Some of these are:

- *Ignorance about credit and money management*: My people are destroyed from lack of knowledge (Hosea 4:6).
- *Intemperance, eating disorders and addictions*: Be not among drunkards or among gluttonous eaters of meat, for the drunkard and the glutton will come to poverty, and slumber will clothe them with rags (Prov. 23:20-21). He who loves pleasure will become poor; whoever loves wine and oil will never be rich (Prov. 21:17);

- ***Early parenthood without adequate preparation***. A prudent man foresees evil and hides himself but the simple pass on and are punished (Prov. 22:3).
- ***Stinginess and unwilling to share with the less fortunate***. A stingy man is eager to get rich and is unaware that poverty awaits him (Prov. 28:22).
- ***Laziness:*** Lazy hands make a man poor, but diligent hands bring wealth (Prov. 10:4) How long wilt thou sleep, O sluggard? When wilt thou arise out of thy sleep? Yet a little sleep, a little slumber, a little folding of the hands to sleep: so, shall thy poverty come as one that travels, and thy want as an armed man (Prov. 6:6-11)
- ***Dishonesty:*** If you have not been trustworthy with someone else's property, who will give you property of your own? (Luke 16:12)
- ***Neglect of God's House***: Ye have sown much and bring in little; ye eat, but ye have not enough; Why? Saith the Lord of hosts. Because of mine house that is waste, and ye run every man to his own house.... I called for a drought upon the land, and upon the corn. Haggai 1:4-11.
- ***Not returning tithes & offerings***: "Will a man rob God? Yet you are robbing Me! But you say, 'How have we robbed You?' In tithes and offerings. "You are cursed with a curse, for you are robbing Me, the whole nation *of you!* "Bring the whole tithe into the storehouse, so that there may be food in My house, and test Me now in this," says the LORD of hosts, "if I will not open for you the windows of heaven and pour out for you a blessing until it overflows. "Then I will rebuke the devourer for you, so that it will not destroy the fruits of the ground; nor will your vine in the field cast *its grapes,*" says the LORD of hosts. "All the nations will call you blessed, for you shall be a delightful land," says the LORD of hosts. Not returning love gifts to God in the form of tithes and offerings and not caring for God's house can lead to poverty (Mal 3:8-12).
- ***Oppression by the powerful over the less fortunate***. So, I returned, and considered all the oppressions that are done under the sun: and behold the tears of such as were oppressed, and they had no comforter; and on the side of their oppressors there was power; but they had no comforter (Ecc.4:1).

ust like a loving father who disciplines his children, there is always
son to be learned and it is always to do you good in the end. Isaiah
) says: *Yet it pleased the Lord to bruise him; he hath put him to grief: when
shalt make his soul an offering for sin, he shall see his seed, he shall prolong
ays, and the pleasure of the Lord shall prosper in his hand.* Do not be
ouraged during adversity or envy the prosperity enjoyed by others.
ng discouragement you are most vulnerable and can be easily
ived. The Psalmist David expressed being envious of people who
ish and are not worshippers of God. He felt that being righteous –
g right and doing right was pointless. It really bothered him. He had
end some time in the synagogue (church) communing with God
t an understanding of this seemingly unfair distribution of wealth.
communing with God, he was able to see that their pleasure was
for a season and that their way led to their eventual destruction.
izing this, he was no longer envious.

Understanding Credit: When I lived in England, I never had
vorry about money because I avoided unnecessary spending and
t. I lived a modest lifestyle and always had enough to meet my every
In the United States however, somehow it didn't matter how much
ned, it seemed never enough. It was this dichotomy that led me
d everything I could get my hand on that addressed the issue of
y. The most useful piece of literature described money as we know
ay as credit, which is virtual currency that gives you purchasing
r. You receive a check from your employer (a promissory note). You
this paper note to the bank and it becomes reserve funds in the
from which you can withdraw cash. The more cash you withdraw,
ss credit you have. The higher the amount of credits you have, the
credit worthy you will be and the more access you will have to
g more things on credit. Ideally, you want to show that you are
sing a small portion of the credit that is available to you. While
is no hard-and-fast rule, financial experts typically recommend
g your utilization of credit below 30%. For example, if your credit
on your open credit accounts total $10,000 and your balances
nt to $2,000, then your credit utilization is 20%. Each time you
ur credit card you will generate a balance, which will be reported
ctored into your credit utilization or rating.

Money in the Bank: People may see money in the bank as a form
urity, but this is a false conception. My sister and I purchased a

- **_Losses as a result of disobedience_**: You
  treasures I will give as plunder, without cha
  your sins throughout your country (Jeremial

- **_Sickness and poor health-without e
  coverage_**. I wish above all things that you n
  in health (3 John1:2). You need health to sus

- **_Failing to save: Spending all your ec
  saving for a rainy day_**. A slack hand caus
  hand of the diligent makes rich (Proverbs 1(
  thou sluggard; consider her ways, and be wis
  guide, overseer, or ruler, provideth her meat
  gathereth her food in the harvest (Prov. 6:6-

- **_Too much bad debt_**: He who oppresses the
  wealth and he who gives gifts to the rich—bo
  (Prov. 22:16). Obtaining loans with high in
  over consumption of consumer items is like
  to the rich. High interest rate loans or credi
  the lender getting a high return. Debt with
  a noose around your neck that gets pulled ti
  you are in a lot of consumer debt, be determ
  another debt. _Deny yourself a thousand things n
  Avoid it as you would the smallpox. Make a sole
  that by His blessing you will pay your debts and the
  if you live on porridge and bread…Take care of the
  will take care of themselves. It is the mites here and
  spent for this, that and the other that soon run up in
  least while you are walled in debts…Do not falter,
  back. Deny your taste, deny the indulgence of appe
  pay your debts. Work them off as fast as possible
  forth a free man again, owing no man anything, y
  great victory (E. G. White, Counsels on Steward_

Poverty can Cause Stress, Depression and L
depression and lack of hope in turn can cause pov
Esther Duflo and the co-author of a study of 2
different countries. Indeed, Poverty is distressing I
lifetime condition. It is something to experience, gc
of and not a life time cycle. God may allow humil

home in Jamaica as an investment property. We subsequently sold the home some years later and I chose to leave my share of the money from the sale in a bank account in Jamaica for it to earn interest. When I withdrew the money after several years, the money was worth little because the Jamaican dollar had devalued considerably over the years. From this experience, I learned that with fluctuating interest rates, you cannot rely on money in the bank as a form of security; owning an income producing property would have been more profitable. Cash money can also easily slip or dwindle away if not invested properly. Your goal therefore should be to combine your knowledge, skills, and material resources to build wealth or substance overtime, realizing that you can lose money and be left with nothing, but if you have wealth in the form of knowledge, skills and resources you will never live in want. When Isaac's enemy stopped up his wells, he simply built more wells. If you are employed by a company that goes belly up or promote someone else over you, you can sell your skills elsewhere or start your own business.

In a society where everything is instant and a click away, the notion of building is not the most inviting because it involves time and effort, whereas the notion of overnight riches is much more attractive. Most rich people gain their riches through one of three ways, inherit it, marry into it; create it by investing in or becoming a product (or selling a product) that everyone wants – this could include personal skills. Is it any wonder that the Bible says labor not to get rich, have the wisdom to show restraint (Prov. 23:4, NIV); In other words, it doesn't matter how hard you work you will probably not get rich simply through hard work alone. Hard work at minimum wage will not grow riches; you must think in a creative manner about how you can utilize your skills to generate wealth. I was driving on the Cross Bronx Express Way on a hot Valentine's day and observed three individuals trying to make money. One had a sign saying "Please help. I am homeless" another was selling bottles of ice-cold water, and the third was selling single long-stemmed roses. Each was being creative in his own way, but at the end of the day, I cannot imagine that the one requesting a handout being better off than the other two who were filling a need.

Invent Something, fill a Need or Solve a Problem: Nathan Myhrvold, a physicist by training and former chief technology officer of Microsoft says that "invention is the closest thing to magic we have." The surest way to wield influence is to invent something useful. You must look for a need and try to fill it or look for a human problem and try to solve it. The many inventions by people of color - the traffic light, the filament in the light bulb, the ironing board, vaccine and blood plasma all came about as a result of a desire to fill a need or solve a problem. Look around you and see if there are any needs that you can fulfill or problems that you can solve. One author pointed out that you are paid based on the amount of problems you can solve or needs you are able to meet. Don't dismiss any idea as too wacky. All it takes is one good idea and a desire to see the idea come to fruition to build wealth. Of course, you may need to pitch your idea to a venture capitalist willing to fund your invention if you do not have the funds to do so yourself. Much of the new technologies that emerged in the San Francisco Bay area were funded by venture capitalists willing to invest in new businesses with high potential for growth.

Overnight Riches: Capitalist societies promote the concept of individualism and the idea that everyone can get rich. This concept is promoted in the media through glossy pictures – mental images of people who have achieved riches, influence and power. The inference is that you too can achieve these things. It is therefore quite easy to believe that if you do not get rich, there is something wrong with you. With easy credit, some may even live on credit to create an illusion of being rich – faking it. They live a lifestyle that is unaffordable to them, but because credit is easily available, they get locked into a viscous cycle of borrowing and spending. Then there are those unscrupulous people who spend days and nights thinking up ideas (legal or fraudulent) to get gullible people to buy their product or to steal their money. I remember receiving a letter in the mail with a legitimate looking bank check for $3,850 just when my mortgage was due. It said I had won $125,000 but I must keep it confidential; the check was supposedly the first of my installment, but I must first pay $2,850 to a tax agent. I called the number and asked about the winning. They said my name was entered in a lottery and I had won. I knew I had not entered any lottery and pointed out that what they were doing was fraudulent and preying on vulnerable individuals. The person immediately hung up on me.

Playing the "Lotto" or lottery is legal and can lead to instant riches if you are that lucky winner out of millions of players but playing the lottery out of habit is also gambling and can become addictive. Of course, you would not know that from the way the lottery is advertised.

It is not packaged to tell both sides. Playing the "lotto" is packaged as something desirable - an opportunity not to be missed and that in buying a lottery ticket you are buying an opportunity to get rich. "You have to be in it to win it" is the catchy advertising slogan. The motivating factor then becomes achieving lots of money and gaining "material things" quickly and without much effort. Through subtlety, the person who is financially desperate, ignorant or experiencing life's challenges gets seduced.

Get-rich-quick schemes are designed to appeal to the lust of the flesh, the lust of the eye and the pride of life – things that separate us from a relationship with God. These desires usually come when you are at your lowest point. You will notice that Satan brought temptations to Jesus after he had fasted, which suggests that Jesus was at his weakest and most vulnerable point when he faced temptation. Satan tempted Jesus in all three areas. Satan told Jesus to make bread out of stones, appealing to the lust of the flesh; he took Jesus to the highest pinnacle of the temple and told him to cast himself down and watch angels bear him up – appealing to his desire for recognition, adulation and popularity through presumption; then Satan took him to an exceeding high mountain and showed him the kingdoms of the world and the glory of them, appealing to his desire for power, and prestige. For each test, Jesus was able to resist through his knowledge of the scriptures. If Jesus had succumbed to the desire for power, prestige and influence, he would have chosen to live the life of an earthly slave to Satan rather than that of a heavenly king.

The desire for fame, fortune, prestige and popularity is ever present in a culture that promotes these values, so it is important to develop a proper perspective on what success means to you and at what cost. The story of "*The ones who walk away fom Omelias*" by Ursula Le Guin is a fictitious story about a happy city where a child suffers so that everyone can remain happy. The city's constant state of serenity and splendor requires that a single unfortunate child be kept in perpetual filth, darkness, and misery. The question Le Guin asks is "how should you feel about the comforts you enjoy if it is at the expense of others?" The story is fictitious, but it raises deep moral questions about your beliefs. Like the citizens in the story, you can either condone wrong while it benefits you, or you can acknowledge it and pay close attention to the sources of your own comforts and the luxuries that you enjoy.

Grow into Wealth: There are those who gamble and gain winnings, which results in getting rich overnight, but riches gained prematurely can sometimes do more harm than good. I grew up in the West Indies where it was not unusual to see people carrying heavy loads of produce on their head to the market. Before carrying the load, they would first test to see if they are able to hoist and balance it on their head. If the load is heavy and thrust upon them prematurely without testing and preparation, before long they would collapse under it. Similarly, if you get the riches of life prematurely, and don't grow into them naturally, before long the weight of it all will crush you and you end up being worse off than before. Imagine having a small apartment that is crammed with stuff. Suddenly someone brings you a whole new set of furniture that you must take right away. You would first need to get rid of the old in order to make room for the new; otherwise, you would be overwhelmed. William Post won $16.2 million in the Pennsylvania lottery in 1988, but in 2010, he was living on his Social Security. Bradley, the author of "Sudden Money: Managing a Financial Windfall" says winners get into trouble because they fail to address the emotional connection to the windfall. He sees that "there are two sides to money - the interior and the exterior. The interior side is the psychology of money and the family relationship to money. The exterior side is the tax codes, the money allocation, etc." Bradley suggests that the goal is to integrate the two. People who can't integrate their interior relationship with money appropriately are more likely to crash and burn," says Bradley.

The widely read and lauded Napoleon Hill's *Think and Grow Rich* book points out that power in the hands of one who did not acquire it gradually is often fatal to success and that quick riches are more dangerous than poverty. He adds that it is one thing to want money, but it is something entirely different to be worth more! It is this latter principle that this book supports. It is for this reason that I support the belief in building wealth overtime rather than getting rich quickly. For me, wealth is resources that are built over time and is sustainable; managed well you will always have enough resources to meet all your needs. Based on biblical principles, it is not unspiritual or unscriptural to desire to be prosperous (wealthy) and be in health (3 John 2). Joshua 1:8 assures us of prosperity and good success if we live by God's word and Matt 6:33 says: Seek first the kingdom of God and His righteousness, and all these things shall be added unto you—not taken from you – added to you. After all, it is God that gives us the power to get wealth (Deut 8:18).

<u>Prosperity Means More Than Being Rich Financially:</u> Being rich is a relative term. A millionaire in the West Indies is not a millionaire in America because of the relative value of the dollar. It is important to remember that becoming rich doesn't change who you are; it simply brings out in greater magnitude your character traits or the behaviors you engaged in before you became rich. If you were a gambler, an alcoholic or an addict before riches came, you will be a bigger gambler or a bigger drug user when you become rich. It is for this reason that you must have a proper perspective on riches and money. *He that trusteth in his riches shall fall: but the righteous shall flourish as a branch (Prov. 11:28).* Riches and wealth without a relationship with God can eventually become meaningless. Kings of the Old Testament like Solomon, Hezekiah, Nebuchadnezzar and Belshazzar are examples of individuals who achieved considerable riches and status, but eventually turned away from God and suffered the dire consequences. They began believing themselves to be the creators of their own success and saw themselves as invincible – even as a god; before long, mental illness and addictions took over. The list of millionaires who commit suicide is endless. If you believe that God is the giver of all that you have, why should suicide be an option? Certain sectors of the entertainment world glorify materialism and many young people yearn for the "bling - bling" (jewelry and material images of success) that is glorified, but these are just *things.* Things can disappear overnight. My experience of Hurricane Sandy in 2012, and observing the devastation caused by Hurricane Harvey in Texas, Hurricane Maria in Puerto Rico in 2017, which destroyed many beautiful beachfront homes, was a compelling reminder that your home and all that you possess can be wiped out in a day. The water surge mounted to several feet engulfing expensive mansions and luxurious beachfront homes and cars. You must have a proper perspective on wealth and riches because disaster can strike at any time. Job is an example of an individual who was not blindsided by his riches. Job had considerable wealth and riches and lost it all through a series of disastrous events. Lynette Khalfani, author of, "The Money Coaches Guide to Your First Million" sees that there are six dreaded "D's" to life: Downsizing, Divorce, Disability, Disease, Death in the family, and Disaster – any of which can result in a family losing all or almost everything. In Job's case, he experienced all six "D's" and his response was simply remarkable. He said, *"The Lord giveth and the Lord taketh away blessed be the name of the Lord."*

Have A Proper Perspective on Riches and Wealth: You do not have to believe in God to become rich or wealthy since not all riches are gained honestly; but if you believe in God and what he can do in and through you, you will gain a proper perspective on wealth and riches and how to expand your usefulness in life with the wealth or riches that you have. It is possible to reverse the order, get rich and fill your life with the most beautiful yacht or the most attractive sports car and material wealth and still not be happy. It is like looking at life through the wrong side of the lens. Essentially, your material wealth – your mammon then becomes your god and you cannot serve God and mammon. In fact, to reverse the order or give up on God after achieving material success, you are more likely to end up self-destructing through your constant feeling of discontent with what you don't have and worrying about protecting what you do have. My mother told me of a lady who had worked for many years in England and decided to retire in Jamaica. She built a beautiful mansion that was very palatial and admired by many. She enjoyed being complimented about her home and spent most of her time taking care of it. Her greatest fear however was that robbers would one day break into her house. Because of her intense fear, she seldom left the house. Her paranoia became so intense that she eventually became a prisoner in her own home. What is the point of having a mansion if you cannot enjoy living in it and sharing it with others? I like the idea of the Fresh Air Fund, where families with large homes in upstate New York would open their home to a poor child from the inner city through the Fresh Air Fund program and give that child a super summer vacation. I recall a child from the Bronx who participated in this program. This child had no ear lobes and through the sponsoring Fresh Air Fund family's wealth and influence they were able to link the child to a plastic surgeon who gave him some new ear lobes and some sense of normalcy. This family is not a celebrity, and no one knows of their good deed because they did not do it for show or recognition. They did it because they were moved with compassion for the boy and had the means and resources to help him. Your material worth should not become a trap but a blessing. Material things of life can become trappings if you define yourself based on your riches, what you own or the position you hold. Material things, power and position should not define who you are. They are what I call incidentals that you should be able to walk away from with ease, when it is time for you to do so. Many women remain in abusive relationships because of the material trappings that they hold on to for dear life. Lot's wife is an example of a woman who defined herself based on her material worth. She lived a life of luxury in Sodom and when it came time for her to leave it behind to avoid her own destruction she could not and in looking back became a pillar of salt.

What is the use of wealth and luxury if it is not used to be a blessing to others? If you Google millionaires, the list is extensive, but the ones we hear of or remember are the ones that are doing something constructive with their wealth to make a positive difference in the lives of those less fortunate. Bill Gates writing in Forbes Magazine (December 2012) notes that there is a great need of innovation for the poor, but there are no buyers for a breakthrough, so he and his wife Melinda have taken on the challenge of returning to society some of the resources they have received. Forbes magazine cited several legends - among them, Oprah Winfrey, Warren Buffett, Bill and Melinda Gates, Steve Case, David Rubenstein and Leon Black - individuals whose altruism is making a difference in the lives of the poor in developing countries. The rest simply die in obscurity leaving their wealth for their lawyers and greedy relatives to fight over and squander. Your wealth should bring glory to God by the blessing it brings.

Think for a moment about your most precious item; have you thought what might happen to it when you die? It might seem morbid, but it is a reality. We carry nothing into this world, and we will carry nothing out. When you die all that you possess will be inherited, distributed, given away or dumped. Nothing is going with you. A U-haul truck will not be attached to your coffin so start thinking about how to be a blessing in this world and leave a legacy of good deeds behind. 1Timothy 6:6-12 says: *Godliness with contentment is great gain. For we brought nothing into this world, and it is certain we can carry nothing out. And having food and raiment let us be content. But they that will be rich fall into temptation and a snare, and into many foolish and hurtful lusts, which drown men in destruction and perdition. For the love of money is the root of all evil; which some coveted after, they have erred from the faith, and pierced themselves through with many sorrows.* It is for this reason that Jesus did not say a rich man could not enter the kingdom of heaven, but rather it is harder for a rich man to enter if he is living for self alone. If you want to enter the kingdom of heaven as a rich person, you must not simply live for your own selfish indulgences; you must do what is right, perform good deeds - learn to tend to the widows, the orphans and the elderly and help the poor and needy become self-sufficient. It is said that a good person will always be great because the means used to bless others will bring returns. *Riches rightly employed will accomplish great good (E.G. White, Christ Object Lessons, p.294).*

When I was a foreign student living in California, I had an opportunity to baby-sit for very wealthy families as a way of helping to pay my way through school. I also had the good fortune of attending prestigious schools in England and the United States. Through my associations with the wealthy, I came to realize that material things and a glamorous life style do not equal happiness. Material things give you a temporary feeling of satisfaction, but once the psychological fix wears off, the need for something more exciting comes back. ***Things do not satisfy the spiritual void that needs to be filled with more of God's spirit***. Money is simply a form of exchange with one purpose - to exchange for goods or services that you want or need. You cannot eat it, sleep in it or wear it. Material things certainly add comfort to your life, and you worry less about survival issues when you have money in the bank but accumulating more and more things can often become a snare and eventually overwhelm you. Living the glamorous life may also attract superficial friends who will leave you when you have nothing to give. Seeking contentment at whatever state of life in which you find yourself will therefore result in greater gain than spending your days laboring or working hard at getting rich simply to hoard it. Contentment is not the fulfillment of what you want, but the realization of how much you already have (Anonymous). So, *keep your lives free from the love of money and be content with what you have, because God has said, never will I leave you. So, we say with confidence,... The Lord is my helper, and I will not fear what man shall do unto me. (Hebrews 13:5 &6).*

The following are ideas for your constructive action plan:

CONSTRUCTIVE ACTION PLAN

1. Take stock of your assets, income, debts and spending
2. Seek financial counseling as needed
3. Make a budget based on your income and expenditure
4. Include your tithe and freewill offering in your budget
5. Save a fixed portion of your income, not to be touched except for emergency – ideally save enough to cover you for 6 months to a year
6. Pay off high interest credit cards first and snowball your debt or consolidate at a lower rate
7. Invest your money wisely and avoid "get rich quick schemes"
8. Give to the poor **through** a registered charity so that you can declare your giving when filing your income tax
9. Join a college/investment savings program for your child

Financial experts suggest that you give away 10% of your income. Save 10% and live off the remaining 80%.

Your 20th Gem

THE KEYS TO SUCCESS

Behold, this was the iniquity of thy sister Sodom, pride, fulness of bread, and abundance of idleness was in her and in her daughters, neither did she strengthen the hand of the poor and needy." (Ezekiel 16:49). Here are presented before us, in the words of Holy Writing, the terrible results of idleness. It was this that caused the ruin of the cities of the plain. Idleness enfeebles the mind, debases the soul, and perverts the understanding, turning into a curse that which was given as a blessing (The Signs of the Times, May 4, 1882; E.G. White, This Day with God).

The soul of the sluggard desireth, and hath nothing: but the soul of the diligent shall be made fat. (Prov.13:4,)

You cannot sit back and do nothing and expect to enjoy wealth and the material rewards or trappings of life that we call success. Enough wealthy and successful people have pointed to the futility of sitting back and expecting success to come to you. The famous botanist George Washington Carver says: "There is no short cut to achievement. Life requires thorough preparation—veneer isn't worth anything." Malcolm Gladwell in his book *Outlier: The story of success* examines the lives of successful people from Mozart to Bill Gates and points out that success is influenced by many factors, so it is not enough to sit back and expect success to come to you. You must take constructive action. Solomon notes that, *"The thoughts of the diligent tend only to plenteousness; but of every one that is hasty only to want." (Prov.21: 5).* Newspaper columnist Ann Landers says, "Opportunities are usually disguised as hard work, so most people don't recognize them." Opportunities are all around you, to become the best that you can be, but are you ready to step forward and reach for them? Are you ready to mount up with wings as eagles?

First and foremost, it is important to realize that money is simply a means of commodity and if you ask God for money and you are in need, in his loving care for you he will supply enough for your need, but you need to ask for more than money. Money comes and goes and that is why sometimes the government gives us money – cash back called stimulus money because the illusion of a windfall leads to greater spending, which in turn stimulates the economy. The Bible is correct when it says of money, "like wings it flies away." God wants you to utilize the gifts that you possess to uncover your purpose; in Maslow's term - become self-actualized and be a blessing to humanity and the world. Use your gifts to make a difference in improving your life and the lives of others. As you become a blessing, you will have more than enough money to supply your need. Louis Braille was blind, yet he invented Braille to help the blind to read. James Young Simpson invented Anesthesia and Charles Drew the blood plasma.

The list of people who have contributed positively to our lives in the fields of science, music, art, medicine and religion are endless. Through their gifts they have risen to a wealthy place. Take some time to think about what you enjoy doing and give some thought to how you can utilize your gift to expand your usefulness and be a blessing. Proverbs 18:16 reminds us that: *A man's gift maketh room for him, and bringeth him before great men.* You must seek to develop an awareness of the gifts that God has given to you so that you can develop and expand your horizon and your usefulness. Spending time with God in daily devotion and going to worship services are possible ways of enhancing your relationship with God and receiving guidance day by day. Sometimes inspiration will come through a prayer, a scripture reading, a discourse or a song.

Like log wood in a coal fire, one stick of log cannot stay ablaze by itself for too long; similarly, withdrawing yourself from worship service or daily devotion will only lead to spiritual lethargy. In Matt.18:20, Jesus said: *"For where two or three are gathered together in my name, there am I in the midst of them."* As you spend time with God, you must ask God to stir up the gifts that are within you so that you can expand your usefulness. As you expand your usefulness, you will never want for money. You will become wealthy. The Bill Gates, Oprah Winfrey and Warren Buffets of this world are rich because of <u>how</u> they utilize their gifts to expand their usefulness. Their wealth and riches did not come overnight.

Sometimes you must take "the road less traveled" in order to uncover your gifts. Think of two individuals who graduate from a prestigious college with similar degrees; one thinks of how to touch many lives and expand his usefulness and the other simply thinks of getting a job and making money. One will settle into a regular paycheck without any eventualities or learning any major life lessons, while the other may go through life's cul-de-sacs, heartaches and detours, but eventually reach his or her goal with a rich experience. Former United States President, Barack Obama is a Harvard Graduate who could easily have settled into a well-paying legal job upon graduating from a prestigious college, but he chose instead to take a less popular and less prestigious path – community organizing and teaching. In doing so, he sharpened his human relations skills, developed patience in dealing with millennials and expanded his usefulness and knowledge of communities until eventually he entered politics and arrived at his destination, President of the United States. It took him over 16 years, but he did not give up in defeat. Similarly, Myron Rolle accepted a Rhode scholarship to attend Oxford University instead of a National Football League draft earning millions of dollars. He made that choice in order to fulfill one of his life-long dreams of entering the medical field and helping needy children in his native island of the Bahamas.

Do not keep praying for God to bless you financially and not do anything to improve your situation. The old Chinese proverb says, "give a man a fish and you feed him for a day but teach a man how to fish and you feed him for a lifetime." How could you possibly say that God is helping you if every day you go to him and he gives you a handout? Or like a vending machine you give an offering to God and He gives you returns? How is that helping you to be the best you that you can be when God has given you gifts and talents that you must develop to bring glory to him? The prodigal son went to his father and pressed him for a hand out. In reluctance, his father gave in. The son then squandered his father's money and ended up being worse off than before. Is it any wonder that so many lottery winners often end up being poorer than before? God wants you to prosper and be in health, but you must first acknowledge that ownership belongs to God and that you are simply a steward of everything that you possess. A steward is basically a caretaker. What type of a caretaker are you?

Use Your Gifts & Talents: The story of the talents told by Jesus is an example of God's desire for us to reach to a higher and broader level of existence by utilizing the gifts that we have. The second part of Proverbs 18:16 says: *A man's gift maketh room for him, and bringeth him before great men..* If you keep asking God to give you a financial breakthrough and you are not receiving any answers, it might be God's way of saying to you "stop asking and stir up or do something-with the gifts that I have given to you." You must embrace your calling if you expect God to bless you. Parker Palmer says in *Let Your Life Speak: Vocation does not come from a voice "out there" calling me to become something I am not. It comes from a voice "in here" calling me to be the person I was born to be, to fulfill the original selfhood given me at birth by God.*

Now get up and stir up the God given gifts inside of you. Start small and like a seed that needs time to grow, nurture that gift. As you do so you will begin to see twigs of success, then leaves of success, strong limbs of success, then branches of success and eventually abundance in your fruits of success. As you enjoy success embrace it because *Let the Lord be magnified, which hath pleasure in the prosperity of his servant. (Ps. 35:27).*

GEMS PART II

STAYING THE COURSE

Your 21st Gem

STOP CHASING AFTER SUCCESS

"Success is not the key to happiness. Happiness is the key to success. If you love what you are doing, you will be successful" ~Albert Schweitzer. God does not bid the youth to be less aspiring. The elements of character that make a man successful and honored among men – the irrepressible desire for some greater good, the indomitable will, the strenuous exertion, the untiring perseverance – are not to be crushed out. They are to be directed to objects as much higher than mere selfish and temporal interests as the heavens are higher than the earth, (E. G. White, Patriarchs & Prophets, p. 562).

George Washington Carver says: **"It** is not the style of clothes one wears, neither the kind of automobile one drives, nor the amount of money one has in the bank, that counts. These mean nothing. It is simply service that measures success." To find lasting happiness—the kind of happiness that is based on and supports your dreams, you must first spend time acquainting yourself with God and focus on how to make a difference for the betterment of humanity in this life instead of focusing on the apparent material trappings that may come with success. To do otherwise is like looking at the telescope from the wrong end. Carver also stated that: "The primary idea in all of my work was to help the farmer and fill the poor man's empty dinner pail. My idea is to help the 'man farthest down'; this is why I have made every process just as simply as I could to put it within his reach."

Austrian neurologist and psychiatrist as well as a Holocaust survivor, Viktor Frankl admonished his students in Europe and America not to aim at success - the more you aim at it and make it a target, he observed, the more you are going to miss it. "For success, like happiness, cannot be pursued; it must ensue, and it only does so as the unintended side effect of one's personal dedication to a cause greater than oneself or as the by-product of one's surrender to a person other than oneself. Happiness must happen, and the same holds for success: you must let it happen by not caring about it. I want you to listen to what your conscience commands you to do and go on to carry it out to the best of your knowledge. Then you will live to see that in the long-run - in the long-run, I say! - Success will follow you precisely because you had forgotten to think about it. Of course, the important part is the...in the long-run..." (Excerpted from *Man's Search for Meaning* by Viktor Frankl).

You must begin today to stop chasing after success and let success follow you. Malcolm Gladwell's book, *Outlier* is an interesting study of the many factors that influence why some people are successful and others are not. His book however does not address how God can miraculously change your life and your circumstances. My life and that of many others I know is a testament that God can make miraculous changes in a person's life. He can change your life for the better – sometimes overnight. The trouble is, you cannot expect to see miracles if you live a paltry Christian life. You cannot keep praying the same high-speed mobile prayers and keep reading the same favored Psalms every day yet expect great things to happen. The closer you get to God, spending time in prayer and meditation on His words, the more like God you will become in character. As you become more like Him, your desires will be in sync with His. Dressing up and going to church to impress others, being revengeful, deceitful, or fighting over positions will not bring you lasting success. Jesus reminded his disciples of the importance of meditative time with God if they expect to be a success. While the disciples engaged in power struggles and focused on recognition, status and prestige, they were powerless to perform miracles.

Power for Successful Living: The prophet Daniel acknowledged that his power to interpret King Nebuchadnezzar's dream came from a meditative life in God's presence. He prayed three times a day. Power for successful living comes through much time in prayer and fasting. Fasting however does not simply mean abstaining from food. It may mean abstaining from those things that take your attention or mind away from God and your purpose. The television, the internet, e-mails, social media and electronic gizmos are all time consumers that can rob you of your time with God and prevent you from becoming the best you that you can be. You must see that *greater is He that is in you than he that is in the world.* Through Christ all things are possible. Jesus approached the lame man at the Pool of Bethesda and asked if he wanted to be healed. The man had been there for 38 years waiting for an opportunity to be first to step into the water after it was believed to have been stirred by an angel. He said in response to Jesus, "I have no one to take me to the water when it is troubled." Jesus offered him an opportunity for healing, but instead of saying yes to the question, he looked to other men and the pool of water to heal him; yet he was in the presence of the healer Himself. Power, position and prestige – the lust of the flesh, the lust of the eyes and the pride of life (1John 2:16) will not heal your mind or bring lasting success. If you look to things or people for validation, then you may find yourself engaging in behaviors that will lead to your ultimate downfall.

Begin Today to Build a Personal Relationship with God

Don't expect immediate transformation. A plant doesn't become a tree overnight. It goes through a growth process. Be patient with yourself and focus on your purpose in life; in so doing, the order in which you grow will be on a solid foundation. You will develop strength of character and moral rectitude. You will be like the evergreen tree. You will notice that the evergreen tree looks like any other tree in the summer, but in the winter, it withstands the storms of winter, the snow and the cold.

Jesus told the parable of the builders. One man built his house on the sand and the other on the rock. The one on the rock stood firm in the storm, but the one on the sand was washed away when the storm came. Similarly, success – which is often equated with riches - without a relationship with God, is to lead a life that is destined for shipwreck because it will not be strong enough to withstand the storms of life. It is the spirit of God in you that makes the difference. When you do not have God in you, you will make a god of yourself, of someone or of something else. Is it any wonder that so many celebrities and millionaires who do not have a relationship with God overdose or commit suicide? The economic meltdown of 2008/2009 saw an increase in the number of murder-suicide pacts. High-profile German billionaire Adolf Merckle killed himself when his business empire collapsed. There were also numerous stories of once rich families living in New York, California and Quebec, who when faced with joblessness and bankruptcy were overcome with depression and took their own lives and the lives of their loved ones. Unless you have a firm spiritual foundation, your riches will not save you when you are assailed by the storms of life. *JOSHUA 1:8 notes: This book of the law shall not depart out of thy mouth; but thou shalt meditate therein day and night, that thou mayest observe to do according to all that is written therein: for then thou shalt make thy way prosperous, and then thou shalt have good success. (Joshua 1:8).*

The Bible outlines all the principles you need for achieving success and prosperity, but you must first give serious thought to what success means to you. You may need to go back to school, attend seminars and trainings or get a mentor. The library is full of books on all types of subjects. Read! Read! Read! Or get audio books that you can listen to when you are driving. It is said: "Show me the books you read, and I will tell you where you will be in the nearest future." Develop a plan, write it down and work towards achieving it; then, go about your business and learn not to worry about your needs. If you find that your means are not enough to meet your needs, rest your case before the Lord. Say the Lord's Prayer everyday as affirmation of your faith and dependence on God to provide for your needs and don't stress yourself. The same God that sent the ravens to feed Elijah by the brook Cherith and cared enough about five thousand people fainting from hunger is the same God that cares about you.

The story was told of two robins sitting on a fence. One asked the other: "Why do mortals worry so?" The other replied, "Because they do not serve the same God that we serve." Call God's attention to your missing finances. If you made financial mistake tell God and confess your desire to make things right; your confidence for success lies in His grace and power to change things. Go about your daily duties and rely on the promises of God. If God cares for the birds of the air and the lilies of the field, why should he not care about you? You are his child. Live a life of expectancy. Expect God to do something miraculous for you. *When you have made God's Service your first interest, you may ask with confidence that your own needs may be supplied. If you have renounced self and given yourself to Christ you are a member of the family of God, and everything in the father's house is for you. All the treasures of God are open to you, both in the world that now is and that which is to come…. The world with everything in it is yours so far as it can do you good. Even the enmity of the wicked will prove a blessing by disciplining you for heaven. "Therefore let no man glory in men. For all things are your's" (1 Cor 3:21, 23; EG White Thoughts from the Mount of Blessing).*

It was Adam and Eve's failure to trust God and their failure to rely on the authority of His words that led to their losing everything they owned. If they had trusted God, life would not have turned out so miserably for them. God desires above all things that you should prosper and be in health, *but as a child who is not yet placed in control of his inheritance, God does not entrust to you your precious possession, lest Satan by his wily arts should beguile you, as he did the first pair in Eden. Christ holds it for you, safe beyond the spoiler's reach. Like the child, you shall receive day by day what is required for the day's need (E.G. White, Thoughts from the Mount of Blessings).*

<u>The Connection with Jesus:</u> While working in poor urban communities in New York and London, I often saw a type of disconnect between an understanding of achieving success or wealth and a connection with Jesus. One urban teenager said he simply couldn't relate to the babe in a manger or the man on the cross. "It's just so wack" (an urban term meaning crazy), he said; how a babe in a manger or a man on a cross can help in my situation. Yet urban youths have more in common with Jesus than they can even imagine. One day when I was telling the nativity story to a group of six and seven-year old children, I asked the question "Why was Jesus born in a stable instead of a palace?" The answers were all relative to their own understanding and experience, but I was struck by the answer of seven-year old Nicholas, who said, "Jesus was born in a stable so that everyone could have access to him. If he were born in a palace, poor people would not be able to see him because the security guards would not let them in. Can you imagine shepherds and their lambs going into a palace?" Wow, what amazing insight I thought. Jesus wants to connect with everyone, so much so that even the place where he was born was accessible to everyone. Maya Angelou, poet and writer relates in her book *Wouldn't Take Anything for My Journey Now* that she changed from being an agnostic to becoming a believer when she came to realize that God loves her. With such realization of God's love for her, she suddenly became aware of her enormous potential to accomplish great things.

As the Son of God, Jesus owned everything, yet he was born poor with a stigma attached to his birth. He was not accepted as the Immaculate Conception or the Son of God, but rather as the illegitimate son of Mary. He was born in a barn or animal shelter and grew up in the hood - a rough neighborhood - so much so that Nathaniel asked, "can anything good come out of Nazareth?" Jesus grew up in "the hood" – a tough neighborhood, but he did not become a hoodlum. Although poor, he spent much time in reading. We know this because at 12 years of age, he was found in conversations with the teachers and city officials. We are told they marveled at his knowledge. Knowledge is gained through experience, study and insight and since he was but a lad, his experience would have been limited by his age, so he must have spent time studying to increase his wisdom, knowledge and understanding. Neuro-surgeon, Dr. Ben Carson in his book Gifted Hands related that he grew up in a poor neighborhood and was performing poorly in school, but he developed a love for books, which helped to turn his life around. You must read and obtain knowledge. Mahatma Gandhi suggests that you should obtain knowledge as though it was your last day on earth. The wise man Solomon throughout his life and writings encouraged readers to get wisdom, knowledge and understanding. Whatever field of employment you are in, master the art of it.

Master the Art of Your Craft: I remember as a university student in England obtaining summer employment in a biscuit (cookie) factory in London. It was my job to stack the cookies on the conveyer belt. My first few days on the job were a total disaster; each day I would jam the rotating belt because I did not know how to stack the cookies on a moving belt at a fast pace. Yet, there I was a third-year college student who could not stack cookies on a conveyor belt. After several failed attempts, I asked an elderly white lady who had been stacking biscuits for over 20 years how she was able to move so quickly. She said "my dear, there is an art in everything - even in stacking biscuits - there is an art." She taught me how to squeeze the biscuits together with my little fingers before stacking them. Once I mastered this skill, I became as good as the lady who taught me how to stack biscuits. Whatever occupation you choose to pursue, do not settle for mediocrity. You must master the art of your craft or occupation. I have yet to meet a successful person who did not spend days and nights working on improving their craft and did not achieve success. Jack Canfield, who used to be a school teacher and became the successful author of the book *Chicken Soup for the Soul* makes some useful suggestions for successful living that I have outlined as your constructive action plan.

CONSTRUCTIVE ACTION PLAN:

1. Seek out a teacher/mentor who knows more than you
2. Realize that on the other side of fear lies your possibilities
3. Avoid negative beliefs, for the only beliefs that make any sense are the ones that will take you from where you are to where you want to go
4. Whatever you're affirming, you're going to get more of so think positive thoughts
5. At the end of each day, ask yourself how you could have improved on your day in relation to your goals and then visualize those changes that you need to make

Your 22nd Gem

BLOOM ABOVE THE DIRT

"But ye are a chosen generation, a royal priesthood, an holy nation, a peculiar people; that ye should shew forth the praises of him who hath called you out of darkness into his marvellous light" 1Peter 2:9.

Although Jesus grew up in Nazareth – a city notorious for poverty, crime and immorality - the "hood" as urban youths would call it, he did not choose to become a hoodlum by succumbing to the violence, alcohol, and crime surrounding him in his neighborhood. Instead he maintained a strong sense of self-worth and a code of conduct becoming of a child of God. How was that possible considering that he grew up in a rough neighborhood? Even Nathaniel who became his disciple questioned if anything good could come out of Nazareth. Like a daffodil bulb that grows from under the dirt and blooms into a beautiful flower, Jesus didn't see himself as just a bulb in the dirt but rather as a daffodil about to bloom; he didn't see himself as a hoodlum but a king in the making.

Although I grew up in relative poverty, I never saw myself as poor. I say relative poverty because by Jamaican standards we were better off than many in my community but compared to western standard we lacked many amenities. Looking back, we did not have many of the creature comforts that my better off neighbors had, but we were always giving food to those who had creature comforts; somehow with all their luxuries they never seemed to have enough to buy food. They spent their money on showy consumer items while their cupboards were bare. *"Wherefore do ye spend money for that which is not bread? and your labour for that which satisfieth not? hearken diligently unto me, and eat ye that which is good, and let your soul delight itself in fatness."* *(Is 55:2)*. As a social worker, I would occasionally come across families whose homes were decked with expensive gadgets and furnishing, but their refrigerators or cupboards would be empty, and their children would have no food to eat. Some of these parents engaged in activities – most often illegal to live a certain lifestyle they could not afford to impress their friends and neighbors who did not give "two hoots" – (did not care) about them. *"Ye shall not steal, neither deal falsely, neither lie one to another."* *(Lev. 19:11)*.

Visualize Your Success: Jesus was not a drifter. Jesus often went into the woods to meditate - clear his head. It is a law of nature that success in any area is created first and foremost in our minds - through goals, beliefs, and a strong sense of self-worth. It sounds simple, but many people never visualize themselves as a success or believe they deserve or think they can succeed. "As a man thinketh so is he." Whenever you are reaching out for something better help will always come your way. *"You will hear a voice behind you saying this is the way walk ye in it."* The urging will be so strong that everywhere you look you will get encouragement to move forward. It is a fact of nature that when it is time for a daffodil to bloom the only thing that stops it from blooming is frost and its succumbing to the elements. When it is your time to bloom, no power on earth but your own thinking can keep you from blooming. If you see yourself as someone of value, a child of the king, you immediately raise your thoughts of yourself above the dirt to a higher level.

Jesus studied the scriptures and used it as a basis for conducting himself. As a young man, he entered the construction business and spent his past time fishing. He knew that he was capable of ministering to a wider audience, so he spent 30 days in focused meditation trying to figure out the direction that his life should take. During those 30 days, we are told that Satan tempted him - more like hounded him. Jesus struggled between the thought of a life of self-pleasing, power and prestige and a life of service. Eventually he decided on entering the ministry and managed to convince 12 "brothers" to join him in his ministry. Working in low-income communities, there was a noticeable difference between those who saw themselves as victims versus those who saw themselves as victors. Those who saw themselves as victims spoke of the unfair card that life had dealt them and expressed resentment at being abandoned by their better off relatives. They seemed stripped of self-worth; some remember being told they would never amount to anything good and believed it. Some simply stopped dreaming.

I have worked with young girls who were sexually exploited and found themselves living a life of prostitution and sex slavery. These girls were groomed by their pimps from as young as 12 and 13 years old; brain washed and trapped in double bind situations and lifestyles, which they did not believe they could change. They had become so beaten down, they could not pull themselves out of their dunghill; Being victimized, they became drug and alcohol involved to numb the pain. In putting up their defense, some became quarrelsome and frequently got into fights with others. They would put down those who were striving to improve themselves, leading to further alienation. Many such individuals had been told by those most important to them that they were worthless and good for nothing and sadly they believed it. In psychology this is called the self-fulfilling prophecy. Conversely, those who saw themselves as victors were aware of their deficits but did not allow negative criticisms or a dysfunctional family life to stop them from aspiring to become the next NBA player or the next teacher, the next poet, inventor, the next doctor, entrepreneur or the next television personality. They had a positive mental attitude that did not repel others and as a result people were drawn to their positive energy and desired to help them. Working in group-homes, I met many young people who had been physically and sexually abused. They were all offered the same opportunity to improve themselves. Some had a vision of bettering themselves and taking themselves and their family out of poverty while others tried to discourage those who tried to improve themselves by making fun of them. Those who saw themselves as victors of their circumstances eventually moved on to achieve considerable success while those who maintained a negative attitude continued to struggle in life always looking for a handout.

People who Become Successful Rise Above Adverse Circumstances Successful individuals have an "I don't care what you say or think about me" attitude. They don't give up when criticized, put down or rebuffed. They accept constructive criticism and dismiss efforts to destroy their self-worth or personhood realizing that a put down says more about the person doing the putting down. It is said that sticks and stones may break your bones, but words will never hurt you, but that is not true. Unkind words do hurt. I still remember unkind words said to me by people whom I respected or were important to me, but a tale of the crow has helped me deal with people who say demeaning things to me. The story goes: A crow with a piece of meat was chased by other crows. The crow had to decide. Fight for the meat or drop it and let all the birds fight over it. The crow decided to drop the meat and continued to soar in the air leaving the chasing crows to fight over it. You do not always have to get into a battle over wrongs done to you or try to defend yourself. Drop it and continue to soar.

I admire tennis stars Venus and Serena Williams for their "don't care what you say about me" attitude. They have risen above slights and put downs to a point where they have become so big that the very people that tried so hard to put them down now look like annoying little cockroaches. The story was told of a donkey that fell in an old well. Its master decided that he couldn't just leave him there and decided to bury him in the well. As he shoveled and poured dirt on the donkey, the donkey would shake it off and stamp on it. The donkey kept repeating this action until it reached a level where he could jump out of the well. *Few people reach what they might in excellence of character because they do not make their aim high. Prosperity and happiness will never grow of their own accord. They are the acquisition of labor, the fruit of long cultivation (Letter 22, June 30, 1875, to W. C. White, her 20-year-old son. This Day with God. E.G. White).*

Have a Strategy: You must develop strategies for rising above adversity. You cannot be lazy and expect to succeed in life. Learn a lesson from the Ants, says the wise man Solomon. Ants gather their food in the summer and store it for the winter. During hard times, don't be too proud to do menial work; accept food from food pantries or shop at a thrift shop in order to survive. Take Joey for example (not his real name), he was a special education student whose mother was a heroin addict; he was placed in foster care because of her neglect of him. Joey said there were times he would ask his mother to take him to school, but she was so often strung out on drugs she would respond to him with expletives to leave her alone. Sometimes he would go to the local supermarket and pack bags just to get enough food to eat. But Joey said he always dreamed of one day having enough to be able to take care of himself and his mother. When he was not working in the supermarket, he was hustling in the street selling cold bottled water and soda. Eventually the authorities took him from his mother. Now an adult, Joey is happily married, with his own home and children and managing a high-end retail business. He is living a healthy life style unlike the one in which he grew up. *"For I know the thoughts that I think toward you, saith the Lord, thoughts of peace, and not of evil, to give you an expected end." Jer. 29: 11.* You must believe that God has something better for your life if you want to lift yourself up. Improve yourself by obtaining an education or a skill. Never think you know enough or remain satisfied with a low standard and can relax your efforts. *Every day you should be learning and putting to practical use the knowledge gained. Remember that in whatever positions you may serve you are revealing motive, developing character. Whatever your work, do it with exactness, with diligence; overcome the inclination to seek an easy task. (E. G. White, Ministry of Healing p.343)*

Your 23rd Gem

SHARE THIS LITTLE BIT OF FOOD

Let none waste time in deploring the scantiness of their visible resources. The outward appearance may be unpromising, but energy and trust in God will develop resources. The gift brought to him with thanksgiving and with prayer for his blessing he will multiply as he multiplied the food given to the sons of the prophets and to the weary multitude (E. G White, The story of Prophets and Kings, p.242).

The story of the five barley loaves and two small fish is often told as a children's story, yet its meaning is so much more profound. The story is told in Matthew Chapter 5 that Jesus had finished teaching five thousand people plus women and children, so an approximate guess of over 15,000 people when He decided to consider their physiological need for food. It seems He was both concerned for their need for food as well as He was testing their understanding of his message of faith and love; He therefore instructed his disciples to feed the people. Puzzled by his instructions they questioned his directives. Where were they supposed to buy enough bread to feed such an enormous crowd? They were poor fishermen. Where were they supposed to get money to buy enough bread to feed 15,000 people? Was Jesus experiencing heat stroke? Is it possible that among fifteen thousand people only one small boy had food or was there only one boy who was willing to exercise faith and share his food with a sea of people? This was no little rich boy who had enough food to share. He was a poor boy with a peasant's lunch – five barley rolls and two small fish. Maybe his mother packed him a little lunch as he went in the company of another family or maybe he was a shepherd boy. Who knows? The Bible doesn't say. The important point here is that the boy could have decided that should he share his lunch with so many people, he would not have had enough left for himself, but in childlike faith he decided to share his lunch. By all appearances he probably didn't look any different from any of the peasant boys in the crowd, but there was something different about him. The lesson here is that you can be from a poor neighborhood and look like everyone in your neighborhood, but you do not have to be like everyone else in the neighborhood. This lad broke the mold. He didn't see himself as just another statistic in the crowd. He stood out from the crowd by acting and his response resulted in his witnessing one of the greatest miracles ever performed. Often in life we do not achieve what we can achieve because we look at our lack rather than our possibilities. Often, we don't feel we can make a difference because of our limitations but this one boy made a huge difference. The story was told of a man walking along a sea shore and observing the numerous starfishes washed upon the shore, he began to pick up the starfish and throw them back into the sea. Another person observed him doing so and remarked, "Why are you doing that? There are so many of them, what you are doing cannot possibly make a difference." The man stopped, picked up a starfish and threw it back into the sea. He said, "it made a difference for that one." *"Successful people are successful because they form the habits of doing those things that failures don't like to do"* says Albert Gray.

You do not need to be afraid to stand out from the crowd for fear of how you might look or what others might think of you. Do not be afraid to improve yourself out of fear of what change might look like or be afraid to make the most of you for fear of standing out in a crowd. Working among the urban poor, I saw many young people who would simply go along with the crowd in order to fit in. They joined gangs or dressed like everyone else, just to blend in. Yet people who rise from the ordinary to the extraordinary do not blend in with the crowd.

While a thermometer adjusts to the temperature, a thermostat controls it. Individuals who rise above the ordinary are like thermostats - they control their environment rather than adjust to it. The story was told of a shoe salesman who went to a foreign country where the people did not wear shoes. He returned disappointed saying that the people do not wear shoes. Another shoe salesman went to the same country and sent back word saying: "business is great! The people do not wear shoes here." The same scenario yet one saw the lack of people wearing shoes rather than the possibilities of people wearing shoes.

Your possibilities are endless if you do not fear being different or seeing things differently. Successful people are not afraid to leave a group if the group stifles their growth or it is toxic to their mental health. As a child of God, you were not meant to just fit in or go along with the crowd. You were meant to stand out. The boy's lunch fed the multitude and the leftovers were so abundant, that it took all twelve disciples to gather them up, in twelve baskets. This is an assurance that God's resources are limitless and when you act from a faith principle, putting God first, he will provide for you abundantly, above all that you ask or think. A lack of temporal prosperity often results from neglecting to put God's interest first. Your prosperity both temporal and spiritual depends largely upon faithful obedience to God's commands. "Honor the Lord with your substance and with the first fruits of all your increase so shall your barns be filled with plenty" (EG White). *"Bring ye all the tithes into the storehouse, that there may be meat in mine house, and prove me now herewith, saith the Lord of hosts, if I will not open you the windows of heaven, and pour you out a blessing, that there shall not be room enough to receive it.." (Mal. 3:10).* Just trust God to fulfill His promise.

Your 24th Gem

EVEN ROOKIES CAN TAKE DOWN GIANTS

Do not ask the Lord to guide your footsteps if you are not willing to move your fee (Anonymous). In every emergency we are to feel that the battle is his. His resources are limitless, and apparent impossibilities will make the victory all the greater (E. G. White, The story of Prophets and Kings p. 202).

The story of David and Goliath is seen as a children's story of a lad who used his slingshot to kill a giant. According to the story, Saul's army, although skilled in military stratagems were fearful of approaching Goliath. They had the skill and the manpower to attack Goliath they were overwhelmed with fear because of his size. David was not trained in military strategies neither had he fought in an army. He did not even have suitable military clothing to go into battle. His own siblings put him down and advised him to go back home and look after sheep. His size was no match for a giant. His resume read like an inexperienced rookie. It is said that he took care of a few sheep and in the process, he had killed two wild animals. With such a skimpy resume what made David gain enough confidence to go up against Goliath? What bold force propelled him forward to challenge a giant? Why was his posture such a contrast to that of the spies that Moses sent to spy out the Promised Land? "We are not able to go up against the people, for they *are* stronger than we." The spies had said. "The land devours its inhabitants, and all the people whom we saw in it *are* men of *great* stature. [33] There we saw the giants (the descendants of Anak came from the giants); and we were like grasshoppers in our own sight, and so we were in their sight." The sight of the giants overwhelmed them with fear, so they resorted to a flight response and was desirous of going back to what is known rather than moving forward in faith by facing the unknown. It took the courage of Caleb and Joshua to say, "The land we passed through to spy out *is* an exceedingly good land. If the LORD delights in us, then He will bring us into this land and give it to us, 'a land which flows with milk and honey.' Only do not rebel against the LORD, nor fear the people of the land, for they *are* our bread; their protection has departed from them, and the LORD *is* with us. Do not fear them."

What giants are you facing in your life today, that overwhelm you with fear? Is it a difficult assignment, a troubled marriage, troubled children, a hostile work environment, a boss or teacher from hell? David, like Caleb and Joshua believed not only in himself but also in the power of God working in and through him. God rewards faith in Him. Of Caleb He said, *"But My servant Caleb, because he has a different spirit in him and has followed Me fully, I will bring into the land where he went, and his descendants shall inherit it."* It takes faith in God to see His miracle working power; a courageous spirit to take the first step and profound confidence in what God can do in and through you to move beyond the ordinary to the accomplishing the extraordinary - to take down the giants in your life. Those who cower in fear will remain stuck, and unable to move forward; they often cannot see past the abuses and put downs that loom large like a ten feet mountainous giant preventing them from moving forward. Abuse be it verbal, sexual or physical can leave you feeling unworthy or defective in some way. You may feel you cannot speak up for yourself or you allow others to use you. Maybe as a child you learned to escape repeated abuse by dissociating while the abuse was occurring. By mentally removing yourself, you were able to get through the abuse and still relate to the abuser. This type of abuse can lead to a whole world view that people can't be trusted, and that people are out to hurt you so it's best to avoid closeness to anyone.

Like the children of Israel facing the giant Goliath, years of abuse and put downs can lead to you taking on a self-defeating attitude. You may remember teachers telling you that you are dumb and stupid; family members telling you that you would never amount to anything good or that you were just like your no-good absent father or drug addicted mother. These put downs can lead to a lack of confidence in yourself or in God. However, if like David you understand the possible underlying cause of your defeatist attitude and you work on bringing about change, you can move forward in faith and shake off negative criticism. In painting a picture, objects closer to you are larger in size and those farther away, smaller in size to show perspective and distance. When you face your giant, you must see that God is bigger than the giant in your life. **Faith must outgrow fear**. You must not withdraw from Him and put distance between you and God. Satan would have you believe God has abandoned you. Like the pimp who tells his sexually exploited victim that no one but he loves her and keeps reminding her of her past indiscretions to keep her trapped as his slave, so too Satan separates you from God by parading all your faults, mistakes and indiscretions before you to make you believe that you are unworthy, and that God has abandoned you. Stop the insanity. Face your giant by encouraging yourself in the Lord, knowing that *Thee Lord thy God in the midst of thee is mighty; he will save, he will rejoice over thee with joy; he will rest in his love, he will joy over thee with singing.. You shall no more be termed forsaken; but you shalt be called my delight; for the Lord delights in you. He will rejoice over you with joy (Zeph. 3:17, Is.62:4 &5,).*

When others try to put you down by pointing out your negative short comings, you will overcome by replacing the negative with positive self-talk. When David was put down by his brothers, he reaffirmed his self-worth by remembering his accomplishments. You too must remember a time when you were at your best and hold that picture in your memory. If you do not have any such memory, imagine a time when you will be at your best. David gained confidence from excelling at small things, which helped to bolster his self-worth and his self-confidence. Change starts with a decision. It might be a decision to first change the way you think about yourself, your circumstances or the situation that you are facing. How you think will affect how you feel. If you focus only on your imperfections, you will beat upon yourself and never move forward; you will adopt a self-defeating attitude. It is said that Thomas Edison made

10,000 unsuccessful attempts at developing his electric light bulb and concluded, "I have not failed. I've just found 10,000 ways that won't work." Edison realized that people do not fail; they just give up trying and when you stop trying you will stop growing. He realized that success means not giving up; why should you? Focus on the challenge you face and ask God to show you how to handle the problem. Being confident of this very thing, that he which hath begun a good work in you will perform it until the day of Jesus Christ: *(Phil. 1)*.

CONSTRUCTIVE ACTION PLAN

1. Refuse to allow negative thinking to overwhelm you
2. Develop a picture in your mind of the outcome you would like to see
3. Read Psalm 34 and encourage your spirit in the Lord

Your 25th Gem

WALK ON WATER

"Somehow I can't believe that there are any heights that can't be scaled by a man/woman who knows the secrets of making dreams come true. This special secret, it seems to me, can be summarized in four C's. They are Curiosity, Confidence, Courage, and Constancy, and the greatest of all is confidence. When you believe in a thing, believe in it all the way, implicitly and unquestionable." ~ Walt Disney. "in quietness and in confidence" says God, (Isa. 30:15) "shall be your strength: and ye would not."

Confidence in one's ability is one of the hallmarks of successful individuals, but to achieve the extra ordinary you must develop confidence in what God can do in and through you. Like Paul, you must believe that *you can do all things through Christ that strengthens you.* I like the title of John Ortberg's book "If you want to walk on water, get out of the boat!" In other words, you must get out of your comfort zone. To be successful in life you must show confidence. Success seems to relate to action. "Successful men [people] keep moving. They make mistakes, but they don't quit," says Conrad Hilton. They don't give up. Successful individuals are not afraid of what others think of them. Noah was the laughing stock of his community. The people had never seen rain so the idea of Noah building an ark because he expected rain seemed psychotic. Your efforts at forging or attempting something out of the norm may be met with ridicule or put down, but don't give up. If Noah had concerned himself with what people thought of him, he and his family would not have survived the flood. Ridicule did not thwart his efforts and self-doubt did not crush his spirit. For Noah, the wait was a faith experience.

Fear can become your biggest road block to developing confidence. Peter saw Jesus walking on water and asked Jesus if he could come to him. Jesus told him to come. Peter stepped out in faith, but before long he started to sink. He shifted his dependence from God unto himself. He became over whelmed with the waves and let hold of the power of God. Often, we step out in faith, but when we meet challenges in life, fear takes over. Fear is the opposite of faith. Fear can cripple your ability to achieve anything in life. The story was told of the famous tightrope walker, Jean-François Gravelet who attracted quite a crowd because he promised to walk on a rope, which extended across the Niagara Falls, in 1859, without the support of a net. The distance was a little over 1,000 feet (305m). Everyone was anxious that he might be endangering his life, but he crossed the tight rope and returned without falling. He offered to take someone across, but no one volunteered. Similarly, it is possible to see evidence of God's miracle working power, but still not believe that God can work in and through you. You must have confidence in what God can do in and through you to achieve your greatest good. When Jesus steps into your life he changes it for the better. Jesus attended a wedding in Cana and to the hosts' embarrassment they ran out of wine. Jesus' mother persuaded him to intervene and in honoring her faith, he stepped in and turned water into wine. Indeed, it was the best wine anyone at that wedding had ever tasted.

People who achieve the extra-ordinary are not in a hurry for recognition. They are usually at peace with themselves because their focus is not on recognition but on making a difference in this life. They have enough faith in God and in themselves to sustain them during any situation. Public speaking is considered the number one fear of most people, but with extraordinary individuals, they embrace a speaking engagement because they focus less on themselves and more on their message and meeting the needs of the audience.

People who achieve the extra-ordinary have enough sense to know that while God looks at the heart, people make judgments based on face validity or the outward appearance; so, in addition to having a connection with God, they are aware of other people's perception of their behavior and appearance. They know how to be appropriate for the occasion. They smile warmly, make eye contact and adopt an open posture. When you go for a job interview or make a presentation for example, it is important to pay close attention to your appearance, grooming, scent, clothing, hair and accessories. Your appearance should be conservative and should not detract from the information exchange process unless you are trying to make a statement by the clothing you wear. Mahatma Gandhi for example wore a loin cloth in order to identify with the peasants of India. Entertainers wear gaudy clothes to focus attention on them and appeal to their audience's idea of stardom, but for a job interview, your clothes and accessory should not be so gaudy that all an interviewer can see are the clothes and your accessories and not the person in the clothes. Avoid profuse ornamentation and overpowering perfume. Smile easily, converse easily and make good eye contact. Be courteous, professional and articulate. *One important key to success is self-confidence. An important key to self-confidence is preparation,"* declared tennis great, Arthur Ashe.

You must do all you can to present yourself in the best light. I remember sharing this information with a staff member that I mentored to move into a higher position. His resume was impressive, and his personality was congenial, and he was always called for an interview, but he was not getting any job offers. Upon his return from an interview, I observed that he was not wearing a tie and the jacket did not match his pants. I pulled him aside and advised him to dress for the position for which he was interviewing. He was interviewing for the position of a director but looked like a line worker. I advised him to invest in a good quality dark colored grey, navy or black single-breasted suit, a white shirt and a conservative tie. He followed my advice and admitted that in dressing appropriately, he felt more confident. It was not surprising that with this small change in his appearance he received several job offers. Women should be careful how they dress for interviews. Don't wear clothing that is tight or revealing. Interviewers look at the way you dress as a predictor of whether you know how or when to be appropriate. While you should not be the last person to get in style, it is not every style that is fashionable will suit you. Not everyone can wear a short skirt and look becoming. Ladies with thick thighs look much better in knee length skirts that stop a little below the knee. Be careful also about the types of fabric that you wear and the styles that you adopt. First Lady Michelle Obama sported knitted twin sets and pearls, which is a European classic, but knitted clothing is not for everyone. Mrs. Obama's arms are slim, but knits can make a person with heavy arms look like a stuffed sausage. If you have heavy arms and feel that you must wear knits, then wear it over something tailored for a sleek look.

Etiquette is Important: Be respectful of people's culture, titles and their way of life. Don't assume that your culture is superior. In fact, you should not look down on any one unless your goal is to lift them up; there is much that you can learn from other people's culture. Working as a social worker in different parts of the world, I have had the opportunity of working with people from different ethnicities and from different strata of society. There are variations in cultures, and it is important to understand and be respectful of them as we move towards the world becoming a global village. I have worked with families with strong cultural traditions from places such as India, Bengal, Vietnam, China and Africa. These people welcomed me into their homes and shared their cultural mores, food and festivities with me and although I was there to teach them, I also learned a great deal from them.

Be respectful of another people's time. Be on time for appointments and call if you are running late. Don't expect traffic to stop for you because you are late. Make it a habit to be on time and practice simple courtesies like holding the door for someone coming behind you; saying please and thank you and always starting your first e-mail correspondence with a salutation and the person's name if you know it. There is nothing sweeter to a person than the sound of his or her name. If you have trouble remembering a person's name, try repeating it to yourself three times or associate the name to an object. My grandmother used to say, the people you pass down the road are the same one's you'll meet coming back so make it a habit to practice courtesy to all and sundry.

If you are a guest in a person's home do not overstay or outwear your welcome. Your presence will become like spoiled fish to your host.

Be respectful of your host's home. Jesus was laid in a borrowed tomb, but he did not leave it a mess. John 20:7 says he folded the cloth that wrapped his head. Leave the place cleaner than you found it. If you are invited to dinner do not be greedy and over eat. *When thou sittest to eat with a ruler, consider diligently what is before thee: And put a knife to thy throat, if thou be a man given to appetite. Be not desirous of his dainties: for they are deceitful meat. (Prov. 23:1-3).* For formal dining, remember the acronym BMW – bread on the left, meal in the middle and water to the right. This will help you avoid drinking someone else's water or eating someone else's bread roll. At the table, start with the outer utensils; Use the knife to assist the fork. Knife in the right hand for cutting and fork in the left and be sure to use your napkin to dab at your mouth. If eating soup, tilt the bowl away from you and soup the spoon sideways. Remember, you eat soup and not drink it. Good posture is important. Stand confidently and do not slouch. It is suggested that you keep your legs aligned with your shoulders and your feet approximately four to six inches apart. This will allow you to distribute your weight equally on both legs. Keep your shoulders back; when seated, sit up straight and don't slouch. Good posture leads to better health and an air of confidence. Take care of your hair, nails, teeth, and oral hygiene and smile with confidence. As a female, you must cross your legs at the ankle and not at the knee when seated in public settings; when getting into a car, sit first, close both legs and lift them together.

Your 26th Gem

YOU MUST SURRENDER

Come unto me, all ye that labour and are heavy laden, and I will give you rest. (Matt 11.28). Father I abandon myself into your hands, do with me what you will; whatever you do, I will thank you; I am ready for all, I accept all, let only your will be done in me, as in all your creatures And I will ask nothing else, my Lord. Into your hands I commend my spirit: I give it to you with all my heart, for I love you Lord and so need to give myself, to surrender myself into your hands, with a trust beyond measure, because you are my father (Charles Foucauld).

It is important to surrender whatever is oppressing you to God. If it is financial lack, surrender it. If it is an oppressive employer, surrender him or her; if it is an unfulfilled desire, surrender it. If it's a parent that you can never please, surrender him or her. The sign of surrender is the outstretched arms with your palms facing outward. Surrender whatever is depressing your spirit. If it is fear or worry, surrender it. If it is an addiction, surrender it daily. At the core of many oppressive feelings is shame. The word shame is associated to ugliness, deformity, and dishonor. It is often symptomatic of early childhood abusive trauma, feelings of abandonment, and not being wanted, or not feeling good enough. Sometimes the feelings run so deep you might be unaware of its presence until it manifests itself in feelings of despair, being different; an inability to develop intimacy in your marriage; an overwhelming feeling of anxiety, powerlessness, or unexplained anger. For some, it might be always striving to achieve and having achieved, never feeling good enough. Shame can cause adult survivors of abuse to dislike themselves and feel unworthy of receiving love, kindness or favor from anyone. They feel so unworthy that instead of seeing themselves as precious gems or sons and daughters of God they see themselves as worthless and worth nothing more than a pile of dung. You must surrender these feelings to God. It is possible to pray to God, get up off your knees and still not surrender yourself or your cares to God. I remember providing my mother with some materials and asking her to make a dress for me because this was one of her life skills. When she did not respond promptly, I took back the material and tried to make the dress myself, but without the skill and experience of my mother, I made a mess of it. Similarly, when you do not surrender your all to God and wait on Him to work in His time and in His way, you can make a mess of your life. Abraham and Sarah made the grave mistake of not waiting on God and provided their own interpretation of the promised child by asking Hagar to bear a child for them. This decision caused multiple emotional problems for their household and for Hagar and Ishmael.

Remember that God loves you: God has your best interest at heart. He will work for you in His time and in His way. He sent His son on an expensive errand just for you. Barabbas who was chosen in place of Jesus was a notorious criminal who terrorized the town. Perhaps he was the child of a prostitute because his name meant son of fathers or a child without a name. His name was not affiliated to a place or a person. Like Jesus, whose birth was questionable, he would have experienced shame and rejection; growing up without a proper name would have left him feeling unloved and not affirmed. Andrew Morrison, a psychiatrist at Harvard Medical School stated that: "A child's sense of not being affirmed or supported in his strivings leaves him feeling the world does not respond to him at all." Is it any wonder that Barabbas became a notorious criminal? Yet even for Barabbas Jesus was prepared to die. Jesus understood Barabbas' shame and he understands your shame because on a chilly night he was stripped of his garment and nailed to a Roman cross with just a loin cloth. With both hands stretched out and nailed to the cross, he could not even cover his naked body from the cold or the shame of exposure. His body writhed with pain from the lashes he received. His crucifixion on a Roman cross was the ultimate Roman symbol of shame and dishonor. This shame he bore for you and through those stripes you are assured of healing. This is a promise for there is power in the name of Jesus. His grace is sufficient to keep you from failing or falling. The opposite of shame is awareness that Jesus loves you and that he paid his life as a ransom for your shame. Now, knowing that you have a loving father who cares for you, shouldn't you surrender to Him? Why not let Him become the ruler of your life? Surrender all to him today. His promise is: *And I will make them and the places round about my hill a blessing; and I will cause the shower to come down in his season; there shall be showers of blessing. (Ez.34: 26).*

Your 27th Gem

A DEMOTION CAN LEAD TO
A BIG PROMOTION

Refrain thy voice from weeping, and thine eyes from tears: for thy work shall be rewarded, saith the Lord; and they shall come again from the land of the enemy. And there is hope in thine end, saith the Lord, that thy children shall come again to their own border. Jer.31:16 &17. God has a purpose in sending trial to his children. He never leads them otherwise than they would choose to be led if they could see the end from the beginning and discern the glory of the purpose that they are fulfilling. All that he brings upon them in test and trials comes that they may be strong to do and suffer for him (The Story of Prophets and Kings p. 578). All who are consecrated to God will be channels of light. God makes them His agents to communicate to others the riches of his grace (E.G. White, Desire of Ages, p.141).

According to the Book of Exodus, Moses was the adopted son of Pharaoh's daughter. It could be said of her that in adopting him she was responding to what is called *the identifiable victim effect.* In other words, she was able to empathize with the one child she could see who would have suffered from her father's edict more so than the entire nation of Israel whose children would suffer. As a result, Moses grew up in Pharaoh's palace. He grew up privileged. Acts 7: 22 states that, *he was educated in all the wisdom of the Egyptians and was powerful in speech and action.* He would have studied psychology, the arts, astronomy, mathematics, and other sciences. He received an Ivy League education and for the first forty years of his life he enjoyed power, prestige and influence. In the eyes of the Egyptians, Moses was the earthly manifestation of a god and the high priest of every temple. His dress, accent and conduct were no different from the Egyptians. The challenge for Moses would have been one of fitting in as a Hebrew. Although he was the adopted son of Pharaoh's daughter, he would have experienced discrimination from those who resented his presence as the son of a slave for it was no secret that he was "drawn from the water." Living between two opposing heritage, there came a point when he had to ask himself "who am I? What do I believe? Where do I belong?" In looking for answers he began to spend more time "hanging out" or associating with the Hebrews. This happens often with adopted children or children from poor backgrounds that grew up privileged. There is a desire to learn more about their own heritage.

Having rejected his Egyptian Heritage in favor of his Hebrew heritage, he began spending more time in the community of the Hebrews and was identifying with their plight. Then one day while in their company, he saw an Egyptian beating a Hebrew; he intervened, tried to exact justice and killed the Egyptian. Fearing for his life, Moses had to flee from Pharaoh's palace after his own kinsman disclosed that he had killed an Egyptian. He fled to Midian where he experienced a demotion in his job status and life style. In his demoted status, he worked for another 40 years looking after sheep. In Egypt he had been accustomed to the pampering of his adoptive mother and all the privileges that go with being royalty. In Midian he was a mere shepherd. He had to become a servant-leader and transfer his dependency from a system of care to a God that cares. This wilderness experience was certainly a demotion that racked his very self-confidence in even being able to express himself. He spent so many days looking after sheep that he had lost his language acquisition skills.

Often, life may flip the script and you end up in a less than ideal situation. You may lose a job where you saw your status as tied to the position, or you valued yourself based on your credential. One day you are a super star and the next you are a "nobody." Overcoming a feeling of grief and loss takes time and a willingness to accept life as a journey rather than a destination. Many individuals who fail to do so often commit suicide at this point. Judas committed suicide when his dreams of fame and fortune through his association with Christ were dashed. Saul committed suicide when he was no longer the star of Israel. Moses could easily have become a bitter and resentful alcoholic or drug addict – self-medicating his loss of status, but instead he used his new experience to build his character and he became one of the greatest leaders ever lived. Moses' experience in the wilderness – the school of "hard knocks" taught him patience, and anger management – all the qualities needed for a future leader. He was changed from a spoiled and arrogant prince to a bold and confident leader. It is said that God promotes you to a better position or saves you from a situation that will get worse. T.D. Jakes in his book *Reposition yourself* uses the analogy of an archer with a bow and arrow. You must pull the arrow as far back as possible to go forward and at a greater distance. The further back you go, the greater the distance in moving forward. So too in life, your setbacks can become your greatest comeback blessing. As Confucius said, "our greatest glory is not in ever falling, but in rising every time we fall."

The story was told of a young woman who was driving along with her father and came upon a storm. The young lady asked her father what to do, he said, "keep driving." Several cars began to pull over to the side as the storm got worse. "What should I do?" the young lady asked. "Keep driving" her father replied. A few feet further up, she noticed that an eighteen-wheeler was pulling over also. She told her dad, "I must pull over, I can barely see ahead. It is terrible out her! Everyone is pulling over." Her father told her not to give up - just keep driving. The storm was terrible, but she never stopped driving and soon she could see a little clearer. After a couple of miles, she was on dry land and the sun was out. Her father said, "Now pull over and get out". She said, "but why now?" He said, "Get out and look back, at all the people that gave up and are still in the storm." You never gave up and now your storm is over.

Joseph received a colorful robe from his father, which stirred up the envy of his brothers. In response they stripped him of his coat and threw him in a pit, left him to die but had a change of heart and sold him into slavery. One cannot help but wonder why Joseph would want to wear his prized coat to the field. Like Joseph, we sometimes become showy about our blessings without giving any thought to the spirit of envy that our behavior might stir up. Joseph was left in the pit to die, but God moved upon the heart of his sibling to return and take him out. God does not leave you in the pit or dunghill to suffer alone. He will make a way. God can move upon the heart of those who have done you wrong. In Joseph's case it was not God's will for him to return to his family. God had a greater plan. Although he was out of the pit, he needed to unlearn some lessons about his past in order to grow into his wealth and purpose. In slavery, Joseph was no longer petted and pampered. His values were certainly put to the test and by standing firm for principle he was thrown into jail. Alone he had to get to know himself better and build his personal relationship with God. From prison he was exalted to the palace.

Whatever you are going through there is a lesson to be learned from the experience or some new skills to uncover. I remember taking a job that did not challenge me. I began to hate even going to work each day. Then one day my pastor, Willis Reed said to me "now that you are in a less demanding job, I hope you are using all the extra time to do some writing." I had published journal articles before but had not done any writing in many years; I had started doing some writing but had not taken it seriously until a magazine published an article that I wrote; the publication of this article motivated me to start concentrating on my writing. It was during this period that my writing skills began to expand. I was able to spend more time developing a skill that I had allowed to go dormant for quite some time. I was able to publish articles and even won a writing contest. One morning on my way to work, I saw a writing contest in the *Amsterdam News* and the prize was a free trip for two to Jamaica - inclusive of all expenses and spa treatment. The trip was offered by *Jet Blue airlines* on their maiden flight to Jamaica. It was offered in collaboration with Starfish Resort and Spa. While traveling on the *F* train to Manhattan, I envisioned myself in Jamaica and wrote the article. When I returned home that evening, I typed the article and entered the contest. To my surprise, I was declared the winner. The position you are in right now might not be your first choice, but if you accept it as God's choice for you and an opportunity for growth and learning it could become the stepping-stone you need to your next venture. Although I did not feel the job was right for me, the experience taught me patience, which I did not have, diplomacy skills, which I was also lacking, showmanship and a love for writing. *There is no limit to the usefulness of one who, by putting self aside, makes room for the working of the Holy Spirit upon his heart, and lives a life wholly consecrated to God…. God will teach them hour-by-hour and day-by-day (E. G. White, Desire of Ages p.250).*

God permits adversities and difficulties to come your way that by your being constant and obedient you may be spiritually enriched, and that through your example you may be a source of strength to others. *The very trials that task our faith most severely and make it seem that God has forsaken you are to lead you closer to Christ, that you may lay all our burdens at His feet and experience the peace, which He will give us in exchange. Not a sigh is breathed, not a pain felt, not a grief pierces the soul, but the throb vibrates to the father's heart"* (E.G. White, The Desire of Ages, p. 356).

CONSTRUCTIVE ACTION PLAN

Below is a self-improvement checklist to help prepare you for your next big promotion. Check the points that are true of you. Any of the areas that are not true of you or needs improvement are areas that you need to work on:

I have - Poise & presence _____Yes _____No _____NI
I have - Good voice tone, volume and quality ___Yes ____No ___NI
I am - Unselfishness _____ Yes _____No _____NI
I wear - Appropriate clothing for the interview ___Yes __No ___NI
I am well-groomed _____Yes _____No_____ NI
I have –Good posture _____ Yes _____ No _____ NI
I have -Pleasant facial expression _____Yes ____No ____NI
I am - Truthful & honest _____ Yes _____No _____NI
I use - Appropriate choice & use of words_____ Yes ___No ___NI
I have – The ability to articulate thoughts and ideas __Yes ___No __NI
I am -Tactful & demonstrate good showmanship ___Yes ___ No___ NI
I am – Confident in my interactions with others ___Yes ___No ___ NI

Your 28th Gem

YOUR DAMASCUS ROAD

Acquaint now thyself with him and be at peace: thereby good shall come unto thee...Receive, I pray thee, the law from His mouth, and lay up His words in thy heart...And the Almighty will be thy treasure... (Job 21:21).

Your Damascus road is the change in your life's journey that can happen overnight. It can come at any time and in the most unusual way. Saul was a man with a brilliant legal mind who was educated at the most prestigious schools of his time. He was a member of the Sanhedrin Council, the supreme theocratic court of the Jews. Saul could debate law and religion with anyone and ridicule their views to the point of embarrassment. He was a young man of great promise and earmarked for greatness by his very elevation to the Sanhedrin counsel. In our time, he would be the smart young aspiring senator or the brash news reporter who would vilify or publish articles that demonized those who get in their way.

The trial of the apostle Stephen troubled Saul. He was not convinced that taking Stephen's life was the way to go, but not wanting to lose his prestigious position or his popularity among his peers, he compromised his integrity and went along with his former teachers. In fact, to prove his allegiance, his opposition against the Christians was heightened. Before long, his narcissism got the better of him and he began to deny his own feelings. Alexander Lowen in his book *Narcissism* notes that narcissistic individuals express their feelings in two forms: an irrational rage and a maudlin sentimentality. The rage is described as distorted outbreak of anger; the sentimentality is a substitute for love. Hitler had intemperate rages, but at the same time he had sentimentality towards his people. There is no real feeling behind the anger because the feelings are controlled through the ego. There is an inability to experience sadness. When such individual seeks to injure or hurt others, he must first deny his own feelings and picture the individual as an image or less than a person. In crime-ridden communities for example, those committing the crime do not see the victim as a person but as an object to prey on. Similarly, individuals who abuse or take advantage of others are often devoid of feelings for those that they hurt. Saul obviously had no feelings for those whom he persecuted. In Saul's case, God had to blind him for a few days to help him to get in touch with his feelings. In his helpless state, shut away from the applause of men or from human sympathy, he had time to reflect and pray. He turned to God for help and God did not disappoint him. God changed his name, gave him back his sight and provided him with a new job of helping to promote the work of the very people that he once persecuted.

God did the same for Samson. Samson insisted on pursuing a wrong course despite receiving counsel from his parents. He insisted on carousing with Philistine women who did not share his beliefs, even though he knew he was being unequally yoked. How can a God-fearing person marry a person who has no love or interest in God? It is like yoking an ox and a donkey together. I recall a young lady marrying a young man who was very handsome indeed but had no love for God. She was counseled against marrying him, but she insisted that she loved him and that she could change him. He attended a few church services to win her affections and seemed to be trying to change, but soon after they were married, he continued his old ways of drinking and carousing with his friends; often he would bring them to their home on her day of worship. This was distressing for her because she came from a family that showed respect for the Sabbath. Eventually they parted ways because he became verbally and physically abusive towards her during his alcoholic binges and rages. Samson's stubborn resolve and disobedience led eventually to Delilah cutting his hair, which left him impotent and helpless and gave the Philistines an opportunity to pluck out his eyes; however, God did not leave him to become the sport of others. His hair began to grow again, and he called on God for help. When you cry out to God for help, like a loving parent he will not leave you to suffer alone. God restored his strength and Samson was able to use it to avenge his enemies.

Your Damascus road may come when you least expect it. It may come in the form of losing a loved one, a job loss, a retirement; children moving on with their lives, conflicts in the home, a divorce, or a failed relationship. Your Damascus road is an opportunity to take an about face look at yourself, your beliefs and your goals in life. It may be time to question if your beliefs, behavior and actions are in harmony with that of God or if you are living up to an image or a set of beliefs that are in contradiction to God's design. Your Damascus road is a time to reflect introspectively, communing with God and allowing him to direct your path. It is at this time, like Saul who became Paul, you must ask, "Lord what do you want me to do?" God did not immediately tell Paul what to do. He first sent him to "church" and there in association with other Christians he obtained knowledge of God and God's will for his life. Sometimes all it takes is just one individual to point you to the new path to success or give you that one referral, that one book that could change your entire future. *When the mind of man is brought into communion with the mind of God, the finite with the infinite, the effect on body and mind and soul is beyond estimate. In such communion is found the highest education. It is God's own method of development. (E. G. White, Acts of the Apostles, p.126)*.

CONSTRUCTIVE ACTION PLAN:

Lord, please direct me to that one person who will influence my life for good.

Your 29th Gem

YOUR TICKET TO HELL AND BACK

"For I know the thoughts that I think toward you, saith the Lord, thoughts of peace, and not of evil, to give you an expected end. Then shall ye call upon me, and ye shall go and pray unto me, and I will hearken unto you. And ye shall seek me, and find me, when ye shall search for me with all your heart." (Jer. 29. 11-13).

The story is told that God instructed Jonah to go to Nineveh, but Jonah decided to buy a one-way ticket to Tar shish, the opposite direction. Well, we all know the storm that Jonah went through; first he was thrown overboard and ended up in the slimy belly of a whale. While in the belly of the fish he made all sorts of promises to God and still ended up having to go to Nineveh. He could have avoided the pain of his experience by simply obeying God's command. Sometimes in life we end up in the belly of the fish when we decide to go against God's expressed design or purpose for our lives. We are all called for a purpose in life, but sometimes we get side tracked with get rich schemes, illegal activity, the wrong crowd, depression or drugs and alcohol, and other addictions. Before long, we end up being worse off than we were before - if not in jail.

When Jonah entered the boat, he did not expect a storm, but a storm did come and almost snuffed out his life and the lives of those around him. Life is full of storms and these storms of life are inevitable, but if you are fulfilling your purpose in life, you are less likely to be devoured by them. You need not be anxious about the outcome if you are fulfilling God's will for your life. Working in poor communities, I have witnessed young people getting shot over their involvement in drug dealing. Many became addicts themselves. Girls contracted AIDS through prostituting their bodies for money to keep up with high fashion. The belly of the whale is any place that destroys you mentally, physically and spiritually. The interesting point of this story is that God did not leave Jonah in the belly of the fish. In fact, God provided the fish as a way of helping Jonah escape from his own poor decision and self-destruction. Samson similarly chose the wrong path and ended up losing his sight, yet God did not forget him in the dungeon. His hair grew back, and he regained his strength. God does not give up on you when you make wrong choices. He may provide a person to give you counseling or provide an opportunity to get away from a destructive situation or even this book to help you get back on track.

You may be in a job that does not challenge you. You might be bored to the point of psychosis and can't find another position; but if you continue to dwell on the negatives of the job you will never grow out of the job. Whatever job you are doing right now may not be your purpose in life, but it might be God's purpose for you at this point in time. God can use that very position to teach you lessons about yourself or use it to prepare you for your next position. We are told, *"Whatever your hands find to do, do it with all of your might"*. Think how you can do the job better. While you are in that position, have a vision of where you would like to be and write it down. We all need a vision of what we want our lives to look like because without a vision you will lose hope. Without a vision you become stagnated. Consult with God before you make any plans. In so doing you are allowing God to plan your life for you and in turn you must trust him to guide you every step of the way. I remember one stage in my career when I had worked for the company for several years and was about to leave to start a new position. Three days before leaving, the president of the company made me an unbelievable financial offer to stay. I had already given my commitment to my prospective employer and on principle could not go back on my word. The question then became do I forfeit the new position and accept the offer, or do I reject the offer and move on to the new position, which offered considerably less money. I felt it would be unprincipled of me to make a commitment and go back on my word, but at the same time the offer of a promotion without having to take on the challenge of a new position was also extremely attractive. I prayed for direction and the answer came: "God wants men [and women] who are more intent upon doing their duty than upon receiving their reward-men who are more solicitous for principle than for promotion (*Ministry of Healing p. 475*).

The new position that I accepted was not what I had hoped for. The first thing I noticed was that my office was a closet that was turned into a make shift office with not enough air. Much of my managerial skills were also underutilized, but the position enabled me to do some pioneering work that contributed to making a difference in the lives of vulnerable children and families in New York City. Within a matter of months my peers nominated me for a special award, which recognized my efforts and my leadership skills. I also learned humility of heart and that a position is not a possession. You can be moved out of a position at any time, so don't hold on to it too tightly. Accept any position you receive as another opportunity for growth. *There is no limit to the usefulness of one who, by putting self aside, makes room for the working of the Holy Spirit upon his heart, and lives a life wholly consecrated to God. If men will endure the necessary discipline, without complaining or fainting by the way, God will teach them hour-by-hour and day-by-day. He longs to reveal his grace. (E. G. White, Desire of Ages p.250).*

Your 30th Gem

LEARN A LESSON FROM JOSEPH'S RISE TO FAME

Then I went down to the potter's house, and, behold, he wrought a work on the wheels. And the vessel that he made of clay was marred in the hand of the potter: so he made it again another vessel, as seemed good to the potter to make it. (Jer. 18:3&4). Believe in the Lord your God, so shall ye be established; believe his prophets, so shall ye prosper. (2 Chron. 20. 14-21).

Joseph grew up in a highly dysfunctional family with siblings who were outright thugs. They were so thuggish that they even conspired to kill Joseph, their own brother. To grow up in such an abusive environment must have caused considerable trauma to Joseph. If anyone had a reason to be angry it was Joseph. If anyone had a reason to want revenge it was Joseph. Yet after achieving considerable success in life, we see Joseph forgiving his brothers, demonstrating unconditional regard and accepting responsibility for the events of his life. He saw that even his life experience, painful as it was, worked for his benefit and the benefit of his family. *Now therefore be not grieved, nor angry with yourselves, that ye sold me hither: for God did send me before you to preserve life. (Gen 45:5).*

Don't compromise with wrong: To rise from the dunghill you must be willing to face challenges with moral fortitude. Many famous movie stars and politicians rose to fame but ended their lives by overdosing on drugs or self-inflected suicide. They focused on their material worth rather than their worth to society. By focusing on themselves, they often compromised their integrity for publicity to the point of their success consuming them. Joseph's life is an example of a young man who did not compromise his integrity to get to the top. He was on an errand to help his brothers when they assaulted him and threw him into a refuse disposal pit before having a change of heart and selling him into slavery. As a slave, he refused to have an affair with his boss' wife, which resulted in his being sent to prison. Sometimes when you do not compromise your integrity you might not fit in with the group. You could end up on the dunghill by either getting fired from a position or denied a promotion, but if you remain true to your integrity, not seeking revenge but standing up for what is right, you will either be reinstated to a higher position or elevated to something better. Joseph stood firm for principle, but he ended up in jail. He could not have been happy to have found himself in jail – knowing that he did nothing wrong or deserving of imprisonment, but God was arranging the circumstances of Joseph's life in order to place him in a wealthy place. This prison experience was also preparing him to deal with different minds for in prison he was trusted with responsibility. Sometimes when challenges come your way, God is giving you a nudge towards your purpose in life. If Joseph had not ended up in prison, he might not have met the butler and the baker and gained the opportunity to interpret their dreams. As a result of his skill in interpreting dreams, he was called to service at the right time and the king, having proven his ability elevated him to a position of honor. God does not always choose for His work, men of the greatest talents, but He selects those whom He can best use. *Before honor is humility. ......If they would cherish true humility, the Lord could do much more for His people; but there are few who can be trusted with any large measure of responsibility or success without becoming self-confident and forgetful of their dependence upon God (E. G. White, Patriarchs & Prophets p.517).*

God can fight your battles: I remember working as the head of a department for a company for several years. The department doubled in size under my leadership and was successful in all its undertakings. Then a new assistant executive director took over and began to dismantle the department. He made some changes that were positive but quite a few that were not even ethical. When I shared with him privately my concerns, he decided that the company no longer needed my services. I felt the decision was a malicious one, but I took assurance from Isaiah 41:10-20, which says: *Fear thou not; for I am with thee: be not dismayed; for I am thy God: I will strengthen thee; yea, I will help thee; yea, I will uphold thee with the right hand of my righteousness….. I will open rivers in high places, and fountains in the midst of the valleys: I will make the wilderness a pool of water, and the dry land springs of water.*

This statement found in the Ministry of Healing by E.G. White also encouraged me: *Study the history of Joseph and of Daniel. The Lord did not prevent the plottings of men who sought to do them harm; but He caused all these devices to work for good to His servants who amidst trial and conflict preserved their faith and loyalty……*

If any are qualified for a higher position, the Lord will lay the burden, not alone on them, but on those who have tested them, who know their worth, and who can understandingly urge them forward. It is those who perform faithfully their appointed work day by day, who in God's own time will hear His call, "come up higher" (E. G. White, Min. of Healing, p.334; 327)

The termination of my services in one department occurred just when a new and higher position was created in another department within the same company and the assistant executive officer over the new department requested my services. Consistent with God's promise, He had made a way for me when I least expected. The new position was less stressful, and I was able to use my creative skills in significant ways to double the size of the department, which expanded services to the community and help build the department to one of significance and prominence. As a result, we earned various congressional and local awards for our accomplishments in the community. The new position required my attending top level round table meetings and from time to time, I had to sit next to the same assistant executive that terminated me; yet I was able to speak to him without any feeling of animosity because I realized that his action, although meant for evil worked out to be a tremendous blessing to me. He even shook my hand and complimented me on the work we were doing. Like Haman, the king's right-hand man in the story of Esther, sadly, the assistant executive director continued in his unethical practices and seditious behavior and his own unethical behavior resulted in his own disgraceful termination.

From this experience, I learned that if you are living right and doing right you don't have to fight your own battles. If you are living according to God's will, he will fight your battles for you because *he will repay, fury to his adversaries, recompence to his enemies; to the islands he will repay recompence. So shall they fear the name of the Lord from the west, and his glory from the rising of the sun. When the enemy shall come in like a flood, the Spirit of the Lord shall lift up a standard against him. (Is. 59: 18).* Not only will God fight for you, he will restore the years that the canker worm has eaten [your losses] and he will heal you of your wounds [your hurt and your pain] (Joel 2:25). Your negative experience can work for your good.

Jesus' crucifixion was a humiliating and brutal experience for him; yet, if Jesus had not died, he could not have risen again. His death has made it possible for us to go directly to God with all our troubles and trials. Jesus acts as our vicegerent and intercedes for us. God will not leave you comfortless in your trials. In the same way that Jesus rose from the grave, you too will rise again from your dunghill experience. No power on earth can keep you down. If you have been fired or down sized, think of this as an opportunity to start something new or even a welcome break from a dead-end situation. In fact, each time you face a new situation you must redefine your purpose. Think of God's purpose for you in that new experience. Each time you face a new experience, you must redefine yourself. This is the opportune time to reassess your skills and competencies, start looking for another position, shore up your skills or even start your own business. Abraham, Sarah, Jacob and Paul are examples of individuals whose encounter with God resulted in a lifestyle change and a redefinition of their name and purpose.

Remember to forgive those who have done you wrong: Forgiving others will free you to soar to new heights. You cannot soar to new heights if you are burdened down with anger and resentment. Try walking a mile with a load on your back and see how much progress you will make without stopping every few steps. Unload your burdens. In the same way that God has forgiven you many times over you too must forgive those who have done you wrong. God's forgiveness or His grace is His unmerited favor or undeserved kindness. Instead of taking deserved action against you, He forgives. You too must forgive those who have done you wrong. Joseph forgave his brothers of the wrong they did to him and Jesus forgave those that persecuted him. Forgiveness is an especially important act that will help you to move beyond the ordinary to achieving the extraordinary. It was after Job had prayed for his accusers that God restored his wealth, health and family. *And the Lord turned the captivity of Job, when he prayed for his friends: also the Lord gave Job twice as much as he had before. (Job 42:10)*

The spirit of revenge and the spirit of forgiveness cannot co-exist together. It is in giving up the power to take bitter revenge that you allow the Holy Spirit to come and dwell within.

CONSTRUCTIVE ACTION PLAN:

I will choose to break free from my unresolved negative emotions by facing up to them, forgiving those who have done me wrong and not dulling my pain and hurt with food, drugs or alcohol.

Today I forgive……………… for…………………………………………..

Your 31st Gem

LEARN FROM DANIEL'S CHOICES

Beloved, I wish above all things thou mayest prosper and be in health, even as thy soul prospers (3 John 2). "A mind devoted to God develops harmoniously: God takes men as they are and educates them for His service…. The weak, vacillating character becomes changed to one of strength and steadfastness" (E.G. White, Desire of Ages, p.251).

It is not unusual for individuals who are in the dunghill of life or down on their luck to resort to intemperate habits. They overeat, drink alcohol, or use drugs to self-medicate. Often this is due to a failure to address negative emotions or the demand for perfection from self or others. Such practices however can only do more harm than good. God created a perfect world but through sin we have become imperfect being. The goal therefore is to restore the image of God in you. To do so, you must develop an awareness of the mind-body and spirit relationship. To soar beyond the ordinary, the importance of following a healthy diet and austere life style cannot be overlooked. I remember working in an office where my work was of a sedentary nature. My previous work had required me moving around a great deal, so I could afford to eat certain high-energy foods. In my new position, I did not change my diet. Although I am a vegetarian, I continued to eat as before and indulged in unhealthy sugary and fatty foods. Within a month, I had gained considerable weight. Diet and exercise go together. A study of the Prophet Daniel's lifestyle choices was helpful to me in getting back on track. Daniel was a foreigner in the courts of Babylon. He got there because of his superior intelligence. In the king's court, he was exposed to all types of indulgences, but he was a very spiritual and meditative person. He did not make decisions without consulting God. He was also keenly aware of the mind body relationship. Working in the palace was primarily sedentary work so Daniel chose a vegetarian diet as opposed to the rich foods at the king's table. Rich foods that are high in fat and carbohydrates cloud your thinking and cause weight gain, which leads to other physical ailments and joint pain - especially if you are doing a sedentary job. This dietary faux pau became even more apparent to me when I moved from a more active position to a sedentary one. Daniel and his friends did not eat the food from the king's table or drink the wine. They realized that in order to make good choices, they must have clear minds to stand up for what they believe in. Michele Obama, wife of President Barak Obama utilized a slogan called "Get up and move" to promote the benefits of exercise. Dr. John J. Ratey in his book *Spark: The Revolutionary New Science of Exercise and the Brain* points out that the brain releases chemicals or neurotransmitters including serotonin and dopamine during exercise and help create an alert brain. It also helps in hormone imbalances, reduces stress and anxiety and helps improves academic performance. The habit of engaging in an exercise routine is therefore a good one.

If you over indulge, use drugs or alcohol, you must bear in mind that the decisions you make are being made while you are under the influence of a brain-altering controlled substance, and you are not in a stable mental state. Knowing this, how can you be sure that you are making the best decisions for your life and future? Daniel and his companions knew this and avoided anything that would affect their acuity in thinking. They prayed often, they studied, they took care of their bodies and they trusted in God. In return, God helped them to have strong minds and make good choices. Heart surgeon Ellsworth Wareham, a Seventh Day Adventist surgeon, at 94-years-old could still be found in the operating room. Dr. Wareham is known to follow a vegan diet, which means he doesn't eat anything with animal products such as meat, milk or eggs. He also spends about 10 hours a week working in his garden. "I've been fortunate, first, but I do try to follow a good lifestyle," he says. You must take care of your body. Dr. David Ireland, founder of Impact Ministries provides some useful tips on using the Bible's stewardship principles to improve your health. He points out that your body is on loan to you and you must care for it. If you loan your new car to a friend you expect him to respect it enough to take care of it, similarly God expects you to care for your body which is on loan to you. Neurosurgeon Deepak Rande notes that ailments like obesity, alcoholism, hypertension and diabetes when they are lifestyle-related, point to the diminishing self-regulatory process. In other words, affluence of the western world has given man the opportunity to indulge like never before. Austerity he says is facing extinction. Yet choosing austerity in your diet is precisely what is needed to live a long and healthy life. Alexander the Great is known for never losing a battle and for expanding the Greek empire to as far afield as the Indus River, yet he died young. One day, after days of heavy drinking he went boating and became quite ill with a fever. It is said he died shortly after. He was only 32 years old. You must seek to exercise self - control over your indulgences and eat to live not live to eat.

As with physical food, you must create balance in your life by including a healthy diet of spiritual food and mindfulness. A study of 399 people by Brown University on Mindfulness, which is the inherent trait of being aware of one's present thoughts and feelings, found that those with higher scores for mindfulness were significantly more likely than people with low scores to have healthy glucose levels. Take time out each day for Bible study and meditation. The body needs a balanced diet of food, air, sunlight, rest and exercise so be sure to take one day for rest and restoration. God ordained the Sabbath as a day of rest – not to be wiled away in bed, but in restorative meditation and worship, in contemplation of his love and his goodness. The Sabbath is precisely for this purpose. West Indian Seventh Day Adventists in Europe and North America tend to spend an entire day of worship in church on Sabbaths, while European Adventists tend to spend a few hours in church and the rest of the day outdoors or with family. Having experienced both approaches to restorative worship, I have seen benefits in both. West Indians, being migrants in a foreign land, spend more time in supportive group fellowship, while Europeans pursue more individual or family pursuits. Whether pursuing individual, family or group endeavor, remember the purpose is restorative in nature. Notice that in the word **rest**oration is rest, which, according to the Hebrew means Shabbat or rest from your work. By your honoring God in resting on the Sabbath and refraining from secular activities you will be lifted from the dunghill and will regain your strength to soar to new heights. This is His promise: *If thou turn away thy foot from the sabbath, from doing thy pleasure on my holy day; and call the sabbath a delight, the holy of the Lord, honourable; and shalt honour him, not doing thine own ways, nor finding thine own pleasure, nor speaking thine own words: Then shalt thou delight thyself in the Lord; and I will cause thee to ride upon the high places of the earth, and feed thee with the heritage of Jacob thy father: for the mouth of the Lord hath spoken it. (Is. 58: 13 & 14). Now unto him that is able to do exceeding abundantly above all that we ask or think, according to the power that worketh in us, (Eph.3: 20).*

CONSTRUCTIVE ACTION PLAN

THE LIFE STYLE CHANGES THAT I NEED TO MAKE ARE:

1. _____
2. _____
3. _____

Your 32nd Gem

LEARN FROM THE COST OF ESAU'S BIRTHRIGHT

When men cast off the fear of God, they are not long in departing from honor and integrity (Patriarchs & Prophets p.556 -557). Through intemperance, Satan works to destroy the mental and moral powers that God gave to man as a priceless endowment. Thus, it becomes impossible for men to appreciate things of eternal worth (E. G. White, Counsels on Diet and Foods, p.150).

Compromising your principles and engaging in negative indulgences are the quickest ways to sabotage your own potential to achieve success in life. Jacob and Esau were twin sons of Isaac. Esau was free spirited, daring and liked immediate self-gratification. His daring personality and his capturing of wild animals captivated the attention of his aging father who had lived a more sheltered life as a young shepherd. I imagine, after Abraham attempted to offer Isaac, Esau's father as a sacrifice, as any protective mother of one child would, I doubt that Isaac's mother, Sarah allowed Isaac, her only son out of her sight; as a result, he probably spent more time with his mother than he did with his father and missed out on the adventures of hunting for food. Is it any wonder that Esau, the more adventurous and freer spirited of the twins was Isaac's favorite son? Through Esau's stories of his hunting exploit, Isaac could live vicariously through him. Jacob on the other hand was a "momma's boy" who was more spiritual, sensitive, caring and concerned for the future. In ancient Hebrew, the birthright was an inheritance, which earmarked the next priest of the family who would be expected to devote his life to God. Esau being the first-born was to receive the birthright, but he desired power, prestige, and the party life. The idea of being the priest was an inheritance that he took lightly. Knowing his propensity to satisfy desire above principle, his mother and brother decided to "set up him" and in one moment of rash self-indulgent desire for some savory soup or a mess of pottage, Esau gave up is birthright.

The annals of history chronicle the names of leading politicians, ministers and high officials, who like Esau have lost their high position for a mess of pottage. Principle is sacrificed for a moment of "censored indulgence" and with easy access to digital cameras, just one click, can potentially expose whatever is done in the dark for all to see. Your poor choices can become fodder for others to capitalize on. Neurosurgeon Deepak Rande notes that indulgence requires neither skill nor intelligence whereas exercising restraint requires a higher form of intelligence. Unfortunately, we live in a society today where love, patience, self-control and contentment are no longer virtues to desire but nice words that are relegated to church sermons.

How easy it is to fail at the point of achieving or having achieved the extraordinary because of compromising one's principles. Working among troubled youth, I met many who were very bright with promising futures but compromised their principles by indulging in drug activity, alcohol abuse or illegal activity believing that if they did not get caught, it didn't matter. I remember a young man who grew up in a group home. He had enormous potential and received various scholarships and awards during his college years. He had the potential to become hugely successful, but at the point of almost graduating from a prestigious university, he compromised his principles because he believed he could get away with dishonest practices. Consequently, he ended up in jail and lost everything. Similarly, Solomon lived a principled life for many years. His success as a leader was known internationally, but he lost sight of the source of his power and became opinionated; he began flattering himself that he could have as many women as he could handle and still maintain his connection with God. Samson similarly gave in to inclination and proclivity for prostitutes and lost his eyesight, his judgeship and his physical strength, resulting in his ending up on the dunghill. The merciful God that we serve did not forget them though. Despite their deviance, God visited them when they cried out for mercy. Samson's hair grew back, and Solomon learned the folly of his ways.

If you have made wrong decisions, God has not forgotten you; he is waiting with open arms for you to realize the folly of your ways. The prodigal son soon realized the folly of his ways and returned to his father. Upon doing so, his father did not reject him. Not a day went by that his father was not on the lookout for him. Upon his return, his father covered him with his robe so that his servants would not see his son's shame. So too when you come to God, he covers you with his robe of righteousness. He does not expose your shame. Shame and addictive behavior – be it chemical addiction (alcohol, cocaine, marijuana and prescription drugs) or process addiction (food, sex, money, gambling, work, spending) often go hand in hand. Addiction is considered a spiritual dis-ease at the core of which is shame. Shame can leave you feeling isolated, without love, not feeling good enough, and never measuring up. As a spiritual disease, it must be treated spiritually. Twelve Steps of Narcotics Anonymous suggests the following principles to live by:

1. Admit that you are powerless over your addiction and that your life has become unmanageable. Believe that a power greater than yourself (God) can restore you to sanity
2. Decide to turn your will and your life over to the care of God
3. Make a searching and fearless moral inventory of yourself
4. Admit to God, to yourself and to another human being the exact nature of our wrongs
5. Be entirely ready to have God remove all defects of character
6. Humbly ask God to remove your shortcomings
7. Make a list of all persons you have harmed and become willing to make amends to them all.
8. Make direct amends to such people wherever possible, except when to do so would injure them or others.

9. Continue to take personal inventory and when you are wrong promptly admit it.
10. Through prayer and meditation, seek to improve your conscious contact with God, as you understand Him, praying only for knowledge of his will for you and the power to carry it out.
11. Having had a spiritual awakening as a result of these steps, try carrying this message to addicts and to practice these principles in all your affairs.

Oh, the long-suffering mercy of God! When His people put away the sins that had shut out His presence, He heard their prayers and at once began to work for them (E. G. White, Patriarchs & Prophets p. 557-558).

Your 33rd Gem

LEARN FROM THE WOMAN WHO WANTED MORE

Come unto me, all ye that labour and are heavy laden, and I will give you rest. Take my yoke upon you, and learn of me; for I am meek and lowly in heart: and ye shall find rest unto your souls. For my yoke is easy, and my burden is light. (Matt 11:28-30)

The story of the woman at the well is a story about a woman who had experienced multiple sex partners and was living with another woman's husband. Her promiscuous life style led to her being scorned by other women in her community. This woman was so ostracized by other women that she avoided them as much as possible. Each day she went to the well at a time of the day when other women would not be there to make their snide remarks about her character. The pain of being ostracized was too much to face until one day she met a man -a Jew at that - asking her for water. Jews were not supposed to have dealings with Samaritans. The Jews looked down on Samaritans and called them dogs. Yet, Jesus went out of his way to meet with her and ask for a drink. As is typical of women who experience sexual abuse, she lived a promiscuous life style - looking for love in all the wrong places and finding only disappointment and abuse all over again. This time she met a man who did not seek to take advantage of her vulnerability; he offered to give her something better. Her immediate desire was for a quick fix. She probably thought, "How wonderful it would be if I never have to come to this well again and face these wretched women who have no idea about the many traumas that I have experienced and have left me with multiple scars." Jesus wanted to take her from a low sense of self-worth to a higher level, so he offered her a life changing experience - a guilt free life where she could think of herself differently. It was Mark Twain who said: *"Keep away from people who belittle your ambitions. Small people always do that, but the really great people make you feel that you too, can become great."* Often, we value ourselves based on other people's opinion of us and our life experience. Growing up in an unhealthy environment of abuse and addictions can lead you to think less of yourself and can affect your sense of self- worth in such a marked way that you cannot imagine yourself doing better or being better. At the core, you feel a sense of shame. As you try to improve yourself, people will begin to take pot shots at you by reminding you of where you came from. They tell you that you will never make it, or they identify you with the stereotypes of your community. The fact remains, some people would rather see you fail than succeed. If you had been in jail or on drugs, as soon as you return from jail or drug treatment the same "so called" friends who dragged you down in the first place often show up to drag you right back down with them. I remember the case of Janice a crack/cocaine addict who desperately wanted to clean up her habit, so she went into an 18-month drug treatment program; as soon as she came out, her drug addicted friends invited her to a celebration party with crack/cocaine on the menu and before the evening was over, she had relapsed. It is for this reason that in your efforts to pull yourself up from the dunghill of life that you must avoid toxic people, places or things that might act negatively to drag you back down. If you have an expensive piece of crystal, you do not treat it carelessly. You know its worth, so you treat it with care. You are a child of God and he has paid a high price for you. Don't sell yourself cheap! *For the time past of our life may suffice us to have wrought the will of the Gentiles, when we walked in lasciviousness, lusts, excess of wine, revellings, banquetings, and abominable idolatries: Wherein they think it strange that ye run not with them to the same excess of riot, speaking evil of you: Who shall give account to him that is ready to judge the quick and the dead.(1 Peter 4; 3-5 NIV).*

Your 34th Gem

BASK IN HIS PRESENCE

God opposes the proud but gives grace to the humble. Humble yourselves therefore, under God's mighty hand, that he may lift you up in due time. Cast all your anxiety on him because he cares for you

(1 Peter 5:5&6). For thus says the Lord God, the Holy one of Israel: In returning and rest you shall be saved. In quietness and confidence shall be your strength (Is 30:15).

Have you taken time out of your day to spend time with God? If you fail to do so each day and you are impatient, and, in a hurry, you will miss out on many precious blessings. The story is told that Jesus visited the home of Martha. Her siblings Mary and Lazarus lived with her. Jesus was always a welcome guest in her home, but on this occasion, Martha lashed out on Jesus. It was the custom of the time to wash the feet of visitors and feed them, so Mary and Martha were busy in the kitchen catering to Jesus and his 12 disciples when Mary slipped away to listen to Jesus, leaving all the chores on Martha. Irked by her sister's abandonment, in frustration Martha told Jesus to tell Mary that she needs to help. Mary ignored her, seemingly unconcerned about the tensions and stresses around her. She remained focused on God's presence in Jesus and Jesus affirmed her choice. Mary and Martha represent contrasting behaviors of hurting individuals.

Often, individuals are angry with God or avoid spending time with God for fear of the emotions that being in the presence of God might conjure up. Martha represents those who are doers and caretakers-caught up in a round of activities, seeming like the perfect child, the perfect spouse, the perfect fundraiser, the perfect student; the prefect employee, all in an unconscious effort to avoid the fear of falling apart. We do not live in a perfect world so to expect perfection from yourself or others is to set yourself up for disappointment and failure. It is the perfectionist who is most prone to develop eating disorder or engage in illicit sexual relationships. Being overly responsible, maybe rigid, industrious, competitive, and very conforming; they often have difficulty coming to terms with their own emotions, so they find solace in food or the thrill of an illicit relationship. Individuals like Martha tend to project their inadequacy unto others, to family, coworkers and friends rather than on themselves. Of course, they see themselves as perfect so why look at themselves? They even blame God when things fall apart. They have difficulty accepting criticism of their work and may display a combative spirit when they perceive they are being corrected or criticized. In Martha's case she was not only disrespectful to Jesus who was a guest in her house; she blamed him and Mary for her inadequacy. This is the same Martha who indirectly blamed Jesus for her brother's death. "If you had been here my brother would not have died," she said. Jesus did not respond to Martha's disrespect or blaming. He responded instead to her pain. Martha had experienced multiple traumas in her life: her brother's death, her sister being sexually abused and sexually exploited, and her relative Simon who had been stigmatized due his being a leper. Her pain ran deep. Her caretaking activities were good, based on Isaiah chapter 58. Indeed, helping others leads to better mental health and Jesus acknowledged this, but Jesus also showed her that taking time out for prayer and reflection was better. In order to grow spiritually and emotionally, you must make a conscious effort to take time out for self-reflection. Spiritual growth takes time. You may have to cut back on some of the committees that you are involved in or give up one of the three jobs that is draining you mentally; shut the computer off and delay answering those e-mails until tomorrow so that you can read the Bible or a book that will deepen your understanding of God and yourself. If your partner does not want to worship with you, you may have to go it alone.

It is possible to live such a self-absorbed life that you seldom look introspectively or even question yourself. Yet your failure to do so keeps you in the dunghill of life. In order to achieve the extraordinary, you must take time out for self-reflection. It is for this reason that God gives us the Sabbath so that we can take time out to de-stress and reflect on him. Every Sabbath that you take time out to rest, you reboot your body, mind and spirit. Do not become so involved in a round of activities - even church activities on the Sabbath - using the day to stay busy to avoid reflecting on your spiritual, physical and emotional condition. *They that wait upon the Lord shall renew their strength; they shall mount up with wings as eagles, they shall run and not be weary, and they shall walk and not faint (Is 40:31).* Mary in contrast to Martha was in touch with the one who knew and understand her pain. Mary was an abused and abandoned woman whose relationship with Jesus was based on his unconditional positive regard and love for her. He lifted her from the dunghill of despair, and she basked in his presence at every opportunity. When Jesus was a guest at her uncle Simon's house, she anointed his feet with expensive oils – a symbolic gesture of her gratitude to him for his saving grace that he extended to her. *Jesus knows the circumstances of every soul. You may say, I am sinful, very sinful. You may be; but the worse you are, the more you need Jesus. He turns no weeping, contrite one away. He does not tell any all that He might reveal, but He bids every trembling soul take courage. Freely will He pardon all who come to Him for forgiveness and restoration (E.G. White, Desire of Ages, p. 568).*

As you begin to spend time with God you may find yourself getting in touch with your feelings. You may even think you are going crazy, but the truth is you are going quite sane. Another feeling that might emerge is anger; you may feel you have been nice for too long and no longer want to be a doormat. Be careful not to go back to your old addictive behavior in an effort to stifle your feelings. Instead, pray, and ask God to forgive those who have done you wrong, whether family, friends, teachers or spouse. Clean out your closet, get enough sleep; exercise and start journaling your thoughts; on one side write your thoughts, feelings and requests and on the other side the answers to prayers.

Your 35th Gem

WHEN THE FISHING NET IS EMPTY

For he satisfieth the longing soul, and filleth the hungry soul with goodness. (Ps. 107:9). To everyone who offers himself to the Lord for service, withholding nothing is given power for the attainment of measureless results. For these God will do great things (E.G. White, Ministry of Healing p.160)

Peter, James and John were fishermen by trade. Peter owned a fishing boat; one night he and the other disciples decided to go fishing. Fishermen fished at night and on this occasion, they fished all night and caught nothing. There was plenty of fish in the sea, but they were not catching any. They came back ashore with empty fishing nets. Naturally, Peter was feeling very discouraged. He had failed at his own profession and he sat discouraged and worried about the future. It was daytime when they reached the shore. Early in the morning, Jesus approached the disciples at the waterfront and decided to join them in the boat. This is a vivid reminder that when you are feeling like an utter failure, God does not leave you alone in your discouragement. You may need a job and see many positions advertised that are suited to your skill;

you forward your resume, but like Peter all the responses say someone else is more suited for the position – that is if you get any response at all. This is a dispiriting feeling, especially if your funds have dried up; but rest assured that God is not about to leave you to suffer alone. E. G. White notes...*I saw that if we do not see immediate answers to our prayers, we should hold fast our faith, not allowing distrust to come in, for that will separate us from God. If our faith wavers, we shall receive nothing from Him. Our confidence in God should be strong; and when we need it most, the blessing will fall upon us like a shower of rain (EG White, Testimonies, Vol. 1, om121).*

God has a way of strengthening your faith by way of a friend, a sermon, a song, a book or through nature. Jesus borrowed Peter's boat and used it as a pulpit to teach the multitude that flocked to hear him. After teaching from Peter's boat, he said to Peter "go fishing again." It is interesting that Jesus taught first before he gave Peter any instruction. Is it possible that Peter needed some encouragement to soften his discouraged brow? The disciples were sitting there mending their nets. It means there were holes in the net and what little fish they caught would have slipped through the net. Maybe they were thinking that by mending the net they might secure a few small fish. You could say they were trying everything in their power to catch some fish – secure their craft. Peter thought it was a crazy suggestion to go fishing during the daytime because fishermen fished at night. But Peter was responding to a command from God and he decided to obey. Peter was in a dejected state of mind, but he still believed Jesus' words. The instruction to launch into the deep was Jesus' simple appeal to him. The Holy Spirit is the medium used by God to appeal to us. Often the appeal comes to us through his ministers, friends or family that is spiritually connected with God. When the appeal comes, we must be willing to listen in order not to lose our blessing. When the disciples tried to pull in the net to shore, the very same net with the holes, they had caught so much fish that the nets began to break.

Like Peter, there are times when your own craft or profession might fail you or it might not yield the increase that you expect. You graduate from college and cannot find a job; you may get laid off, even terminated or you may have to give up some pet interest that is no good for you; your ever loving, all knowing heavenly father does not leave you alone to wallow in despair. It is interesting that, Jesus sought out Peter and entered his boat at a time when Peter was at his lowest ebb. If you are at your lowest point right now, be it in your career, your education or occupation, or even marriage don't give up in discouragement; stop the negative self -talk. Start mending your net and ask God for his guidance. The right side is the side of faith. It is reaching a point of total dependence on God. Often in life we acknowledge God's blessings, but we fear to trust Him fully. David Stoop in his book *"You are what you think"* notes: *"That which we make an absolute is what we trust;"* in other words, what you worry about happening in the future is really your way of identifying the object of your trust. If you worry about your job, then you are saying that one of the major objects of your trust for your future is your job. You are trusting in that job to protect your future. Or if you are worrying about money, you are placing your faith for the future in money. Thus, whatever you are worrying about is your security blanket. Stock markets go up and down and businesses go out of business, so you cannot put your trust in any of these things. You will notice that written on the back of the United States dollar bill is the statement "IN GOD WE TRUST," which suggests that money does not expect you to trust in it. It is for this reason that Jesus said you should not be anxious about your life. Worry is reaching into the future to play God. It is Satan's work to discourage the soul; it is Christ's work to inspire with faith and hope (Desire of Ages p.208). *When God opens the way to accomplish a certain work and gives assurance of success, the chosen instrumentality must do all in his power to bring about the promised result (The Story of Prophets and Kings, p.263).*

Your 36th Gem

LORD I NEED A MIRACLE

When the poor and needy seek water, and there is none, and their tongue faileth for thirst, I the Lord will hear them, I the God of Israel will not forsake them. (Is 41:17-20).

Many people sometimes fail to reach their potential through lack of faith, self-doubt or discouragement. They give up on God and stop praying when things don't work the way they expect. This is where God's will come in. It wasn't Peter's will or desire to go fishing again. Moreover, fishermen do not fish in the daytime. It was God's will and he obeyed, and God honored his obedience. Sometimes God wants us to stretch our faith in him. I remember when I left London, England to attend University in California many people questioned my decision since I had already achieved considerable success in England. Yet, making that change was the best decision that I could have made. It was a faith decision and God has blessed me beyond my wildest dreams. He has enriched my spiritual life, strengthened my faith, blessed me with a beautiful family and he has supplied all my needs. The blessings did not come all at once, however. Like Peter, I experienced some serious down moments, empty nets and some heartbreaking tsunamis. Upon arrival in California, I found that as a foreign student I could not obtain employment. I feared that I would never survive my first semester let alone two years, but I remembered the bible text "whatever your hands find to do, do it with all of your might" so I did odd jobs just to survive. Baby-sitting was the only regular job available to me, so I would comb the notice boards around campus looking for baby-sitting jobs. The rates offered to me were below the going rate, but I was grateful for even a less than minimum wage job and I took good care of the children in my charge. After a while, I became known as one of the best baby sitters around. I helped children with their homework, I made sure babies did not get diaper rash and I allowed "parentified" children (meaning children who were used to parent their younger siblings because their parents worked long hours) enjoy being a child in my presence. One set of children that I baby sat for an extended period (some 20 years later) still remind me of the fun they had with me making green cookies. Before long, word got around that I was a wonderful baby sitter and without putting out any advertisement, I was bombarded with calls. Little did I know that that the humble role I played as a babysitter would prepare me for a more exalted position in the field of child welfare! George Washington Carver, the great inventor says: "Learn to do common things uncommonly well; we must always keep in mind that anything that helps fill the dinner pail is valuable."

Exercising good money management in the financial affairs of your life is also especially important. As a child I read the novel *David Copperfield* by Charles Dickens and was struck by a statement made by the character Mr. Micawber, (which we now call *the Micawber Principle*). Micawber had lost his wealth through lack of frugality and concluded based upon his observation that if your "Annual income is twenty pounds, annual expenditure nineteen pounds nineteen and six pence, result happiness. Annual income twenty pounds, annual expenditure twenty pounds ought (plus) and six, result misery." In other words, you must live within your means. That principle has always stayed with me. *All should learn how to keep accounts. Some neglect this work as nonessential, but this is wrong. All expenses should be accurately stated; many, very many, have not so educated themselves that they can keep their expenditures within the limit of their income. They do not learn to adopt themselves to circumstances, and they borrow and borrow again and again and become overwhelmed in debt, and consequently they become discouraged and disheartened,* says Ellen White in the book *Adventist Home (p.374).*

Our fishing nets will remain empty when we remain ignorant about money management and we accumulate too much consumer debt and consumer items. What is the point of having a closet stuffed full of clothes and no money in the bank to pay the bills? *If you have extravagant habits, cut them away from your life at once. Unless you do this, you will be bankrupt for eternity…Let us not spend our means in gratifying desires that God would have us repress. Let us fitly represent our faith by restricting our wants (Adventist Home, p.375).*

Be wise in your use of loans when you are in debt; loans can either generate assets or become a liability. The story of Elijah and the widow who had nothing left but a cruse of oil is a good example of how to use loans to generate asset. The story is told that a certain woman of the wives of the sons of the prophets went to Elisha and asked for help, saying: *"Thy servant my husband is dead; and thou knowest that thy servant did fear the LORD: and the creditor is come to take unto him my two sons to be bondmen;"* Elisha instructed the widow to borrow containers from all of her neighbors, even empty vessels; and *"borrow not a few in which to put the oil. And when thou art come in, thou shalt shut the door upon thee and upon thy sons, and shalt pour out into all those vessels, and thou shalt set aside that which is full."* It is interesting that Elisha told the woman to close the door while filling the vessels. Similarly, it is not always wise to share your investment ideas with others in case they beat you to it. I remember sharing my thoughts about a business opportunity with a colleague and this person ran a head with the idea and usurped the opportunity, so keep your investment plans private. The widow followed Elisha's instructions and the oil multiplied.

If you borrow money do not waste it on consumer items, unless the item will generate income or increase your asset. Elisha then instructed the widow to sell the oil. In this instance, the widow borrowed to invest, and she multiplied her resources. One investment that always brings return is investment in your education, your children's education or a job skill. The wise man Solomon says: "Get wisdom and in all your getting get understanding." The Bible says: "The love of money is the root of all evil." This suggests that there is nothing wrong with money of itself. Money can be a blessing in the right hands. It is what you do to get it and what you do with it when you get it that will dictate how you relate to it. I recall a young man who was criminally involved in drug dealing. He wanted to stop selling drugs but had become accustomed to an affluent life style. I suggested that he think about a skill that he enjoys and can perform well. He remembered liking carpentry in school, so he decided to pursue this craft. This interest led to one of his friends linking him to a contractor who taught him interior finishing in the building trade and today he has his own interior finishing and repair company, which generates enough income for him to enjoy a comfortable life style. It is said that if you take time doing what you love the money will eventually come. Indeed, many successful businesses started from scratch in some one's living room, kitchen or garage. *In all thy ways acknowledge him, and he shall direct thy paths. (Prov.3:6).*

Money matters can sometimes make or break a family or a relationship. If you are starting out in a marital relationship, there should be a common pot or a partnership where money matters are concerned and the one most frugal should manage it. Consider this, if one spouse dies the other will inherit all that is owned by the deceased so why not enjoy it together while you are alive. It will go so much further and together you will accomplish a lot more. Ecclesiastes 4:9-12 says: *Two are better than one; because they have a good reward for their labour. For if they fall, the one will lift up his fellow: but woe to him that is alone when he falleth; for he hath not another to help him up. Again, if two lie together, then they have heat: but how can one be warm alone? And if one prevail against him, two shall withstand him; and a threefold cord is not quickly broken.*

I recall a story that was told of two groups of people being placed in two separate rooms with a huge pot of soup and an exceptionally long ladle that was several feet long. In one room the people grew skinny and malnourished while in the other, they grew fat. What made the difference, you may ask? In one room everyone tried to feed himself with a ladle that was too long to reach from the pot to their mouth, but in the other they took turns to feed each other with the ladle. When in a marriage or working with a group, you must adopt a team spirit to achieve success. If you are a boss, do not only concern yourself with "feathering your own nest" at your staff's expense by taking all the credit for the work they do. Be concerned for those that work under you and seek to elevate them as you rise.

God has a thousand and one ways of providing for your needs. He is like the master chess or domino player looking down on the board.

If you make a bad move, He is there to tell you how to make your next move. *"And thine ears shall hear a word behind thee, saying, This is the way, walk ye in it, when ye turn to the right hand, and when ye turn to the left." (Is. 30:21). I will instruct thee and teach thee in the way which thou shalt go: I will guide thee with mine eye. Be ye not as the horse, or as the mule, which have no understanding: whose mouth must be held in with bit and bridle, lest they come near unto thee. (Ps 32:8&9).*

If you think you know it all and don't need guidance, then you won't hear God's voice. You cannot hear God's voice unless you are in tune with him. Now I am not referring to auditory hallucination, which can be symptomatic of a mental illness such as schizophrenia, drug induced psychosis, dementia, or delirium. Being in tune with God requires a meditative spirit and knowledge of the scriptures. When Jesus was in the wilderness, Satan came to him to tempt him with all sorts of inducements. Through his study of the scriptures, Jesus was able to overcome Satan's wiles. So too, your decision-making must be guided by the word of God. Jesus' disciples asked him to teach them how to pray. They observed that he was in tune with God and accomplished great feats after spending time in prayer. You too must spend time in prayer and in studying God's words, if you wish to receive guidance from God. Pray until something happens (PUSH). Your prayers can be conversational as in talking to a friend, or as petitions that call to mind the power and promises of God. I recall attending a prayer meeting service at the Campus Hill church while at Loma Linda University where the speaker suggested the use of the acronym ACTS to help structure your prayer if you do not know where to begin. "A", represents the word Acclamation or giving glory to God; "C" represents Confession or confessing your sins; "T" represents Thanksgiving and "S" is supplication or making your request known to God.

Daily Devotion: Each day take some time out to read the bible and devotional books that will help to keep your mind in tune with God. Make it a habit to read your bible before breakfast. As with Peter, when you need a miracle God will give you an instruction. The wise man Solomon says (Prov. 12:14): *A man shall be satisfied with good by the fruit of his mouth: and the recompence of a man's hands shall be rendered unto him.them reward.* You must speak good things into your life. I remember in the early days of being married, my husband's old Honda began costing us more in repairs than it was worth. I asked my husband what type of car he wanted. He responded dismissively that we can't afford one, so it was not worth mentioning. I said just go ahead and say it. "A Volvo would be nice," he said. I prayed there and then. "Lord, please give us a Volvo that we cannot afford at a price we can afford." I had heard T. D. Jakes mention that he had prayed this prayer and God answered his request. He also said God has a way of bringing down the prices of things for his children to afford them and I have found this to be true, especially as a tithe payer. It was less than a week later that my husband came home excited saying he had seen a new Volvo on sale at an unbelievable price that we could afford. I remember also that when the recession hit in 2006 and the housing market went down, people were paying more for mortgage than their homes were worth; President Obama introduced the home refinancing program which allowed us to refinance at a lower rate. God can make a way when there is no way or when all that you can see a head are just road blocks. God will bulldoze a way and make the impossible possible.

A Delay to Answered Prayer: Don't get discouraged if you have prayed and you have not received an immediate response or answer. From the moment you begin to pray God dispatches his angels to help you (*see Daniel 9:20-23*). When Daniel prayed God sent the angel Gabriel *swiftly* to his aid. On another occasion the answer to Daniel's prayer was delayed because Gabriel was blocked by the evil one. So fierce was the blockade that he was held up 21 days to the point that Michael, one of the chief princes of heaven had to intervene (*Daniel 10:12-14*). This suggests that answers to your prayers can be delayed for any number of reasons unknown to you. It doesn't mean God has forgotten you. God will come through for you, but you must continue to pray. In Daniel's case he continued praying and fasting until his prayer was answered. It is the delay to your seemingly unanswered prayers that can lead to cynicism, resorting to pseudo-science or to the worshiping of things that you can see. The children of Israel turned to idolatry when Moses delayed his return from his encounter with God and they suffered the dire consequences. Don't let delay cause you to give up on God. Wait patiently for him. The story was told of a little boy who was waiting for a bus to arrive. Everyone told him the last bus had already left, but he said, "if the last bus has gone, my father is the bus driver and I know he will come back for me" and sure enough the bus did come back. God is your heavenly father and He cares for you. He will not leave you stranded. On one occasion my teenaged daughter went with her friends to a birthday party. She did not like the turn of events at the party and asked her father to come and pick her up. He did not hesitate. He responded right away. God will not hesitate to answer when you need Him the most.

If embarking on a spiritual journey that is new to you, it is important to be aware that physiologically, there are two sides to your brain, left and right sides. Knowing this is important because left-brained individuals are more concrete thinkers and tend to want to see immediate response. Right-brained thinkers are more reflective and more spiritual so if you are a left "brainer", not seeing an immediate response to your prayer can be discouraging in your spiritual walk. You can develop your right brain by being more conscious of the "still small voice" within; through meditation and prayer. The still small voice is often referred to as intuition – the feeling side of the brain. By operating in the right brain, you will be better able to grasp concepts without words and feeling them; while allowing the left-brain, which deals with logic to wait. Owen Waters, in his article "Whole brain thinkers," suggested developing the right side of the brain by feeling your way into a deeper experience. The right brain uses symbols and pictures, not words. Symbols can be visual. Listening to music, especially classical music can help you to develop your right brain. If you are new to paying attention to your intuition, then you will need a little practice. Practice makes perfect; you'll achieve good results a lot sooner than you might expect. Pay attention to your intuitive insights and you will grow to realize how profoundly correct they are. As you keep track of all your insights, you'll be amazed at their accuracy.

Your 37th Gem

JUST SPEAK TO YOUR MOUNTAIN

For verily I say unto you, That whosoever shall say unto this mountain, Be thou removed, and be thou cast into the sea; and shall not doubt in his heart, but shall believe that those things which he saith shall come to pass; he shall have whatsoever he saith. (Mark 11:23).

We all have problems in life that we must face; some of our problems are like little pebbles that we can easily handle or cast off, while others are like huge mountains that seem insurmountable. Your problem may even feel like it's pressing you down and without supernatural intervention it would crush you.

Queen Esther had a huge problem that seemed more like Mount Everest. How could she ever move that mountain alone? Her people were about to be wiped out and according to her cousin Mordecai she was their only hope. He told her she must go to the king and beg for mercy. She was the king's wife, so she was in the best position to appeal to the king, but in the palace, there were rules of conduct that if breached could lead to death. Esther was scared for her life. It would be easier to ignore the problem of her people than to put her own position in jeopardy, she thought.

Mordecai reminded Esther that she is a Jew and just because she is in the king's palace doesn't mean she wouldn't get killed along with all the other Jews. If you remain silent, he said, help might come another way, but you and the rest of our family will die. "Who knows? Maybe God chose you to be queen to save us from this time" he reminded. Esther knew that being in a position of power isn't always enough to move the mountain that she faced. She needed the help of a higher power, so she told her cousin Mordecai to get all the Jews in Susa to pray and fast for three days (attend a focused 3-day prayer and fasting meeting). It was Jesus who reminded his disciples after they failed miserably at trying to heal someone that if they wanted to see God's miracle working power and glory, they had to do some serious fasting. After praying and fasting for three days, Esther made her decision. She said even though it's against protocol, I will go to the king and if I die, I die.

Esther knew that after you have prayed you must do your part. She dressed to impress and walked to the door of the throne room. She stood nervously waiting. When the king saw her, he welcomed her and asked, "What can I do for you my queen?" I imagine it wasn't the right time to speak to her mountain, the words could not come out right, and so she invited him and the enemy of her people, Haman to a banquet. They all had a great time at the banquet, but it still wasn't the opportune time to speak to her mountain, so she invited them again to another banquet.

The king was no fool and Esther knew that she couldn't keep inviting him to banquet with her for no apparent reason. He wanted to know her motive. Finally, she plucked up enough courage to speak to her mountain, to paraphrase: "My king, if you really love me, please let me live and let my people live also. I have been told that my family and I are all going to be killed". The king was shocked. "What! My queen! Who would do that?" This was Esther's opportunity to tell the whole story. At this, Esther pointed to Haman, the man who conspired to destroy her people.

How you handle the mountains and pebbles in your life will determine your success or failure. Stones and pebbles are the little problems or annoyances that show up in family relationships, on the job, or on the road when you are driving. Rocks and mountains are the big problems that you cannot move by yourself alone. The mountains might be a financial difficulty, a job loss; struggles in your family, your marriage, your job, challenges in school or problems with a rebellious child; problems in your life that seem insurmountable.

How You Speak to Your Mountain is Important: Like Esther, pray about it first, calmly consider the situation, and think it through. Get into the habit of writing hurt feelings in your personal journal or sleeping on it before responding rashly or taking any action. The wise man Solomon says: *A soft answer turns away wrath, but a foolish answer stirs up anger.* Speak to the person that has offended you or is causing you pain. Don't explode, get into a fight, or send an angry e-mail that you might regret, or post inappropriate stuff on social network - Face book or Twitter that the whole world can see. Simmering over some wrong that has been done to you will only fester and make you bitter and morose. It is much better to go directly to the individual that has done you wrong and tell that person how hurt you feel by their action. In doing so, use "I" instead of "you" statements. Using "I" statements means you are not blaming, and you are taking responsibility for your feelings. The person will be less likely to react defensively. An example of an "I" statement is: "I am upset at what you said. It really hurts my feelings." In so doing you are taking responsibility for your response to how the person's behavior made you feel. Once you have settled the issue, let them know you have forgiven them of the wrong done to you and move on with your life. If you have caused pain or hurt to someone, ask for forgiveness; apologize, it will also free you to move forward with your life. If you make a mistake don't hide it. Be sure to give advance notice to the person impacted or affected by the outcome of your mistake. In a work environment, give your boss the heads up on a matter that could prove an embarrassment. If you make a request, don't be offended if the answer is "no," move on in search of another opportunity.

Ask for Help: Don't be afraid to call a professional and ask for help. I needed a mentor for my doctoral dissertation, and I reached out to several people that I knew, but no one was able to help, or they were charging exorbitant fees. I decided that if I must pay then I must pay for the best, so I called Harvard University and spoke to an individual whose work I respected and asked him to be my mentor. He was kind and gracious and did not charge me a dime.

During my doctoral studies, I had a professor whom I thought was unnecessarily unkind until I saw how God used her to be a blessing to me. She rejected my final term paper for her class many times and wrote deflating comments in big bold letters on the cover page each time she returned it to me. Being the only person of color in that class, all the negative statements about people of color flooded my mind. I kept trying to improve and even consulted with another professor with expertise in the subject area to get some help, but the paper was just never good enough. I kept wondering if or where the blockage was that I couldn't seem to grasp her instructions. I delayed in approaching her because she was abrasive and not very approachable. Finally, I plucked up enough courage to ask her to show me where I was going wrong. To my surprise, she was neither rude nor hostile. She told me that I had done more than she had asked and that she kept returning my paper instead of giving me a failing grade because I had given too much information and that I should simply stick to answering the question. Sometimes we fear situations that a simple question might resolve. If Queen Esther had not plucked up enough courage to speak to her husband, the King her people would have been annihilated. *If you have no confidence in yourself, you are twice defeated in the race of life. With confidence, you have won even before you have started*, says Marcus Garvey.

In the end, God used my repeated rejected paper experience to prepare me for the final comprehensive doctoral exam. Through the repeated submissions, I had become so familiar with the subject matter that I could write about it with ease. On reflection, after six years of study, I would have failed the final written comprehensive exam and essentially the doctoral course if I had not passed that one subject on the final comprehensive exam. The daughters of Zolephehad were about to be disinherited based on tribal laws so they went to Moses and pointed out that the tribal laws discriminated against females. Moses consulted with God on the matter; God agreed and instructed Moses to change the rule. God can change polices that are not working in your best interest. He can change your most difficult situation and turn it to your advantage if you but ask.

God spoke the world into existence; don't you think he can move your mountain by the power of his word? He can change things in the "twinkling of an eye." Jesus was placed in a sealed tomb. His persecutors thought they had seen the last of him when they placed him in that tomb, but God wasn't finished with him yet. He sent an angel to remove the stone and on the third day He rose again. In three days, He moved from death to life. In three days, His change came. In three days, your change can come. God is not finished with you yet either. If you are down in the dunghill you will rise again. If you feel caged in, He will make a way of escape for you to fly; if you are blocked in on every side, he can airlift you out. Or like Daniel and his companions, if you are in the fiery furnace, He will stay in the fire with you and help you bear whatever you are going through until you sense His presence and witness His power. *God will do great things for those who trust in Him. The reason why his professed people have no greater strength is that they trust so much to their own wisdom, and do not give the Lord an opportunity to reveal His power in their behalf. He will help his believing children in every emergency if they will place their entire confidence in Him and faithfully obey Him (E. G. White, Patriarchs and Prophets p. 454).*

God told Moses to speak to the rock, which represented the rock Christ Jesus; but Moses struck the rock instead. His rash act displeased God because he destroyed the image of Christ - their provider and sustainer, in the minds of the people. If Moses had spoken to the rock, the people would have seen that when they face mountains of difficulty, all they must do is simply ask God for blessings in the name of Jesus and He would answer in His time and in His way. They do not need to perform any antics or act out aggressively. They are His children and He will provide for their needs. When you are going through mountains of difficulties be careful how you respond to others because how you respond to your mountain can either draw others to Christ or turn them away from him. Your negative response could also destroy your opportunity for future advancement because people will remember your behavior under pressure.

Jesus was clear in saying: *"For verily I say unto you, That whosoever shall say unto this mountain, Be thou removed, and be thou cast into the sea; and shall not doubt in his heart, but shall believe that those things which he saith shall come to pass; he shall have whatsoever he saith."* (Mark 11:23). Speaking to your mountain means you must pray – express audibly in words what you want God to do for you. Command a removal in the name of Jesus; declare a removal in the name of Jesus. In Luke 10:19, Jesus said: *"Behold, I give unto you power to tread on serpents and scorpions, and over all the power of the enemy: and nothing shall by any means hurt you."* Jesus has already given you the authority to move mountains, so if in faith you speak to the mountain and ask for it to be moved it will be done. Whatever mountains of problems you face today don't be afraid to ask for help to move that problem. Ask in the name of Jesus, and God can do more for you - more than you can ask or think.

God can move your mountain in the most remarkable way. My husband had a blocked artery. He was scheduled to have an angiogram to check the extent of the blockage; his cardiologist placed him on aspirin therapy prior to the procedure. My daughter and I prayed with him and asked the church to pray also. Some prayer warriors came to our house and prayed with him the day before the procedure. As he was getting ready to go to the hospital, his surgeon called and postponed the procedure. Twice the procedure was postponed. On the day of the procedure, I was able to speak to the cardiologist and ask a few questions; after speaking to the cardiologist I feared the worse, but my husband seemed at peace. When my husband returned from the procedure, the cardiologist said excitedly "great news, there is no blockage!" I responded, "Thank you God!" I believed that God had delayed the procedure so that the aspirin therapy could work. If God can remove a blocked artery don't you think he can remove your mountain?

Trust God to remove the mountains of difficulties you are facing and watch him work on your behalf. *Throughout the history of God's people, great mountains of difficulty, apparently insurmountable, have loomed up before those who were trying to carry out the purposes of Heaven. Such obstacles are permitted by the Lord as a test of faith. When we are hedged about on every side, this is the time above all others to trust in God and in the power of His Spirit. The exercise of a living faith means an increase of spiritual strength and the development of an unfaltering trust. It is thus that the soul becomes a conquering power. Before the demand of faith, the obstacles placed by Satan across the pathway of the Christian will disappear; for the powers of heaven will come to his aid. Nothing shall be impossible unto you (Matt.17:20; E. G. White, Prophets and Kings, p. 595).*

Your 38th Gem

IT'S TIME TO CROSS YOUR RED SEA

*I will go before thee and make the crooked places straight; I will break
in pieces the gates of brass and cut in sunder the bars of iron: And I will
give thee the treasures of darkness, and hidden riches of secret places,
that thou mayest know that I the Lord, which call thee by thy name,
am the God of Israel (Is. 45:2&3).*

The Israelites left Egyptian bondage in hopes of making a better life for
themselves but looming before them was a vast bed of water and behind
them was their pursuing oppressors. In front was death and behind was
bondage. They were caught literally between the devil and the deep blue
sea. They had to decide fast. Either they return to bondage or move
forward, so at the command of Moses they moved forward. *In marching
down to the very water, they showed that they believed the word of God as spoken
by Moses. They did all that was in their power to do, and then the mighty One of
Israel divided the sea to make a path for their feet. The great lesson here is for all
time. Often the Christian life is beset by dangers and duty seems hard to perform.
The imagination pictures impending ruin before and bondage or death behind. Yet the
voice of God speaks clearly, "Go forward" (Patriarchs and Prophets p.289-290).*

If the children of Israel had not taken that first step in faith, they would have been forced to return to Egyptian bondage and would have missed out on the Promised Land. They had to make the first step of faith towards their future destiny for God to part the Red Sea. It was Confucius who said: *"The journey of a thousand miles begins with a single step."* Many times, in life we do not accomplish all that we can accomplish because of fear. What is it that you need to do to move forward? What is your red sea? Is it going back to school, starting a business, purchasing that home, writing or publishing that book, or is it moving forward with your invention? You have probably tried many times and failed, but don't give up. The children of Israel were weary and terrified, but their faith in God encouraged them to move forward. There was no promised land in sight. All they could see before them was a bed of water, but they trusted God to make a way out, of no way and God honored their faith. He parted the Red Sea before their very eyes. God is ready to part your red sea if you are willing to make that first step forward. You may have failed in the past; you may be feeling discouraged because you have never finished anything. Your resources might be limited, but do not fear. If you are moving in the path that God directs, he will provide the resources you need to see you through to the end of your journey.

In deciding to leave England and attend Loma Linda University in California, I did not have enough money for two years of tuition, but I stepped out in faith. In my first year at Loma Linda, I did baby-sitting jobs and other odd jobs on campus; in my second year, God provided the tuition in the form of a paid internship opportunity. Similarly, when I decided to send my daughter to a Christian school, the school fees were prohibitive, but each semester, God provided opportunities for me to earn extra income to cover her tuition.

Jesus told his disciples to get in a boat with him and go to the other side of the lake. While they were on the lake a storm arose. The disciples tried in vain to handle matters by themselves, but to no avail. It was when they were about to perish that they remembered to call on Jesus. They forgot that it was Jesus who suggested that they should go to the other side of the lake in the first place. Jesus being all knowing and all powerful, would have known that a storm was about to billow its way across the lake, yet he told his disciples to get in the boat. The fact is Jesus was in the boat with them and while Jesus was with them no evil could befall them. When they called on Jesus, he arose and stilled the storm. He then asked them "where is your faith?" While Jesus is with you no evil that is formed against you will stand. As you attempt to achieve new heights, be it in pursuing an education, taking on a new position or a promotion, you will meet challenges that may seem like tsunamis; but, if you have faith that God will ride through the storm with you, you will eventually get to the other side. There is a poem by Patience Strong that has always stayed with me. It says: *"Keep going keep showing you are not beaten yet. Keep moving keep proving though things are upset, it's all coming right as in time you will see it's all for the best and the best is to be. Keep praying keep saying the dream is coming through a wonderful future is waiting for you."* The following statement by Ellen White has also been a source of encouragement to me: She notes, *"We should obey this command, even though our eyes cannot penetrate the darkness, and we feel the cold waves about our feet. The obstacles that hinder our progress will never disappear before a halting, doubting spirit. Those who defer obedience till every shadow of uncertainty disappear and there remains no risk of failure or defeat, will never obey at all... The path where God leads the way may lie through the desert or the sea, but it is a safe path"* (Patriarchs and Prophets p. 289-290).

Your 39th Gem

POT SHOTS AT YOU

Trust in the Lord with all thine heart; and lean not unto thine own understanding. In all thy ways acknowledge him, and he shall direct thy paths. (Prov. 3:5&6).

As you cross your red sea and achieve success in life –living right and doing right - for the glory of God; loving justice and practicing mercy and truth (Prov. 3:3 &4), you will find favor with both God and man. This does not mean everyone will like or support you. My grandmother used to say, "the higher the monkey climbs is the more he gets exposed and the more people will take potshots at him." In other words, you will become more visible as you become more successful in life. Like a black dot on a white sheet of paper; people will notice everything you do and say. You must be responsible about the things you say and do publicly and privately. As a child growing up in Jamaica, I recall that we had several different types of mango trees in our yard; the sweetest of all the trees was the Bombay Mango, so during mango season, people would ignore the other trees and spend hours throwing sticks at the Bombay tree to get at the ripe mangoes. Pastor Carl Ming, speaking at a North

Eastern Conference Youth Camp meeting, recalled the story of his boyhood days and how he was picked on by bullies. When he reported this to his mother she would simply say, "School boys don't throw stones at green mangoes." He did not understand her response until one day the same boys were trying to knock down a single ripe mango among some green ones from a mango tree and asked for his help.

As you achieve success, people who knew you when you were in the dunghill - your lowest point will try to pull you down or try to steal your joy but rise above it and shake off their negative criticisms and put-downs.

Dealing with Resentments and Hostility: Thomas Sowell in his article "Race and Resentment" points out that resentments and hostility toward people with higher achievements are one of the most widespread of human failings and is deadlier than envy of the wealthy. The hatred of people who started at the bottom, and worked their way up, far exceeds any hostility toward those who were simply born into wealth. Inherited wealth is not considered an achievement. He points out that the sultans who inherited extraordinary fortunes in Malaysia are not as hated as the Chinese, who arrived there destitute and have risen in rank; the inheritors of the Rockefeller fortune do not experience the same hostility as Jewish immigrants who rose from poverty on Manhattan's Lower East Side to prosperity in a variety of fields. Others who started at the bottom and rose to prosperity—the Lebanese in West Africa, the Indians in Fiji, the Armenians in the Ottoman Empire, and the Jamaicans in Brooklyn for example—have likewise been hated for their achievements; similarly, resentment or anger directed at you by others results from their feeling that they had similar and sometimes better opportunities but did not make the most of their chances. In the words of Longfellow: *If we could read the secret history of our enemies, we should find in each man's life sorrow and suffering enough to disarm all hostility, says H. W. Longfellow.*

Jesus, although his fame was widespread, faced similar resentment when he returned home during his ministerial years. In Mark 6:1-5 we are told the people who knew him were amazed at his wisdom [his achievement] but instead of embracing him they said, (in trying to put him down), "isn't this Mary's son and the brother of James, Joseph, Judas and Simon? Aren't his sisters here with us? They failed to even acknowledge Joseph as his father and took offense at him. Jesus remarked that only in his own town is a prophet without honor. His own people rejected him. They had no faith in him because they could not get beyond his similar poor background and rise from poverty, or in their eyes, his illegitimate birth. In their resentment of his rise to notoriety they lost out on their blessing. Jesus wanted to do more for his people, but his own people rejected him. It is said he could not do any miracles except heal a few people.

Don't cower in defeat because others are jealous or resentful of your success. The "emotional plague" is a common ailment of people who are jealous of others. Just accept that many will be jealous of you as in Isaac, Daniel, and David's cases. Isaac was a very prosperous foreigner; he was so prosperous that his neighbors tried to sabotage his success by stopping up his wells. Even the king Abimelech resented Isaac's prosperity. He feared that Isaac was more powerful than he and so he asked Isaac to go *"away from us, for you are much mightier than we."* Daniel's ability to interpret dreams resulted in king Nebuchadnezzar sparing the lives of the wise men of the king's court. These so called "wise men" ought to have been eternally grateful to Daniel for saving their lives, but instead they planned his assassination through their hidden agenda. Similarly, David killed Goliath and defeated the Philistine army; King Saul ought to have been grateful to David that his people were spared death and plunder, but as the people sang David's praises Saul became the more enraged with jealousy and tried to hurt David. There are individuals that I have helped who have disappointed me when I needed their support the most. Some have even tried to humiliate me publicly, but I have learned to love them anyway and have helped them in their time of need. Prov. 25:22 says in doing them good *"For thou shalt heap coals of fire upon his head, and the Lord shall reward thee.."* You must not let the negative feelings of others towards you dictate your attitude or treatment towards them. While Jesus was on the cross, the very people he healed, or fed should have been the first to speak in his defense, but they abandoned him when he needed them the most. Why do you think your experience will be any different?

Dealing with Yellow Journalism: Unfortunately, you will meet people who will try to belittle you and try to cut you down to their size. Some will demonize you to make your good intentions look bad. Some will even make tabloid news of your past indiscretions to achieve success at your expense. If you take a stand on an issue that upholds principles of truth, justice and mercy, be prepared to deal with yellow journalism in the form of scandal mongering, half -truths, untruths and sensationalism. It will start with negative name calling, then labeling, followed by repeated drum beats of the label. If that doesn't stop you or kill your spirit, the drum beat will become louder with inflammatory references so hurtful that even friends will abandon you. Joseph, Moses, David, Job, Daniel and Jesus all experienced yellow journalism, yet God did not prevent these attacks on them; after some malicious bruising, God moved in their favor and caused them to rise again from the dunghill of life to accomplish incredible success. Let Romans 8:28 be your assurance that God will cause all things to work together for your good because you are called according to His purpose. As a royal child of God, you must expect evil forces to revolt against you. You have a calling and destiny to fulfil, so expect to be attacked. If you are in the company of others, expect to be singled out for an attack. Samson was on his way to Timnah with his parents when he was attacked by a lion. His parents were not attacked. He was attacked. He was attacked because God's anointing was upon him. He was the one with the gift. The evil one worked through the lion to snuff him out, but God who is in control gave him the strength to kill the lion. Key players on a team are always under the attack of the opponent. They expect and accept this. Carry yourself with dignity and don't go tweeting in response to every negative comment or criticism stated or posted on social media about you. In the words of former first lady, Michelle Obama, "when they go low, you go high."

You will also meet individuals who will befriend you to get what they can from you or just to tear you down. Sadly, these individuals may include your very family and close friends. Jacob was hustled twice by his scheming uncle Laban, but God gave Jacob wisdom to outsmart his uncle. Laban told Jacob to take the spotted sheep knowing that there were very few spotted sheep, but God told Jacob what to do. God will give you wisdom to handle those that try to hurt or hustle you, so love them any way and forgive them. Forgiving someone doesn't mean you forget the wrong done to you, but rather that you are giving up your right to retaliate against that person. As you forgive or give up that right, they will either become a blessing to you or they will fall into their own treacherous trap. *He (God) will thwart the purposes of wicked men and will bring to confusion the counsels of those who plot mischief against His people (E. G. White, Prophets and Kings p. 176).*

The story was told of a little bird flying south for the winter. It was so cold the bird froze and fell to the ground into a large field. While the bird was lying there, a cow came by and dropped some dung on it. As the frozen bird lay there in the pile of warm cow dung, it began to realize how warm it was. The dung was thawing it out! The bird lay there all warm and happy, and soon began to sing for joy. A passing cat heard the bird singing and came to investigate. Following the sound, the cat discovered the bird under the pile of cow dung. The bird felt relieved that the cat had come to help him, but the cat promptly dug him out and ate him. The moral of the story is that sometimes even the wrong done to you can be for your own good and not everyone who pulls you out of trouble is your friend. People can steal your ideas so be sure to copyright your original inventions and ideas. Don't be too eager to join money making schemes and groups that claim to have your best interest at heart. My grandmother used to say, "it's not everyone that skins their teeth with you is laughing with you." I have seen many cases of poor inner-city youths caught up in the clutches of drug dealers who pretend to be helping them but are using them as drug carriers in exchange for a few dollars. Similarly, gangs and secret societies recruit members under the pretense of providing them with a family and protection.

When you are getting out of the dunghill of life and things are beginning to go well for you, it's sometimes best to keep your mouth shut, about your success, especially when in the company of those who do not have your best interest at heart. Only share your story of success with those who might benefit or upon request. It is said that Billionaire Warren Buffett offers his advice only to those who request it. Be mindful that not everyone will accept you. Some will hate you just because of how you look or because you are more successful than they. If Jesus was not accepted by the people of his own town, why do you think you will be treated any differently? Just remember, *"A prophet is not without honor except in his own country"*. Often, it is only when others give you recognition that your own people will claim you as their own. Even so: *Let all bitterness and wrath and anger and clamor and slander, be put away from you, along with all malice. Be kind to one another, tender-hearted, forgiving each other, just as God in Christ also has forgiven you. (Ephesians 4: 31-32).*

Your 40th Gem

LETTING GO AND STARTING OVER

Now unto him that is able to do exceeding abundantly above all that we ask or think, according to the power that worketh in us, (Eph. 3:20).

Letting go of a relationship that has ended, clothes or shoes that don't fit, a job in which you once excelled or a home country to which you have no intention of returning can be a challenge. The children of Israel left Egyptian bondage with the goal of moving to the Promised Land, but when the Promised Land did not emerge immediately after their Red Sea experience, they became disenchanted and longed for the fleshpots of Egypt. They forgot the pain of slavery and the reason they wanted to get out in the first place and began reminiscing about what they considered the pleasures of the past. For you to grow, you must let go of the past and move forward in faith believing that God will open doors of opportunity for you. When the door is open, do not be like the monkey that had his hand caught in the cookie jar with a handful of nuts. All it had to do was let go of the nuts, but it held on for dear life and was caught and trapped by monkey hunters. What are you trapped in and do not wish to let hold of? Whatever you are holding onto might be holding you back from reaching your God ordained position in this life.

I remember the case of a 14-year-old teenaged boy in the Bronx whose mother was drug addicted and had abandoned him. He longed to be adopted by a wealthy family. One day a wealthy family saw his picture in an adoption catalogue and their teenaged son chose his picture. He wasn't the most attractive looking child, but he had an engaging smile. The family met with him and decided that they wanted him to join their family. He was excited that his long-held desires had been granted. The family treated him kindly, but after being with them for three months, he ran away. Everyone was shocked and puzzled since this was the opportunity that he had longed for. After a few days, he resurfaced in his old neighborhood. When I asked what had happened, he said, "I miss being here. I miss the very smell of my old neighborhood." He came from a very rustic high crime and drug infested neighborhood and although he longed for something better, he could not bear to leave the old neighborhood behind. After returning for a couple of weeks, he again wanted to leave because the neighborhood had not changed, but his exposure to a better life style had changed his outlook on life. It is possible to give up an old position, a toxic relationship or oppressive lifestyle and although the new situation might be better, like the children of Israel who had been enslaved in Egypt, you may yearn for the fleshpots of the past without appreciating the blessings of the present.

Stop Looking Back on What Was Lot's wife turned a pillar of salt when she looked back with regret on the life she left behind. She regretted leaving Sodom and Gomorrah. Sodom was a place of luxury and wealth, with plenty to eat, and an abundance of leisure time. The people engaged in violence and all sorts of sensual perversions with a total disregard for the poor and needy. Lot's wife did not want to leave her luxurious home, the lifestyle to which she had become accustomed and enjoyed and the family members who were also engaging in perversions; as a result, she suffered the dire consequences of her choice. Our God is a loving God who (if we allow him) monitors our lives. He not only opens doors of opportunities for us; he may also close some that might do us more harm than good. Before the children of Israel could enter the Promised Land, they had to go through their wilderness experience. This was a necessary experience because in slavery they had developed a slave-like mentality. Slaves are dependent on their master for everything. God wanted the Israelites to transfer their dependency from their slave master to Him.

The question is: Who is your master? Is it money, materialism, position, power or prestige? Until you get to that point where you are totally dependent on God, you will never leave your wilderness. The Children of Israel wandered in the wilderness for 40 years and some did not make it to the Promised Land. If you look at a Bible map you will see that the distance from Egypt to the Promised Land was not far, yet it took them 40 years to get there. They spent 40 years wandering about in the wilderness because they held on to the mentality of a slave and needed to unlearn many of the lessons learned in slavery. As soon as things became challenging, they began desiring to go back into slavery. On the very borders of the Promised Land, the older generation distrusted God and forfeited their right to enter the land that God had promised them. The 10 spies brought back a favorable report about the land, but only Caleb and Joshua took God at his word.

Facing Life's Challenges – Fight, Flight or Freeze: Within each person is a fight, flight or freeze temperament response, which evidences when faced with challenges. How you respond to a challenge – be it to fight, freeze or take flight can determine your future success or failure. Challenges are opportunities to gain greater self-knowledge and make changes, but a change will not come until you see the need to change. I sometimes see married couples that are in a crisis in their marriage use the crisis to learn about the relationship and create inner change; however, I have also seen others engage in a "blame game" and eventually decide to quit the marriage - only to repeat the same mistake in another marriage. They repeat the same behavior simply because they carried the same attitude and character flaw into their next marriage. Challenges are opportunities to discover major character flaws that you can change and enable you to grow and elevate your level of being. The children of Israel had left slavery, but they were still psychologically enslaved. Their passing through the wilderness was an opportunity for change and growth, but many of them missed the opportunity. Of the thousands of Israelites that left Egypt only a handful made it to the Promised Land. If you choose to always run away from challenges, you will always be psychologically enslaved.

If right now you are in the wilderness of your experience, it is time to give some serious thought to making some radical changes in your life. Start today by getting rid of destructive habits, negative beliefs, old unhealthy relationships and even old clothes and shoes that you don't wear anymore and are weighing you down. Call up a charity and give them away so that you can move into something new and better - even your promised land. Steve Jobs in his commencement address to the students at Stanford University on June 12, 2005 stated that he started Apple with his friend Woz and the company grew from just the two of them to 4,000 employees. Just after they released Macintosh, Jobs got fired by his board of directors from the very company he started with his friend in his father's garage. Jobs said it was devastating but getting fired from Apple was the best thing that could have ever happened because the heaviness of success was replaced by the lightness of being a beginner again, less sure about everything. He added that it freed him to enter one of the most creative periods of his life. He started a company named NeXT, another company named Pixar, fell in love, and created the first computer-animated feature film, "Toy Story," which is perhaps the most successful animation studio in the world. In a remarkable twist of events, Apple bought NeXT and Jobs returned to Apple. In the words of Jobs, "sometimes life's going to hit you in the head with a brick. Don't lose faith." Alexander Graham Bell, inventor of the harmonic telegraph, from which idea sprang the invention of the telephone once said: *We so often look so long and so regretfully upon the closed door that we do not see the ones which are open for us.*

Your Next Job Interview: If you go for a job interview and you are not accepted, don't become depressed, dejected and despairing – feeling rejected and doubting your abilities. Employers reject prospects for any number of reasons. Your qualifications might be topnotch, but you might not be the right fit for the company. You might be overqualified, which means you are lowering your standard and might become bored in the position. The company might be looking for a younger or an older person to complement the existing team. The company might be looking for diversity or uniformity. It is not always about you. In the bee kingdom there are worker bees, queen bees and drones. The work environment is remarkably similar. The company might be looking to replace a worker bee, a queen bee or a drone or they may be looking to change the culture of the organization. It is for these reasons that you should research the organization to which you are applying and learn about its culture, ideology and the vacant position even before applying. If you are asked to tell something about yourself, do not tell stories about your cats, family or love of hiking. Tell the interviewer about your competencies and why you would be the right fit for the position. This is another reason to first do your research. Don't be afraid to ask the interviewer about the culture of the organization and the qualities that they are looking for in the person they are seeking to hire. This will help you determine if the position is the right fit for you. A job interview is a two-way process. The interviewer is interviewing you, but you must also interview the interviewer to see if the position is the right fit for you. You might be desperate for a job, but like a pair of good-looking shoes that don't fit well, you will not be happy in the position. If the position is not the right fit and if you are not happy in it, you will not be as creative as you can be. If you cannot expand your creativity, your spirit will eventually die and before long you will start experiencing all sorts of depressive symptoms.

You may have achieved considerable success in your chosen field and are now wondering what next to pursue. Why not channel your energies into creating or doing something that will be a blessing to humanity? If you are a gold medal Olympian for example, and the glory of winning has lost its sting, it makes no sense dwelling on the glory you once enjoyed. Why not create other Olympians by starting a school or sponsoring some young athletes. Bill Gates left the world of computers after making millions of dollars to do philanthropic work. Bill Clinton, former US president decided to direct his energies into relief work in developing countries.

Success Despite Adversity: Jim Crow laws, which enforced racial segregation particularly in the Southern states of America, were enacted post emancipation until 1965. These laws were introduced at a time when African Americans began to enjoy remarkable and meritorious rise from the depths of slavery to accomplishing great feats, serving as educators, politicians, scientists and bankers. Jim Crow established color lines of separation (redlining) in virtually all areas, including education, hospitals, housing and even water fountains. Although Jim Crow was introduced to disenfranchise people of color, and to pull the proverbial rug from under their feet, the opposite occurred. African Americans enjoyed considerable growth and success despite Jim Crow. Relegated to live within the color line, there was a sense of interdependence. They all lived in the same community so those who were more fortunate used the opportunities they enjoyed helping the less fortunate. The talented helped those less talented and the "haves" helped the "have not;" their motto was "lifting as we climb." They supported each other through adversity and some of the best Black colleges, trade schools and universities came out of this era. Similarly, when the children of Israel began to grow in number and in wealth, the Egyptians felt threatened by them and enslaved them. Pharaoh feared that one among them would become a deliverer and so he tried to destroy all the new-born male children. Yet Moses, the deliverer grew up and was groomed in the very home of the same person who sought to destroy the prospect of a deliverer. God has an amazing sense of humor.

Man's Extremity is Indeed God's Opportunity: God can turn your adversity into prosperity. The very people who revolt against you can become your greatest blessing. You might not like where you are right now, but don't feel defeated and down cast. Sing praises to God; trust him to come through for you. Paul and Silas were jailed without justification, yet in prison neither one asked: "Why me Lord? What did I do to deserve this when I have done so much to proclaim your name?" Instead, right there in prison they started a song service that led to their deliverance. Even the very jailor dressed their wounds and wanted to know more about Jesus. Indeed, God can change difficult circumstances for *These things saith he that is holy, he that is true, he that hath the key of David, he that openeth, and no man shutteth; and shutteth, and no man openeth; I know thy works: behold, I have set before thee an open door, and no man can shut it: for thou hast a little strength, and hast kept my word, and hast not denied my name. (Rev. 3:7&8).*

Learn a Lesson from the Acorn: You might feel poor and insignificant and even feel like giving up on life; you might be at your wits end, but God can help you grow into your wealth and purpose. Think of the acorn for example, it looks like a little tiny green egg in an eggcup, yet this small seed grows into a mighty oak tree, standing tall and dignified. The oak tree can grow to an enormous height. Some grow as tall as 130 feet in height and 40 feet in girth. Because of its size, all types of animals and insects can nest in every part of it. As God blesses, you too must become a blessing to others through your wealth, wisdom knowledge and understanding. My grandmother who was always sharing what little she had with others would often say: "to whom much is given much is expected." Be careful though, of adopting codependent behavior. Codependents tend to misinterpret the scriptures about giving and doing for others and tend to work themselves into a frenzy of good deeds. This type of behavior is reflective of a false belief that "doing for others" leads to love, success and acceptance. True service does not involve neurotic self-denial. It is having self-respect and self-worth. Reciprocal giving leads to disappointment when the return is not equitable. When you give expecting nothing in return blessings result. Like the oak tree, the animals and insects in the oak tree help the oak tree to reproduce itself. The insects feeding on its bark help it to shed its bark and allow for new ones to grow. The animals provide waste matter, which go back into the soil as nutrients and produce more acorns. Similarly, as you help others the blessings will come back to you in many ways, shape and form. Former president William (Bill) Clinton created Economic Empowerment Zones in low income communities while he was in office; upon leaving office, he had difficulty finding office space and was eventually able to re-establish himself in Harlem, New York, in one of the very Economic Empowerment Zones he helped to create. In the book of Proverbs, the wise man Solomon gives some useful counsel on being mindful of the less fortunate. He says in *Prov. 22:9: He that hath a bountiful eye shall be blessed; for he giveth of his bread to the poor* In Prov. 28:27: *He that hath a bountiful eye shall be blessed; for he giveth of his bread to the poor.* In Prov. 19:17: *He that hath pity upon the poor lendeth unto the LORD; and that which he hath given will he pay him again.*

Success is meaningless if you cannot be a blessing to others. After all, what can one do with billions of dollars if not to improve the lives of others less fortunate? How many cars can you drive in a day, how many outfits or shoes can you wear in a day? How much food can you eat in a day? When is enough, enough? Since the industrial revolution, we have been producing more goods than we need; as a result, advertisers are constantly thinking up ways to get us to buy more stuff than we need. Often our excesses become a snare. When the stock market crashed, and gas prices spiked, I saw many people who had lost money in the stock market trying to scale back by getting rid of some of their consumer items, but no one was buying because people had less money to spend on consumer goods. Inevitably, their excesses became a liability and a snare.

You Must not Dwell on Your Past Successes: or on the "good old days" when things went well for you. Do not define yourself based on a position you once held. I have met many individuals from foreign countries who held prestigious positions in their country of origin and upon arrival in their new country experience depression because no one cared about them or the status they held back home. Worse yet, those who knew them from back home do not even acknowledge them. Then there are those who left one job with status only to find that the new position does not offer any status or recognition. These individuals rather than humbly accept their lot and make the best of a bad situation become very bitter and morose - regretting their decision to leave their country or their job while forgetting that if things had been that great in their former position, they would not have left in the first place. If migration or your new job does not turn out as expected, do not sit and dwell on what was or could have been. Consider it a detour or a cul-de-sac and act. Size up your skills and level of competence; establish some new goals and determine who could support your goals and just move forward. If you have been downsized, see it as an opportunity to try something new rather than sit around moping about the unjust practices of the company. My grandmother would often say "time and tide wait for no one" so keep moving. If you were once a celebrity and now no one cares or even remembers who you are; do not dwell on what used to be. Seek instead to help someone less fortunate rather than focus on your past glories or losses. There are orphaned children that need parenting and seniors in nursing homes that feel abandoned and need care; become a substitute parent, visit the sick or volunteer at a senior citizen's home. Just remember that the world revolves on its axis it does not revolve around you. *How far you go in life depends on your being tender with the young, compassionate with the aged, sympathetic with the striving, and tolerant of the weak and the strong because someday in life you will have been all of these,* says George Washington Carver.

Be Considerate of Others: It is said that the great humanitarian Mahatma Gandhi was boarding a train when one of his shoes slipped off and fell between the train and the platform. Unable to retrieve the shoe, he promptly removed the other shoe and threw it next to the missing shoe. When asked why he did that, he responded: "What good is one shoe to a poor chap who is in need and finds it. Now he will have both shoes." We are not to live for self alone…. *It is only by self-forgetfulness,* *by cherishing a loving, helpful spirit, that we can make our life a blessing. The little attentions, the small, simple courtesies, go far to make up the sum of life's happiness, and the neglect of these constitutes no small share of human wretchedness (E. G. White, Patriarchs and Prophets, p. 139).* "The greatest use of life is to spend it for something that will outlast it" -says William James, psychologist and philosopher. Now, be sure to enjoy the blessings of the moment but realize that life can flip the switch at any time. You must seek in some way to be a blessing to humanity and the world. Letting go does not mean forgetting from whence you came or your past accomplishments, but to dwell on past successes (or failures) will only limit your ability to move forward and achieve your personal best.

Now tell yourself ....
..When I feel depressed, I will sing a happy song
...When I feel discouraged, I will read my Bible
...When I feel weak, I will ask God for strength
..When I feel sad, I will laugh.
...When I feel afraid, I will step out in faith.
...When I feel inferior, I will seek to accomplish new feats
...When I feel blocked, I will clean out my closet
..When I feel poverty, I will think prosperity
..When I feel incompetent, I will remember past successes
...When I feel friendless, I will become a friend
...When I feel lack, I will count my blessings with gratitude to God
...When I feel insignificant, I will dream again
...Today I will move forward in confidence being the absolute best that God wants me to be.

Finally, I am Leaving You with this Blessing: *The Lord hear thee in the day of trouble; the name of the God of Jacob defend thee; Send thee help from the sanctuary, and strengthen thee out of Zion; Remember all thy offerings, and accept thy burnt sacrifice; Selah. Grant thee according to thine own heart, and fulfil all thy counsel. We will rejoice in thy salvation, and in the name of our God we will set up our banners: the Lord fulfil all thy petitions. (Psalm, Ch. 20:1-5).*

Index

Bibliography/Source Materials/Acknowledgements

Allen, C. (1953) *God's Psychiatry*, Spire Book

Angelou, M. (1993) *Wouldn't Take Nothing for My Journey Now*, Bantam books

Arden, P. (2006) *It's Not How Good You Are, It's How Good You Want to Be*. Phaidon Press

Aronson Deb, Profiles: *The Strengths of Sampson*, Alumni 2008

Arno, Richard Gene; Arno, Phyllis Jean (2002). *The Missing Link: Revealing Spiritual Genetics*. pp. 83, 105, 140, and 156.

Alcoholic Anonymous: Twelve Steps and Twelve Traditions (1953), AA World Service, Inc.

Awake, September 2010: From a Tiny Acorn to a Mighty Oak, Watchtower

Barras, C. (2014) The Abominable Mystery. How Flowers Conquered the Earth. *BBC Earth. October 16, 2014*

Buber, Martin (1950) *The Way of Man*, Routledge & Kegan Paul Ltd.

Bible Promises to Live By (*New Living Translation*) 2007, Tyndale House Pub

Blackwell, Wiley, (July 27, 2010, Background Music Can Impair Performance, cites new study. *Science Daily, July 28, 2010*)

Bitton, Y. (2013) *Awesome Creation. A Study of the first three verses of the Torah*. Gefen Publishing House Ltd

Blanchard, K. (2016) *Lead like Jesus*. Lead Like Jesus Publication

Bloomfield, H. & McWilliams, P. (1994) *How to Deal with Depression*, Prelude Press

Boeree C. G, (2008) *Personality theories (on line text)*,

Braden, N. (1969) *The Psychology of Self-Esteem*, Bantam Books

Bradley, S. (2000) *Sudden Money*, John Whiley & Sons

Bryant, J. (2009) *Love Leadership*. Jossey-Bass

Burkley-Frost, M. (2010) *Making Life Healing Changes*. NCCA

Carson, B (2008) *Take the Risk*. Zondervon.com

Charles Dickens (1849) David Copperfield, *eBooks @ manybooks.net*

Colbert, D. (2009) *The New Bible Cure for Depression and Anxiety*, Siloam A Strange
    Company

Corcoran, B. (2003) *Use What You've Got*. Penguin Books

Covey, S. (1989) *The Seven Habits of Highly Effective People*. Franklyn Covey

DeGruy, J. (2012) *Post Traumatic Slave Trauma*. Joy DeGruy Publications Inc.

Eareckson- Tada, J. (1988) *Secret Strength*, Multnomah School of the Bible

Felder, C. (1989) *Troubling Biblical Waters*, Orbis Books

Feuerbach, L. (1957) *The Essence of Christianity*. Frederick Ungar Pub. Co.

Flamming, J. (2001) *The Prayer of Jabez: A Sermon*, First Baptist Church, Richmond,
    Virginia January 7, 2001

Frankl, A. V. (1993) *Man's Search for Meaning*, Buccaneer Books

Funk, W. (1953) *Six weeks of word power*, Pocket Books

Gladwell, M. (2008) *Outliers: The Story of Success*. Little, Brown and Co. Pub.

Goldstein, E, 8 Lottery Winners Who Lost Their Winnings. *Bank rate.com*
    (retrieved 9. 18. 2010)

Goldstein, R. (2014) Alice Coachman, 90 Dies: Groundbreaking Medalist, *New
    York Times, July 15, 2014*

Gossett, D. (1976) *What You Say Is What You Get*, Whitaker House

Hill, N. (1937) *Think and Grow Rich*. Aventine Press

Hill, N. (1928) *The Law of Success in 16 Lessons*. Create Space

Ireland, D (2006) The Bible and Your Body, *Impact Ministries International*

Jack Canfield, @jackcanfield http://lewishowes.com/143

Jakes, T.D. (2007) *Reposition Yourself*. Atria Books

Jeff, R. (2011) Bereshit: In the Beginning of What? Blog 10/18/2011

Jeremy Lin is the Knicks' faithful phenom - NY Daily News
http://www.nydailynews.com/sports/basketball/knicks/jeremy-lin-rooted-
    christian-faith-ny-knicks-point-guard-centered-article-

Jones, D (2011) *Will Power, Blog*

Kelemen, L. (1990) *Permission to believe –Four rational approaches to God's existence*,
    Targum Press

Khalfani, L. (2007) *The Money Coach's Guide to Your First Million*, McGraw-Hill

Kidder, V. (2008) *Meet Me at the Well*, Moody Pub.

Koenig HG. Religion, spirituality, and medicine: research findings and implications for clinical practice. *Southern Medical Journal. 2004;97(12).*

Kristof, N. (2015) The Power of Hope is Real. *The New York Times Op-Ed,* Thursday, May 21, 2015

Kushner, H. (2004) *When Bad Things Happen to Good People.* Anchor Books

LaCour, J. M. (1996) *Counseling the Codependent.* NCCA

LaHaye, Tim (1984). *Why You Act the Way You Do.* Tyndale House Publishers. pp. 81–82. ISBN 0-8423-8212-7.

Lewis, C. S (1952) *Mere Christianity*, Macillian

Leadershipnow.com –Quotes on Self Discipline

Lowen A. L. (1985*) Narcissism*, Simon & Schuster

Mann, C. *The Birth of Religion.* National Geographic Vol.219:No.6 June 2011

Marx, K. Critique of Hegel's Philosophy of Right German economist & Communist political philosopher (1818 - 1883)

McGonial, K (2011) *The Willpower Instinct*

McMinn, M. (1991) *Cognitive Therapy.* Word publishing

Moseley, Stacey, Adult Anorexia - the forgotten tragedy of lives lost to illness, July 18, 2010

Mwanje, F. (2004) *Walking in the Spirit.* Florence Mwanje.

Nast, P. (2012) Get up and move, A little exercise may boost learning. *Neatoday Spring 2012*

Nelson, T. (1982) The New King James Version (NJKV)

Nelson, Greg (2010) Friday Night Live, Elmont ~ Sermon about Zacchaeus

NNPA from the San Diego Voice & Viewpoint – Ant-drowning Device Saves Children from Drowning/*The Final Call June 3, 2014.*

Newberg, A. &Waldman M. R. (2010) *How God Changes Your Brain: Breakthrough Findings from a Leading Neuroscientist,* Ballantine Books.

Newberg, A. MD, & Waldman, M. R. (2010) *Too Many Gods in our Brain? Center for Spirituality and the Mind*, University of Pennsylvania

Norton, J. (2011) The iron axe-head that swam. *The Biblical Illustrator, Electronic Database by Biblesoft, Inc.*

Obadare, A. Discover Your Natural Abilities, *USI News Columnist, and Vol.4 No.54. Sept 1, 2010*

Orkin, J. (2003) This Far by Faith – Thomas Dorsey. *The Faith Project – PBS.* www. pbs.org/thisfarbyfaith/people/thomas_dorsey.html (1/26/11)

Pagels, E. (1995) *The Origin of Satan.* First Vintage Books

Pausch Randy (2008) *The Last Lecture*, Hyperion

Peale, N. V. (1974) *You can if you think you can*. Simon & Schuster

Ratey, J. Spark (2008) *The Revolutionary New Science of Exercise and the Brain* Harvard

Richards, C & K. (1998) *Praying Bible Promises*

Sedler, M. (2003) *When to Speak Up*, Chosen Books

Smith Pegues, D. (2009) *Confronting Without Offending*, Harvest House Pub.

Shubentsov, Yefim (1998) *Cure Your Cravings*, GP Putnam & Sons

Stoop, D. (1996) *You Are What You Think*, Mass Market

Sources: Biography.com and Alan Loy McGinnis, <u>The Friendship Factor</u>

Sowell, T (2010) *Race and Resentment (On line text)*

Swindoll, C. (1994*) Growing Strong in the Seasons of Life ("No Place for Pride") on pages 62-65)*. Harper Collins

The Bible –King James Version, New International Version, New Living Bible

The Living Bible Translation, Fleming H Revell

The Economist (Jan 22-28, 2011) The Rich and the Rest, NY N.Y., US

*TodaysTQ@ThinkTQ.com*Tolstoy, L (1894) The Kingdom of God Is Within You. Posting Date: July 8, 2011 [EBook #4602] Release Date: November 2003 [This file was first posted on February 17, 2002] Produced by Jack Eden

Walters, R. (1987) *Counseling for Problems of Self-Control*, NCCA

Williams, P (2012) *Full Recovery of Schizophrenia, Brain Blogger May 29, 2012*

Woodward, B. (1999*) Shadow*. Simon & Schuster

Zeiss, Y. T. (2000) Awesome Creation: A Study of the First Three Verses of the Torah, in *Becoming Influential*. Triumphant Publishing International

Acknowledgements

1. History & Development of The Arno Profile System, http://www.apsreport.com/Benefits.html
2. Permission obtained from the Ellen G. White Estate for the use of her books and manuscripts. *Disclaimer: The quotations from Ellen G. White's writings are this writer's own interpretation.*
3. Permission obtained from Ada Mui of Columbia University to share my experience of her teaching strategies.
4. Permission obtained from Marianne Williamson to include her poem "Our Deepest Fear"
5. Permission obtained from Pastor Jerome Barber to retell his story.
6. 3ABN Today "God's Beautiful Heavens" (Guest: Jim Burr)
7. The Authorized Version **or** King James Version (KJV), 1611, 1769.
8. Permission obtained from Pastor George A. McKinney to retell his story

Daphne Valcourt PhD, CPsyD, MA, MS, LMFT, LMHC, CQSW, BCPC,

G.E.M.S

In the ancient traditions, inspirational life lessons and words of wisdom were passed on from one generation to the next through the oral tradition; modern technology (television, electronic games, gizmos, and social media) however has replaced these oral traditions resulting in important life lessons and impactful stories that help to strengthen character and build resilience not being passed on. This book was written as a legacy to my daughter to help preserve these life lessons for generations to come; in so doing, these lessons will not be lost or forgotten. In times of crisis or distress, most people tend to revert to a more primitive form of existence to seek for strength, but conceivably, if the life lessons were never learned then there would be nothing to revert to; it is then that they give up in defeat. This book has valuable life lessons, impactful stories and research discoveries, which are called "G.E.M.S" and is shared to encourage and strengthen you in your personal journey. Enjoy the Journey!

Daphne Valcourt PhD, CPsyD, MA, MS, LMFT, LMHC, CQSW, Notary public

A PICTURE OF DR. VALCOURT AND HER FAMILY
TAKEN AT THE START OF WRITING THIS BOOK

Dr. Valcourt is a sought-after speaker with extensive experience as an educator, administrator and clinician; a New York State licensed mental health practitioner and New York State licensed marriage and family therapist; a United Kingdom certified social worker and trained teacher. She has devoted over 30 years to working with vulnerable children and families in both the public and private sectors of England and the United States. She obtained her undergraduate and graduate professional qualifications from Universities in London, England, in the areas of Education and Youth & Community Studies with distinction (Whiteland's Teachers College, Surrey University) and in Sociology & Social Policy, specializing in Medicine, Education & Society as well as a Diploma in Social Work/CQSW (University of North London). In the United States, she obtained her graduate professional degree in Marriage & Family Therapy (Loma Linda University) and doctoral degrees in Social Work (Fordham University) and in Christian Psychology (Scarborough Seminary). Her motto in life is: *"I can do all things through Christ who strengthens me." Dr. Valcourt seeks only to be a blessing, especially to young adults. She can be reached at: 917-582-7391; drdvalcourt@gmail.com*

Lightning Source UK Ltd.
Milton Keynes UK
UKHW040620170120
357144UK00001B/197